ALL THE WORLD'S ANIMALS

MARSUPIALS & INSECTIVORES

ALL THE WORLD'S ANIMALS

MARSUPIALS & INSECTIVORES

TORSTAR BOOKS
New York · Toronto

CONTRIBUTORS

MLA M. L. Augee
University of New South Wales
Kensington, NSW
Australia

CJB Christopher J. Barnard BSc
DPhil
University of Nottingham
England

JWB Jack W. Bradbury PhD
University of California
San Diego, California
USA

CRD Christopher R. Dickman PhD
University of Oxford
England

GG Greg Gordon
Queensland National Parks
and Wildlife Service
Brisbane, Queensland
Australia

MLG Martyn L. Gorman PhD
University of Aberdeen
Scotland

TRG Tom R. Grant
University of New South Wales
Kensington, NSW
Australia

DJH Donna J. Howell
Southern Methodist University
Dallas, Texas
USA

MAK Margaret A. Kuyper BSc MSc
Sidmouth, Devon
England

AKL A. K. Lee
Monash University
Clayton, Victoria
Australia

GFM Gary F. McCracken
University of Tennessee
Knoxville, Tennessee
USA

JMcI John McIlroy PhD
Division of Wildlife and
Rangelands Research
CSIRO
Lyneham, A.C.T.
Australia

RM Roger Martin
Monash University
Clayton, Victoria
Australia

MEN Martin E. Nicoll BSc PhD
Smithsonian Institution
Washington DC
USA

MAO'C Margaret A. O'Connell PhD
National Zoological Park
Smithsonian Institution
Washington DC
USA

WEP William E. Poole
Division of Wildlife and
Rangelands Research
CSIRO
Lyneham, A.C.T.
Australia

EMR Eleanor M. Russell
Division of Wildlife and
Rangelands Research
CSIRO
Midland, Perth
Western Australia

MJR Michael J. Ryan
Milwaukee Public Museum
Milwaukee, Wisconsin
USA

AS Andrew Smith PhD
University of New England
Armidale, NSW
Australia

RES Robert E. Stebbings PhD
Monks Wood Experimental
Station
England

DCT Dennis C. Turner ScD
Universität Zürich
Zurich
Switzerland

MDT Merlin D. Tuttle PhD
Milwaukee Public Museum
Milwaukee, Wisconsin
USA

AW Andrew Wroot
Royal Holloway College
University of London
Egham, Surrey
England

ALL THE WORLD'S ANIMALS
MARSUPIALS & INSECTIVORES

TORSTAR BOOKS INC.
41 Madison Avenue
Suite 2900
New York, NY 10010

Project Editor: Graham Bateman
Editors: Peter Forbes, Bill MacKeith, Robert Peberdy
Art Editor: Jerry Burman
Picture Research: Linda Proud, Alison Renney
Production: Clive Sparling
Design: Chris Munday

Originally planned and produced by:
Equinox (Oxford) Ltd
Littlegate House
St Ebbe's Street
Oxford OX1 1SQ, England

Editor
Dr David Macdonald
Animal Behaviour Research Group
University of Oxford
England

Artwork Panels
Priscilla Barrett

Library of Congress Cataloging in Publication Data

(All the world's animals)
Bibliography: p.
Includes index.
1. Marsupialia. 2. Insectivores. I. Title:
Marsupials and insectivores. II. Series.
QL737.M3M35   1986   599.2   86–43332

ISBN 0–920269–72–9 (Series: All the World's Animals)
ISBN 0–920269–80–X (Marsupials & Insectivores)

On the cover: Red kangaroo
Page 1: Koala
Pages 2–3: Feathertail glider
Pages 4–5: Sugar glider
Pages 6–7: Water shrew
Pages 8–9: European hedgehog

9 8 7 6 5 4 3 2 1

Printed in Belgium

In conjunction with *All the World's Animals*
Torstar Books offers a 12-inch raised
relief world globe.
For more information write to:
Torstar Books Inc.
41 Madison Avenue
Suite 2900
New York, NY 10010

CONTENTS

FOREWORD

Animals that can fly, as well as those that burrow, run and swim, animals that can navigate, hunt and communicate with sounds and echoes way beyond human perception—such are the selection of startling creatures (all of them mammals) to be found in *Marsupials & Insectivores*.

Marsupials probably means merely kangaroos and wallabies to most laymen; readers may, therefore, be surprised to learn that this group actually includes over 260 species in all manner of shapes and sizes, from the American opossums through bandicoots, gliders and wombats to the ever popular koala.

Of the more common insectivores considered in this book, the hedgehog has always enjoyed a close relationship with man, although our attitude to moles and shrews is markedly less benevolent. Shy, secretive, often nocturnal creatures, insectivores are not easy subjects for field study, yet fascinating details emerge here about their lifestyles and habitats.

Marsupials & Insectivores also includes studies of edentates (toothless mammals) the most familiar of which is the anteater; of the primitive mammalian order called monotremes—unique among mammals in laying eggs rather than giving birth to live young; and of bats, the only vertebrates, apart from birds, capable of sustained flight. Although bats comprise over one quarter of mammal species, knowledge of their lifestyles has, until recently, been relatively slim; within these pages are the most up-to-date insights into how their strange, often mysterious societies work.

How this book is organized
Animal classification can be a thorny problem—one on which even the experts sometimes find it difficult to agree. This book has taken the views of many taxonomists, but in general it follows the classification of Corbet and Hill (see Bibliography) for the arrangement of families and orders.

Marsupials & Insectivores is structured on two main levels. First, general essays highlight the common features and main variations of the biology, ecology, behavior and evolution of insectivores, edentates, bats, monotremes and marsupials. These essays are introduced with a summary of species or species groupings, a map showing distribution and, in the case of insectivores, bats and marsupials, include a description of the skull, dentition and any unusual skeletal features of representative species. The main text is devoted to individual species or groups of species and covers details of physical features, distribution, evolutionary history, diet and feeding behavior. The animals' social dynamics, spatial organization, conservation and relationship with man are also discussed.

Before the textual discussion of each species or group of species, readers will find an information panel. This gives basic data about size, lifespan and distribution. A map shows areas of natural distribution, while a scale drawing compares the size of each species with a six-foot man or, where more appropriate, with part of a six-foot man or a twelve-inch human foot. When silhouettes of two animals are shown, they are of the largest and the smallest representatives of the group. If the panel covers a large group of species, those listed as examples in the panel are those referred to in the text. Detailed descriptions of the remaining members of a group are to be found in a separate Table of Species. Unless otherwise stated, dimensions given are for both males and females. Where there is a difference in size between the sexes, the scale drawings show males.

In many cases the text is enhanced and amplified by specially commissioned color artwork showing representative species engaged in characteristic activities. Simpler line drawings illustrate particular aspects of behavior or clarify anatomical distinctions between otherwise similar species. Particular care has been taken to select color photographs that really bring the text to life by showing creatures in their natural habitats and, where possible, displaying typical behavior.

While bats are fortunate in that in many countries they are protected by legislation, for many of the species described here the future is less certain. The most famous monotreme, the duck-billed platypus, for example, belongs to an order which is seriously imperiled. The *Red Data Book* of the International Union for the Conservation of Nature and Natural Resources (IUCN) lists at least 30 of the species considered here as at risk. Some are also listed in the Appendices I through III of the Convention on International Trade in Endangered species of Wild Flora and Fauna (CITES).

In this book the following symbols have been used to show the status accorded to species by the IUCN at the time of going to press: $\boxed{E}$ = Endangered—in danger of extinction unless causal factors are modified (these may include habitat destruction and direct exploitation by man). $\boxed{V}$ = Vulnerable—likely to become endangered in the near future. $\boxed{R}$ = Rare, but neither endangered nor vulnerable at present. $\boxed{I}$ = Indeterminate, insufficient information available but known to be in one of the above categories. The symbol $\boxed{*}$ indicates entire species, genera or families, in addition to those listed in the *Red Data Book*, that are listed by CITES.

INSECTIVORES

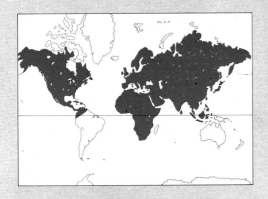

ORDER: INSECTIVORA

Six families: 60 genera; 345 species.

Tenrecs
Family: Tenrecidae
Thirty-three species in 11 genera.
Includes **Aquatic tenrec** (*Limnogale mergulus*),
Common tenrec (*Tenrec ecaudatus*) **Giant otter
shrew** (*Potamogale velox*).

Solenodons
Family: Solenodontidae
Two species in a single genus.
Includes **Hispaniola solenodon** (*Solenodon
paradoxurus*).

Hedgehogs and moonrats
Family: Erinaceidae
Seventeen species in 8 genera.
Includes **European hedgehog** (*Erinaceus
europaeus*).

Shrews
Family: Soricidae
Two hundred and forty-six species in 21
genera. Includes **Eurasian water shrew**
(*Neomys fodiens*) **European common shrew**
(*Sorex araneus*) **Vagrant shrew** (*Sorex vagrans*).

Golden moles
Family: Chrysochloridae
Eighteen species in 7 genera.
Includes **Giant golden mole** (*Chrysopalax
trevelyani*).

Moles and desmans
Family: Talpidae
Twenty-nine species in 12 genera.
Includes **European mole** (*Talpa europaea*),
Pyrenean desman (*Galemys pyrenaicus*),
Russian desman (*Desmana moschata*). **Star-
nosed mole** (*Cordylura cristata*).

ALL of the approximately 345 species of insectivores are small animals (none are larger than rabbits) with long, narrow snouts that are usually very mobile. Most use a walk or run as their normal style of movement, although some are swimmers and/or burrowers. Body shapes vary widely—from the streamlined form of the otter shrews to the short, fat body of hedgehogs and moles. All walk with the soles and heels on the ground (plantigrade). In general, the limbs are short, with five digits on each foot. The eyes and ears are relatively small and external signs of both may be absent. Most members of the order are solitary and nocturnal, feeding mainly on invertebrates, especially insects, as the name of the group suggests.

The insectivores are often divided into three suborders to emphasize the relationships between the families. The Tenrecomorpha comprises tenrecs and golden moles; the hedgehogs and moonrats (the latter considered the most primitive of the living insectivores) are placed in the Erinaceomorpha; and the Soricomorpha consists of shrews, moles and solenodons.

Although the order as a whole is very widely distributed, only three families can be said to be widespread. These are the Erinaceidae (hedgehogs and moonrats), Talpidae (moles and desmans), and Soricidae (shrews) which between them account for almost all of the worldwide distribution. The other three have very limited distributions indeed! The Solenodontidae (solenodons) are found only on the Caribbean islands of Hispaniola and Cuba. The Tenrecidae (tenrecs) are also found mainly on islands—Madagascar and the Comores in the Indian Ocean—with some members of the family (the otter shrews) found only in the wet regions of Central Africa. Because of their differences in distribution, lifestyle and habitat, the otter shrews were at various times considered to be in a separate family, the Potamogalidae, although their teeth indicate that they are true tenrecs. The golden moles occur only in the drier parts of southern Africa.

As a group, the insectivores are generally considered to be the most primitive of living placental mammals and therefore representative of the ancestral mammals from which modern mammals are derived. This was not the original purpose of the grouping. The term "insectivore" was first used in a system of classification produced in 1816 to describe hedgehogs, shrews and Old-World moles (all primarily insect-eaters). The order soon became a "rag-bag" into which fell any animal that did not fit neatly into the other orders of mammalian classification. In 1817, the naturalist Cuvier added the American moles, tenrecs, golden moles and desmans. Forty years later, tree shrews, elephant shrews, and colugos were included. All were new discoveries in need of classification but none looked much like any other members of the group.

Confronted in 1866 by an order Insectivora containing a number of very different animals, the taxonomist Haeckel subdivided it into two distinct groups that he called Menotyphla and Lipotyphla. Menotyphlans (tree shrews, elephant shrews and colugos) were distinguished by the presence of a cecum (the human appendix) at the beginning of the large intestine; lipotyphlans (moles, golden moles, tenrecs and shrews) by its absence. Menotyphlans also differ greatly from lipotyphlans in external ap-

◄ **Leafy setting** for a Eurasian water shrew. Although they sometimes forage on land, they are usually found near water.

▼ **The best-known** of the insectivores is the European hedgehog. It is also the only insectivore to have a favorable relationship with human beings.

pearance: large eyes and long legs are only two of the more obvious characters. The colugos are so different that the new order Dermoptera was created for them as early as 1872. In 1926 the anatomist Le Gros Clarke suggested that the tree shrews are more similar to lemur-like primates than to insectivores, but the most modern view is that tree shrews comprise a separate order, the Scandentia. The elephant shrews also cannot be readily assigned to any existing order, so they have become the sole family in the new order Macroscelidea. Modern analyses (of skull features in particular) show that the remaining, lipotyphlan members of the Insectivora are probably descended from a common ancestor. This conclusion does not apply to the fossil members of the Insectivora, which includes a vast assortment of early mammals and remains very much a "waste-basket" group. Many of these early forms are known only from fossil fragments and teeth; they are assigned to the Insectivora largely as a matter of convenience, having insectivore affinities and no clear links with anything else.

Not all of the insectivores are primitive mammals. Most living insectivores have evolved specializations of form and behavior which mask some of the truly primitive characters they possess. "Primitive" characters are those features which probably would have been found in those animals' ancestors. These are contrasted with "derived" (or advanced) characters, found in animals which have developed structures and habits not found in their ancestors. The cecum is a primitive character, and its lack is therefore a derived character, a feature of the Insectivora as it now stands. There are, however, a number of characters considered to be primitive which are more commonly found in the Insectivora than in other mammalian orders. These include relatively small brains, with few wrinkles to increase the surface area, primitive teeth, with incisors, canines and molars easily distinguishable, and primitive features of the auditory bones and collar bones. Other primitive characteristics shared by some or all insectivores are testes that do not descend into a scrotal sac, a flat-footed (plantigrade) gait, and possession of a cloaca, a common chamber into which the genital, urinary and fecal passages empty (*cloaca*: from the Latin for sewer). Some of these primitive features, such as the cloaca and abdominal testes, are also characteristic of the marsupials, but insectivores, like all Eutherian (placental) mammals, are distinguished by the possession of the chorioallantoic placenta which permits the young to develop fully within the womb.

Many insectivores have acquired extremely specialized features such as the spines of the hedgehogs and tenrecs, the poisonous saliva of the solenodons and some shrews, and the adaptations for burrowing found in many insectivore families. A number of shrew and tenrec species are thought to have developed a system of echolocation similar to that used by bats.

If all these derived characters are ignored, it is possible to produce a picture of an early mammal, but only in the most general terms. They would have been shy animals, running along the ground in the leaf litter but capable of climbing trees or shrubs. Small and active, about the size of a modern mouse or shrew (the largest known fossil is about the size of a Eurasian badger), they probably fed mainly on insects; some may have been scavengers. They would have looked much like modern shrews, with small eyes and a long, pointed snout with perhaps a few long sensory hairs or true whiskers. A dense coat of short fur would have covered all of the body except the ears and soles of the paws. Perhaps they had a dun-colored coat, with a stripe of darker color running through the eye and along the side of the body—a common pattern, found even on reptiles and amphibians. The development of the ability to regulate body temperature, combined with the warm mammalian coat, meant that the early mammals could be active at night when the dinosaurs (their competitors and predators) were largely inactive due to lower air temperatures.

From this basic stock, two slightly different forms are believed to have developed,

THE INSECTIVORE BODY PLAN

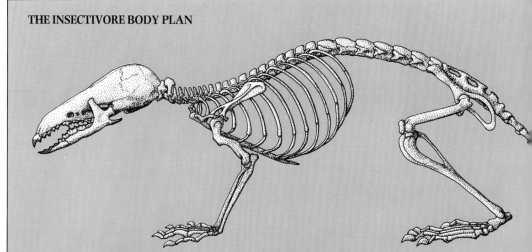

▲ **Skeleton of the Vagrant shrew,** a typical insectivore. The skull is elongate and flattened. Typical characteristics of insectivores include a small brain case, and the absence of a zygomatic arch (cheek bone), in all except hedgehogs and moles, or auditory bullae (bony) prominences around the ear opening). The teeth of shrews are well differentiated into molars, premolars and canines, with pincer-like front incisors. The dental formula of the Vagrant shrew is I3/1, C1/1, P3/1, M3/3 = 32. The teeth are partially colored by a brownish-red pigment.

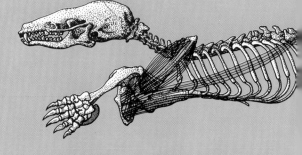

▲ **Burrowing moles** have drastically modified forelimbs. The bones are relatively massive and the palm of the hand is supported by an additional (falciform) bone (red). In the digging stroke the humerus is rotated by the *teres major* (green), *latissimus dorsi* (blue) and *pectoralis posticus* (mauve) muscles. The elbow is flexed by the triceps (pink) to assist the digging stroke.

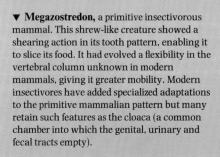

▼ **Megazostredon,** a primitive insectivorous mammal. This shrew-like creature showed a shearing action in its tooth pattern, enabling it to slice its food. It had evolved a flexibility in the vertebral column unknown in modern mammals, giving it greater mobility. Modern insectivores have added specialized adaptations to the primitive mammalian pattern but many retain such features as the cloaca (a common chamber into which the genital, urinary and fecal tracts empty).

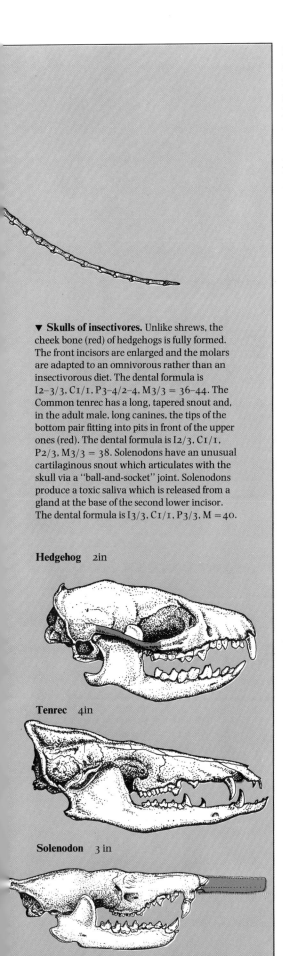

▼ **Skulls of insectivores.** Unlike shrews, the cheek bone (red) of hedgehogs is fully formed. The front incisors are enlarged and the molars are adapted to an omnivorous rather than an insectivorous diet. The dental formula is I2–3/3, C1/1, P3–4/2–4, M3/3 = 36–44. The Common tenrec has a long, tapered snout and, in the adult male, long canines, the tips of the bottom pair fitting into pits in front of the upper ones (red). The dental formula is I2/3, C1/1, P2/3, M3/3 = 38. Solenodons have an unusual cartilaginous snout which articulates with the skull via a "ball-and-socket" joint. Solenodons produce a toxic saliva which is released from a gland at the base of the second lower incisor. The dental formula is I3/3, C1/1, P3/3, M =40.

Hedgehog 2in

Tenrec 4in

Solenodon 3 in

known today only from teeth and fragments of bone dating from the late Cretaceous (80 million years ago). These two groups are characterized mainly by very different teeth. From the evidence available, it appears that one group, the Paleaoryctoidea, eventually gave rise to the creodonts, a type of early carnivore, while the Leptictoidea were thought to have produced the modern insectivores. Recent research on leptictoid fossils suggests instead that most of them were less closely related to the Insectivora, and were perhaps "dead-end" offshoots from the main branch of insectivore evolution.

Despite the evolutionary relationships between the families, insectivores have little in common other than their apparent primitiveness. It is perhaps this diversity which is responsible for the success of the three larger families. The family Talpidae contains both the true moles, which spend practically all of their lives in their subterranean burrows, and the desmans, which spend much of their time in the water and construct burrows in stream banks only for shelter. Similarly, the mainly terrestrial family Tenrecidae also includes the rice tenrecs, which are said to burrow in the banks of rice paddies, while the Aquatic tenrec leads a semi-aquatic life along stream banks and the shores of lakes and marshes. The Soricidae show adaptations to every type of habitat—in addition to the "standard" shrew, running along the ground, there are also species, like the American short-tailed shrew, that are reported to burrow like miniature moles, and those like the European water shrew that swim much like the tenrecid otter shrews.

The order Insectivora is rich in examples of convergent evolution (where animals not closely related have adapted in similar ways to fit the demands of a specific habitat or way of life). Moles and golden moles, for example, are not closely related within the order yet both have adopted similar burrowing lifestyles and even look much alike. According to the fossil record, moles developed from an animal which resembled a shrew, whereas golden moles appear to be more closely related to the tenrecs. The similarity between golden moles and the Marsupial mole of Australia is even more remarkable. In this case, the lineages have been separate for 70 million years; one is placental, the other pouched—yet the golden mole is more similar in appearance to the Marsupial mole (even in the texture of its fur) than to the true mole. The eyes of both Marsupial and golden moles are covered by skin—the eyelids have fused, whereas the minute eyes

of the true moles are still functional. Comparisons can also be made between the otters (order Carnivora, family Mustelidae) and the otter shrews, members of the Tenrecidae. Hedgehogs are well known for their spiny coat and their ability to curl up into a ball when threatened. Several genera of tenrecs have also independently developed a similar coat of spines, and some members of three genera have acquired the ability to curl up as well.

The ability to curl up, combined with a dense coat of spines, is an obvious deterrent to predators. Some non-spiny species (moles and shrews for example) have strongly distasteful secretions from skin glands which may have a similar effect. Many of the other specializations are more likely to be the result of competition for food. If two or more species compete for food or some other resource, then either the worst competitor will become (at least locally) extinct, or all will evolve to specialize on different aspects of the resource and reduce the competition. Moles, for example, may have developed their burrowing life-style to avoid both predation and competition with surface-dwelling insectivores. Some species of both shrews and moles have become semi-aquatic, probably to exploit a different source of invertebrate food.

The tenrecs are thought to have been one of the first mammalian groups to arrive on Madagascar. Like the Australian marsupials, they provide a fascinating example of adaptive radiation, having evolved, in the absence of competition with an established fauna, a variety of forms which use most of the available habitats.

Insectivores rely heavily on their sense of smell to locate their prey, as would be expected from the relatively large center of smell in the brain. Invertebrates are the main food—most are thought to feed on insects and earthworms, although some of those associated with water also eat mollusks and possibly fish. Where food habits have been closely studied, the animals appear to eat almost anything organic they find or can catch, and many will attempt to kill prey which are substantially larger than themselves: hedgehogs, for example, can kill chickens; water shrews can kill frogs. The poisonous saliva of solenodons and some shrews may have evolved to enable these animals to catch larger prey than their body size would normally permit. The poison acts mainly on the nervous system, paralyzing the victim.

Shrews, in particular, have a reputation for gluttony, consuming more than their own body-weight daily, but recent studies indicate that their food is less nutritious than the dry seeds eaten by rodents of a similar size, so they need to consume a correspondingly greater bulk. High food requirements also result from the high metabolic rates of the shrews, which in the case of some northern shrews may be an adaptation to a highly seasonal climate. All but the otter shrews and some true shrews are active mainly at night, dawn and dusk.

Reported litter sizes vary widely in those species that have been studied. Females of the genus *Tenrec* have been caught with up to 25 developing embryos, of which probably only 12–16 survive to birth. Other tenrec species, and moles, hedgehogs, and shrews have litters of 2–10; solenodons have only one or two young per litter. The timing of the breeding season is governed mainly by food availability and thus the young of animals living in arid areas are usually born in the rainy season (winter), while temperate species breed in the spring and summer. Some tropical species (the moonrats, for example) are thought to breed throughout the year.

Many insectivore species are known only from a few museum specimens, and some have not subsequently been found in the original locality. In general, insectivores do not lend themselves to field study; most are nocturnal, secretive creatures of retiring habits. Shrews, for example, are relatively common but rarely seen in the wild. They are also often difficult to catch and keep in captivity, and many occur in areas where field research is difficult. It is not surprising, therefore, that very little is actually known about the social biology of insectivores. Those few species that have been the subject of research (mainly shrews, some hedgehogs and tenrecs) are solitary, with little communication between adults except at breeding times. Studies of European hedgehogs indicate that individuals do not defend territories, although shrews do.

Shrews are territorial in that their home ranges—about 5,400sq ft (500sq m) in the European common shrew—are mutually exclusive. When shrews meet they behave aggressively towards each other. Moles, such as the European mole, are even less sociable and, once the juveniles have been expelled from a female's burrow system, she will not normally tolerate another mole in her home burrow except for a few hours in the spring when she is ready to mate. Moles usually do not trespass into each others' tunnel systems, though they will quickly take over a territory if its occupant is removed. It is likely that scent plays an important role in keeping the animals apart and they are probably circumspect about entering unfamiliar places smelling of other moles. This pattern of mutual avoidance is probably common among some other insectivore groups too. Mole home ranges are essentially linear, being constrained by tunnel walls. The burrow system acts as a pitfall trap which collects soil invertebrates as prey and in poor soils, longer burrow systems are needed to supply sufficient food. Thus a mole's linear home range may vary from 100–400ft (30–120m) or more, depending on soil type and food density. Surface activity, especially among dispersing juveniles may extend this home range considerably. Hedgehogs, such as the European hedgehog, which forage over an area from 2.5–12.5 acres (1–5ha) in a night, may use a home range of up to 74 acres (30ha) in a season; males travel further and have larger ranges than females. Unlike some small rodents, insectivores do not normally seem to make use of a three-dimensional home range by climbing into bushes and trees. In desmans, the home range is linear, along a stream edge; in tenrecs it is an area around the burrow or den; but for many species there is no detailed ecological information at all.

A number of species, including the tenrecs and solenodons, are now facing a major problem: the introduction by man of new competitors and predators, such as rats, mice, cats and dogs, which are effective generalists and can thrive almost anywhere. These competitors also have high reproductive rates, bearing several litters in a year, and can thus quickly build a sizeable population which overwhelms native species before they have any chance to adapt to the changed situation. Solenodons were the principal small carnivores in the Antilles until the 17th century, when the Spaniards brought with them dogs, cats and rats. Mongooses were introduced in the late 19th century to combat Black rats. The latter two proved to be highly effective as competitors for food and all apparently added solenodons to their diet. These pressures, combined with the clearance of jungle for cultivation, are now proving too great for the solenodons. *Nesophontes* (a solenodon-like insectivore from the Caribbean and the sole member of the family Nesophontidae) is thought to have become extinct in the last 50 years, and the two species in the Solenodontidae are unlikely to survive much longer in the wild.

The Russians are at present trying to preserve the remnants of their Russian

▲ **Insectivores in the Middle Ages.** TOP Hedgehogs, one encrusted with fruit, depicted in a bestiary from about AD 1300. The incorrect notion that hedgehogs deliberately carry fruit on their spines derives from the Roman author Pliny and has been handed down ever since. ABOVE The mole, depicted in *Le Bestiaire d'Amore* by Richard de Fournivall; early 14th century. According to this author: "The mole is blind with eyes under his heart, but he makes up for it by his acute hearing. So with all of the senses: if one is defective there is always another which surmounts it. Also the mole lies purely in earth, being one of those animals which live only in one element."

▶ **A rash of mole-hills** ABOVE on an upland pasture in Herefordshire, England, shows just how much of a nuisance moles can be, turning a significant proportion of the pasture into spoil heaps.

▶ **The fate of moles.** For centuries, moles have been trapped, both to reduce their effects on farmland and for their pelts. Now, eradication campaigns are still waged when they become serious pests but their pelts are no longer valued.

(especially in Madagascar and the West Indies) and the smaller ones are probably rarely noticed.

Most insectivores are too small and too scarce to be any use for food, and equally are unlikely to be serious economic pests. Many are, however, extremely abundant, and it has been suggested that if all shrews were to disappear suddenly, the number of insect pests in fields and gardens would increase noticeably. Other insectivores are more likely to become accidental victims of human activities than to be blamed as pests or praised as allies.

Some species have been economically exploited. The Russian desmans have a dense lustrous coat and, in the past, numbers of these animals were caught in nets and traps. They were also chased from their burrows and shot or clubbed. A century ago, a fortunate hunter might obtain 40 desman skins during the month-long hunting season at the time of the spring thaw. Despite their value, desman pelts were never a major commodity and the "industry" seems to have been opportunistic.

Mole-skins have been used for hats and trimming since Roman times. In the 17th and 18th centuries many were used in Germany for purses, caps and other things. Fashions are fickle and although moles were caught in sufficient numbers in Germany at the end of the 19th century to cause fears of extinction, the market had dwindled by 1914. Demand from America in the 1920s is said to have caused the export of some 12 million moles from Europe and, even as late as the 1950s, a million mole-skins a year were being trapped in Britain. Mole-skins are graded and valued according to size and whether or not they show signs of molt. Until the late 19th century many English parishes employed a professional mole catcher to rid the fields of troublesome moles. Some of these men claimed to kill a thousand or more moles each winter. However, mole-skins are no longer an economic proposition; they are worth comparatively little and cheaper synthetic substitutes are readily available.

A large proportion of insectivore species are found only in tropical countries where the emphasis is on development and exploitation of resources rather than preservation of wildlife. Few, if any, of the nature reserves have been designed with insectivores in mind; they are generally unprepossessing animals and, with the exception of a few species like the hedgehogs, a threat of extinction is unlikely to receive wide public attention.   AW

desman population. This was once a staple of the fur trade, with tens of thousands of skins exported annually to western Europe, but hunting, combined with pollution of their aquatic habitat and competition from introduced coypus and muskrats, has drastically reduced the population. The small population of Pyrenean desmans in the Pyrenees is threatened by water pollution. Several species of golden mole are also threatened by various changes in their habitat.

The only insectivore which has a favorable relationship with man is the hedgehog. The folklore of both Europe and Asia contains tales of hedgehogs and although they are regarded as pests by some English gamekeepers, householders in the urban areas of western Europe provide them with bowls of bread and milk. Elsewhere in the world, the larger insectivores are eaten occasionally

TENRECS

Family: Tenrecidae
Thirty-four species in 11 genera.
Distribution: Madagascar, with one species
introduced to the Comoros, Mascarenes and the
Seychelles; W and C Africa.

Habitat: wide-ranging, from semi-arid to rain
forest, including mountains, rivers and human
settlements.

Size: ranges from head-body length 1.7in
(43mm), tail length 1.8in (45mm) and weight
0.18oz (5g) in *Microgale parvula* to head-body
length 10–15in (250–390mm), tail length
0.2–0.4in (5–10mm) and weight 18–53oz
(500–1,500g) in the Common tenrec.

Gestation: relatively uniform within the
Oryzoryctinae and Tenrecinae where known
(50–64 days); unknown in Potamogalinae.

Longevity: up to 6 years.

Coat: soft-furred to spiny, brown to gray to
contrasted streaks.

Tenrecs
Subfamily Oryzoryctinae
Twenty-five species in 4 Madagascan genera,
including **Aquatic tenrec** (*Limnogale mergulus*),
rice tenrecs (3 species), genus *Oryzoryctes*;
long-tailed tenrecs (20 species), genus
Microgale; **Large-eared tenrec** (*Geogale aurita*).

Subfamily Tenrecinae
Six species in 5 Madagascan genera: **Greater
hedgehog tenrec** (*Setifer setosus*), **Lesser
hedgehog tenrec** (*Echinops telfairi*), *Dasogale
fontoynonti* (possibly based on mistaken
identification), **Common tenrec** (*Tenrec
ecaudatus*), **streaked tenrecs** (*Hemicentetes
semispinosus* and *H. nigriceps*).

Otter shrews
Subfamily Potamogalinae
Three species in 2 African genera: **Giant otter
shrew** (*Potamogale velox*), **Ruwenzori least
otter shrew** (*Micropotamogale ruwenzorii*),
Mount Nimba least otter shrew (*M. lamottei*)

Tenrecs and otter shrews are remarkable in having a greater diversity than any other living family of insectivores. Yet this has been achieved in virtual isolation, since tenrecs themselves are confined to Madagascar, and the otter shrews to West and central Africa. Tenrecs retain characters which were perhaps more widespread among early placental mammals. These conservative features include a low and variable body temperature (see box), retention of a common opening for the urogenital and anal tracts (the cloaca) and undescended testes in the male. Some of the family comprise a more conspicuous part of the native fauna than temperate zone insectivores, being either an important source of food, relatively large and bold, or conspicuously colored. Even though detailed studies of the family are few and restricted to a handful of species, they provide an excellent basis for the elucidation of mammalian evolution.

The earliest fossils date from Kenyan Miocene deposits (about 25 million years ago), but by then the Tenrecidae were well differentiated, and had probably long been part of the African fauna. The tenrecs were among the first mammals to colonize Madagascar. The only survivors of this ancient group on the African mainland, the otter shrews (Potamogalinae), are sometimes regarded as a separate family.

Eyesight is generally poor in these largely nocturnal species, but the whiskers are sensitive and smell and hearing are well developed. Vocalizations range from hissing and grunting to twittering and echolocation clicks. The brain is relatively small and the number of teeth ranges from 32–42.

The aquatic Tenrecidae are active creatures of streams, rivers, lakes and swamps. The Giant otter shrew and Mount Nimba least otter shrew are confined to forest, but the Ruwenzori least otter shrew and the Aquatic tenrec are less restricted. All four species have a sleek, elegant body form with a distinctive, flattened head which allows the ears, eyes and nostrils to project above the surface while most of the body remains submerged. Stout whiskers radiate from around the muzzle, providing a means of locating prey. The fur is dense and soft, and frequent grooming ensures that it is waterproof, and traps insulating air during dives. Grooming is accomplished by means of the two fused toes on each hindfoot which act as combs. All otter shrews and the Aquatic

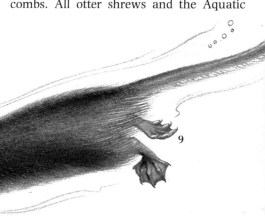

often figures as part fish and part mammal in African folklore, giving rise to such names as "transformed fish." The unmistakable deep, laterally flattened tail, which tapers to a point, is the main source of such beliefs even though it is covered by fine, short hair, but the animal's proficiency in water no doubt plays a part. Sinuous thrusts of the powerful tail extending up the lower part of the body provide the propulsion for swimming, giving rise to startling speeds and great agility. Although most of the active hours are spent in the water, the agility extends to dry-land foraging. The Boulou of southern Cameroun call the Giant otter shrew the *jes*: a person is said to be like a *jes* if he flares up in anger but just as rapidly calms down.

The long-tailed and Large-eared tenrecs are shrew-like, and the former have the least modified body plan within the Tenrecidae. Evergreen forest and wetter areas of the

▲ **Species of tenrecs.** (**1**) Lesser hedgehog tenrec (*Echinops telfairi*). (**2**) Common tenrec (*Tenrec ecaudatus*). (**3**) Streaked tenrec (*Hemicentetes nigriceps*). (**4**) Long-tailed tenrec (*Microgale melanorrachis*). (**5**) Greater hedgehog tenrec (*Setifer setosus*). (**6**) Rice tenrec (*Oryzorictes tetradactylus*) (**7**) Giant otter shrew (*Potamogale velox*). (**8**) Ruwenzori least otter shrew (*Micropotamogale ruwenzorii*). (**9**) Aquatic tenrec (*Limnogale mergulus*).

tenrec have a chocolate brown back; the Aquatic tenrec has a gray belly and otter shrews have white bellies. The Madagascan Aquatic tenrec shows strong convergence with the least otter shrews, with a rat-size body and a tail approximately the same length. The Ruwenzori least otter shrew and the Aquatic tenrec have webbed feet, which probably provide most of the propulsion in the water, and their tails are slightly compressed laterally, providing each with an effective rudder and additional propulsion.

The Mount Nimba least otter shrew is probably the least aquatic, having no webbing and a rounded tail. However, all are probably agile both in water and on land. The Giant otter shrew, which is among the most specialized of the aquatic insectivores,

central plateau of Madagascar are the primary habitats for long-tailed tenrecs, and only one species extends into the deciduous forests of the drier western region. These tenrecs have filled semi-arboreal and terrestrial niches. The longest-tailed species, with relatively long hindlegs, can climb and probably spring among branches, while on the ground live jumpers and runners, together with short-legged semi-burrowing species. The Large-eared tenrec is also semi-burrowing in its western woodland habitat, and is apparently closely related to one of the oldest fossil species.

The rice tenrecs with their mole-like velvet fur, reduced ears and eyes, and relatively large forefeet fill Madagascar's burrowing insectivore niche. In undisturbed areas of northern and western Madagascar, these tenrecs burrow through the humus layers in a manner similar to the North American shrew mole, but the extensive cultivation of rice provides new habitats for them.

The subfamily Tenrecinae comprise some of the most fascinating and bizarre insectivores. The tail has been lost or greatly reduced, and varying degrees of spininess are linked with elaborate and striking defensive strategies. Both the Greater hedgehog tenrec and its smaller semi-arboreal counterpart, the Lesser hedgehog tenrec, can form a nearly impregnable spiny ball when threatened, closely resembling the Old World hedgehogs. Continued provocation may also lead to them advancing, gaping, hissing and head-bucking, the latter being common to all Tenrecinae. The brown adult Common tenrec, qualifying as the largest living insectivore, is the least spiny, but it combines a lateral open-mouthed slashing bite with head-bucking which can drive spines concentrated on the neck into an offender. A fully grown male with a gape of 4in (10cm) has canines measuring up to 0.6in (1.5cm) and the bite is powered by the massively developed masseter (jaw) muscles. A pad of thickened skin on the male's mid-back also provides some protection. The black-and-white striped offspring relies less on biting but uses numerous barbed, detachable spines to great effect in head-bucking. Common tenrecs have better eyesight than most Tenrecidae, but may also detect disturbances through long sensitive hairs on the back. Disturbed young can communicate their alarm through stridulation, which involves rubbing together stiff quills on the mid-back to produce an audible signal. Streaked tenrecs are remarkably similar to juvenile Common tenrecs in coloration, size and possession of a stridulating organ. Like juvenile Common tenrecs, they forage in groups, and their main defense involves scattering and hiding under cover. When cornered, they advance, bucking violently, their spines bristling.

Tenrecs and otter shrews are opportunistic feeders, taking a wide variety of invertebrates, as well as some vertebrates and vegetable matter. Otter shrews scour the water, stream bed and banks with their sensitive whiskers, snapping up prey and carrying it up to the bank if caught in the water. Crustacea are the main prey, including crabs of up to 2–3in (5–7cm) across the carapace. Rice tenrecs probably encounter most of their invertebrate prey in underground burrows or surface runs, but also consume vegetable matter. Fruit supple-

ments the invertebrate diet of the more omnivorous species such as the Common and hedgehog tenrecs. Common tenrecs are also large enough to take reptiles, amphibians and even small mammals. Prey are detected by sweeping whiskers from side to side, and by smell and sound. Similarly, semi-arboreal Lesser hedgehog tenrecs and long-tailed tenrecs perhaps encounter and eat lizards and nestling birds. The streaked tenrecs, one of which is active during daytime, have delicate teeth and elongated fine snouts for feeding on earthworms.

Tenrec reproduction is diverse and includes several features peculiar to the family. Where known, ovarian processes differ from those in other mammals in that no fluid-filled cavity, or antrum, develops in the maturing ovarian follicle. Spermatozoa also penetrate developing follicles and fertilize the egg before ovulation; this is known in only one other mammal, the Short-tailed shrew.

Most births occur during the wet season, coinciding with maximum invertebrate numbers, and the offspring are born in a relatively undeveloped state. Litter size varies from two in the Giant otter shrew and some Oryzoryctinae to an extraordinary maximum of 32 in the Common tenrec, and apparently reflects survival affected by the stability of the environment. For example, oryzoryctines inhabiting the comparatively stable high rain-forest regions are apparently long-lived and bear small litters. Similarly, average litter size of Common tenrecs inhabiting relatively seasonal woodland/savanna regions with fluctuating climatic conditions is 20, compared to 15 in rain-forest regions and 10 in Seychelles rain

▲ **The striped coat** of a young Common tenrec is a form of camouflage enabling it to accompany its mother on daylight foraging trips.

◄ **Very like a hedgehog,** this ball of spines is in fact the Lesser hedgehog tenrec, a species native to Madagascar.

forests within 5° of the equator. Variation in weight within the litter can reach 200–275 percent in Common and hedgehog tenrecs.

The Common tenrec feeds her offspring from up to 29 nipples, the most recorded among mammals. Nutritional demands of lactation are so great in this species that the mother and offspring must extend foraging beyond their normal nocturnal regime into the relatively dangerous daylight hours. This accounts for the striped camouflage coloration of juveniles, which only become more strictly nocturnal at the approach of the molt to the adult coat. Moreover, adult females have a darker brown coat than adult males, presumably because it affords better protection for daylight feeding throughout their brief spell of lactation. The striking similarity between juvenile Common tenrecs and adult streaked tenrecs suggests that a striped coat associated with daylight foraging has been an important factor in the evolution towards modern streaked tenrecs.

Rain-forest streaked tenrecs form multi-generational family groups comprising the most complex social groupings among insectivores. Young mature rapidly and can breed at 35 days after birth, so that each group may produce several litters in a season. The group, of up to 18 animals, probably consists of three related generations. They forage together, in subgroups, or alone, but when together they stridulate almost continuously. Stridulation seems to be primarily a device to keep mother and young together as they search for prey.

The primary means of communication among the Tenrecidae is through scent. Otter shrews regularly deposit feces either in or near their burrows and under sheltered banks. Marking by tenrecs includes cloacal dragging, rubbing secretions from eye-glands and manual depositing of neck-gland secretions. Common tenrecs cover 1.2–5 acres (0.5–2ha) per night, although receptive females reduce this to about 2,150sq ft (200sq m) to facilitate location by males. Giant otter shrews may range along 0.5mi (800m) of their streams in a night.

Common tenrecs have been a source of food since ancient times, but are not endangered by this hunting. Undoubtedly, some rain-forest tenrecs are under threat as Madagascar is rapidly being deforested, but some species thrive around human settlements. Forest destruction is also reducing the range of the Giant otter shrew and perhaps also of the Mount Nimba least otter shrew and the Ruwenzori least otter shrew.

MEN

Tenrec Body Temperature

Body temperature is relatively low among tenrecs, with a range of 86–95°F (30–35°C) during activity. The Large-eared tenrec and members of the Tenrecinae enter seasonal hypothermia, or torpor, during dry or cool periods of the year when foraging is difficult. This hypothermia ranges from irregular spells of a few days which are opportunistic, to continuous periods lasting six months; then it is integral to the animal's physiological and behavioral cycles, as in the Common tenrec in the hot, humid rain forests of the Seychelles within 5° of the equator. So finely arranged are the cycles of hypothermia, activity and reproduction that the Common tenrec must complete such physiological changes as activation of the testis or ovary while still torpid, since breeding begins within days of commencing activity.

The Giant otter shrew, some Oryzoryctinae and the Tenrecinae save energy at any time of year because body temperature falls close to air temperature during daily rest. In this way, the animals save energy otherwise used to keep the body at a higher, constant temperature. Interactions between these fluctuations in body temperature and reproduction in the Tenrecidae are unique. For example, during comparable periods of activity in the Common tenrec, body temperatures of breeding males are on average 1.1°F (0.6°C) lower than those of nonbreeding males. This is because sperm production or storage can only occur below normal body temperature. Other mammals have either an elaborate mechanism for cooling the reproductive organs or, in a few rare cases, tolerate high temperatures. Normally, thermoregulation improves during pregnancy, but female Common tenrecs, and no doubt others in the family, continue with their regular fluctuations in body temperature dependent on activity or rest, regardless of pregnancy. This probably accounts for variations in recorded gestation lengths, as the fetuses could not develop at a constant rate if so cooled during maternal rest. Although torpor during pregnancy occurs among bats, it is well regulated, and the type found in tenrecs is not known elsewhere.

SOLENODONS

Family: Solenodontidae
Two species in a single genus.

Hispaniola solenodon [E]
Solenodon paradoxurus
Distribution: Hispaniola.
Habitat: forest, now restricted to remote
regions; nocturnal.

Size: head-and-body length 11–13in (284–
328mm), tail length 8.5–10in (222–254mm),
weight 25–35oz (700–1,000g).

Coat: forehead black, back grizzled gray-brown,
white spot on the nape, yellowish flanks; tail
gray except for white at base and tip.

Cuban solenodon [E]
Solenodon cubanus
Distribution: Cuba.
Habitat, activity and size as for the Hispaniola
solenodon, except that the tail is slightly
shorter.

Coat: finer and longer than in the Hispaniola
solenodon, dark gray except for pale yellow
head and mid-belly.

[E] Endangered.

▶ **A threatened species,** the primitive
Hispaniola solenodon falls prey to carnivores
and suffers competition from rodents
introduced to its sole location on the island of
Hispaniola.

THE extraordinary solenodons of Cuba and Hispaniola face a real and immediate threat to their survival. They are so rare and restricted that the key to their survival lies in prompt governmental effort to provide adequate management of forest reserves in remote mountainous regions. Without such efforts, these distinctive ancient Antillean insectivores are likely to follow the West Indian shrews, the Nesophontidae, which may have declined to extinction upon the arrival of Europeans.

The solenodons are among the largest living insectivores, resembling, to some extent, large, well-built shrews. The most distinctive feature is the greatly elongated snout, extending well beyond the length of the jaw. In the Hispaniola solenodon, the remarkable flexibility and mobility of the cartilaginous appendage stems from its attachment to the skull by means of a unique ball-and-socket joint. The snout of the Cuban solenodon is also highly flexible but lacks the round articulating bone. Solenodons possess 40 teeth, and the front upper incisors project below the upper lip. The Hispaniola solenodon secretes toxic saliva and this probably occurs also in the Cuban species. Each limb has five toes, and the forelimbs are particularly well developed, bearing long, stout claws which are sharp. Only the hindfeet are employed in self-cleaning and can reach most of the body surface by virtue of unusually flexible hip joints. Only the rump and the base of the tail cannot be reached, but because these areas are hairless they require little attention. The tail is stiff and muscular and possibly plays a role in balancing.

As in most nocturnal terrestrial insectivores, brain size is relatively small, and the sense of touch is highly developed, while smell and hearing are also important. Vocalizations include puffs, twitters, chirps, squeaks and clicks; the clicks comprise pure high-frequency tones similar to those found among shrews, and probably provide a crude means of echolocation. Scent marking is probably important, as evidenced by the presence of anal scent glands, while contact perhaps plays a role in some situations.

In addition to the living genus, solenodons are known from North American middle and late Oligocene deposits (about 32–26 million years ago). Their affinities are difficult to ascertain owing to their long isolation, but their closest allies are probably the true shrews (Soricidae), or the Afro-Madagascan tenrecs. Some mammalogists have also considered the extinct West Indian nesophontid shrews to be within the Solenodontidae.

Solenodons were among the dominant carnivores on Cuba and Hispaniola before Europeans arrived with their alien predators, and were probably only occasionally eaten themselves by boas and birds of prey. Soil and litter invertebrates constitute a large part of the diet, including beetles, crickets and various insect larvae, together with millipedes, earthworms and termites. Vertebrate remains which have appeared in feces may have been the result of scavenging carrion, but solenodons are large enough to take small vertebrates such as amphibians, reptiles and perhaps small birds. Solenodons are capable of climbing near-vertical surfaces, but spend most time foraging on the ground. The flexible snout is used to investigate cracks and crevices, while the massive claws are used to expose the prey under rocks, the bark of fallen branches and in the

soil. A solenodon may lunge at prey and pin it to the ground with the claws and toes of the forefeet, while simultaneously scooping up the prey with the lower jaw. Occasionally the prey is pinned to the ground only by the cartilaginous nose, and must be held there as the solenodon advances. These advances take the form of rapid bursts to prevent the prey's escape, and a maneuvering of the lower jaw into a scoop position. Once it is caught, the prey is presumably immobilized by the toxic saliva.

The natural history of solenodons is characterized by a long life span and low reproductive weight, with a litter size of 1–2, as a consequence of having been among the dominant predators in pre-Columbian times. The frequency and timing of reproduction in the wild is not known, but receptivity lasts less than one day and recurs at approximately 10-day intervals. Events leading up to mating involve scent marking by both sexes, soft calling and frequent body contacts. In captivity, the scent marking involves marking projections in the female's cage with anal drags and also defecating and urinating in locations previously used by the female. The young are born in a nesting burrow, and they remain with the mother for an extended period of several months, which is exceptionally long among insectivores. During the first two months, each young solenodon may accompany the mother on foraging excursions by hanging onto her greatly elongated teats by the mouth. Solenodons are the only insectivores which practice teat transport, and carrying the offspring in the mouth is more widespread within this order. Initially, the offspring are simply dragged along, but as they grow they are able to walk with the mother, pausing when she stops. Teat transport would undoubtedly be useful if nursing solenodons change burrow sites regularly. More advanced offspring continue to follow the mother, learning food preferences from her by licking her mouth as she feeds, and getting to know routes around the nest burrow. The mother-offspring tie is the only enduring social grouping among solenodons; adults are otherwise solitary.

There are no accurate estimates of solenodon numbers in Cuba or Hispaniola, although the Cuban solenodon appears to be the rarer species. The low reproductive rate is one factor in the decline in solenodon abundance, but more important factors accounting for their rarity are habitat destruction and predation by introduced carnivores, against which solenodons have no defense. Mongooses and feral cats are the main predators on Cuba, whereas dogs decimate solenodon populations in the vicinity of settlements on Hispaniola. There is little hope for the Hispaniola solenodon in Haiti, the nation comprising the western half of Hispaniola, but protected areas of dense forest now exist in remote regions of the neighboring Dominican Republic, and on Cuba. These require prompt, efficient management to ensure the solenodon's survival. Such is the pressure for new land which accompanies the human population explosion on these islands that the solenodons' survival may ultimately rest upon the efforts of zoos. MEN

▼ **The solenodon's snout** is a unique feature, a cartilaginous appendage extending well beyond the jaw. In the Hispaniola solenodon, but not the Cuban solenodon, the snout articulates with the skull by means of a ball-and-socket joint, and is used to investigate cracks during foraging and to pin down prey.

HEDGEHOGS

Family: Erinaceidae
About seventeen species in 8 genera.
Distribution: Africa, Europe, and Asia north to
limits of deciduous forest but absent from
Madagascar, Sri Lanka, and Japan. Introduced
to New Zealand.

Size: ranges from head-body length 4–6in (10–15cm), tail length 0.4–1.2in (1–3cm) and weight 1.4–2oz (40–60g) in the Lesser moonrat to head-body length 10–18in (26–45cm), tail length 7.8–8.3in (20–21cm) and weight 2.2–3lb (1,000–1,400g) in the Greater moonrat.

Habitat: wooded or cultivated land (including urban gardens), tropical rain forest, steppe, and desert.

Gestation: known only for European hedgehog (34–49 days) and Long-eared hedgehog (37 days).

Longevity: up to 6 or 8 years (10 in captivity).

Moonrats or gymnures
Subfamily Echinosoricinae
Five genera with 5 species: **Greater moonrat**
(*Echinosorex gymnurus*), **Lesser moonrat**
(*Hylomys suillus*), **Hainan moonrat**
(*Neohylomys hainanensis*), **Mindanao moonrat**
(*Podogymnura truei*) [v], **Shrew-hedgehog**
(*Neotetracus sinensis*).
Southeast Asia, China.

Hedgehogs
Subfamily Erinaceinae
Twelve species in 3 genera, including **Western
European hedgehog** (*Erinaceus europaeus*),
W and N Europe; **long-eared hedgehogs**
(*Hemiechinus* spp), Asia and N Africa; **desert
hedgehogs** (*Paraechinus* spp), Asia and
N Africa.

[v] Vulnerable.

▶ **Grist to the mill.** Hedgehogs will eat almost any invertebrate prey. Here a South African hedgehog is devouring a grasshopper.

▶ **A white moonrat, foraging.** The Greater moonrat is usually black with whitish head and shoulders but some individuals are white all over.

THE hedgehogs are among the most familiar small mammals in Europe, distinguished by their thick coat of spines and ability to curl up into a ball when threatened. Hedgehogs have always enjoyed a close and rather friendly relationship with man. They figure prominently in folk tales and in many places are treated as free-ranging pets. Nevertheless, only the European species have been studied closely.

Even less is known about the moonrats or gymnures (sometimes considered to be spineless hedgehogs), which are found in Southeast Asia and China. These five species are very diverse in appearance: the Greater moonrat is the size of a rabbit, with coarse black hair and white markings on the face and shoulders; all the others are smaller and have soft fine hair (rather like large shrews). All of them have very elongated snouts.

With the exception of the spines and their associated musculature, the body plan of hedgehogs and moonrats is very primitive. The eyes and ears are well developed, the snout is long and pointed and extends a long way in front of the mouth. The front of the skull is quite blunt, however, so that the tip of the snout is unsupported and capable of great mobility. The teeth vary from 36 to 44 in number, usually with both upper and lower first incisors (the "front" teeth) larger than the others. In the hedgehogs, the first upper incisors are separated by a wide gap into which the blunt, forward-projecting lower incisors can fit (when a hedgehog closes its jaws on an insect, the lower incisors act as a scoop and push upward between the upper teeth to impale it). The rest of the teeth are either pointed (incisors, canines, and first premolars) or broad with sharp cusps (last premolars and molars).

All species but one have five toes on each foot, the exception being the Four-toed hedgehog which has only four on the hindfeet. The hedgehogs have powerful legs and strong claws and are good at digging (those species occupying dry areas often live in burrows). The five species of moonrats look and behave rather like large species of shrews, tending to move abruptly and quickly. Hedgehogs can run at up to 6.5ft/sec (2m/sec), but usually move with a slow shambling walk.

Among the five species of moonrats, two species, the Mindanao moonrat and the Hainan moonrat, are quite distinct. Of the other three species, all of which have similar geographic ranges and apparently occupy fairly similar habitats, the Greater moonrat is readily distinguished by its large size and striking coloration. Despite the superficial

similarity of the Lesser moonrat and the Shrew-hedgehog, the latter has fewer teeth.

About 12 species of hedgehogs are usually recognized, divided into three genera on the basis of shape and pattern of spines and length of ears, as well as skull morphology. The long-eared hedgehogs do not have a narrow spineless tract on the crown of the head while the other two genera do. Desert hedgehogs differ from woodland hedgehogs in having longitudinal grooves on their spines. Differences between the species within a genus often involve the color of the spines and the length of the toes or ears. In general, the division of a hedgehog genus into species rests upon their geographical ranges. Even this criterion fails when considering the two species of European hedgehogs: it is unclear whether there are one,

two, or perhaps even 12 species present. The problem is that hedgehogs vary considerably in size, shape and color, and that groups of individuals from different parts of Europe tend to be quite different in appearance. Animals from Spain are paler in color, those from Crete and Britain are smaller, those from the western parts of Europe have mostly brown underparts while eastern European animals tend to be white on the breast. It is not known whether these subgroups are sufficiently and consistently different in appearance to be considered as subspecies. Even the division into eastern and western species of European hedgehog accepted here is not based on an inability to interbreed: hybrids have been produced in captivity and intermediate forms are occasionally found in areas where the two species meet. Nevertheless, the two are considered to be separate species because there are minor differences in the skull and, perhaps more importantly, there are differences in the appearance of their chromosomes.

Like other insectivores, hedgehogs and moonrats eat a wide variety of prey. European hedgehogs (in both Europe and New Zealand, where they have been introduced) eat virtually any available invertebrate. The major prey is the earthworm, followed by beetles, earwigs, slugs, millipedes and caterpillars. In addition, hedgehogs will scavenge the remains of any animal found dead and take eggs and young from birds' nests. Despite a reputation for killing frogs and mice (among others) and for destroying the eggs of ground-nesting birds, it is unlikely that they are a significant predator on any vertebrates. In contrast, the Daurian hedgehog of the Gobi desert has been reported to feed mainly on small rodents, perhaps because there is little else to eat in that area. The Greater moonrat enters the water quite readily, and eats crustaceans, mollusks and even fish. Little is known of the diets of the other species of moonrats, or of most of the non-European hedgehogs.

Hedgehogs will eat seeds, berries or fallen fruit. Stomach contents or droppings frequently reveal abundant plant matter, especially grasses and leaves, largely undigested.

There is no information on breeding for the Hainan and Mindanao moonrats, and little for the other three species. Both the Greater and Lesser moonrats breed all year round in the Tropics, while the Shrewhedgehog may have either a long breeding season (April to September) or two breeding seasons: one in April/May and the other in

▼ **Species of hedgehogs and moonrats.**
(1) Desert hedgehog (*Paraechinus aethiopicus*).
(2) Algerian hedgehog (*Erinaceus algirus*).
(3) Shrew-hedgehog (*Neotetracus sinensis*).
(4) Lesser moonrat (*Hylomys suillus*).
(5) Long-eared hedgehog (*Hemiechinus auritus*).
(6) Mindanao moonrat (*Podogymnura truei*).
(7) Greater moonrat (*Echinosorex gymnurus*).

August/September. Greater and Lesser moonrats have two or three young in a litter, the Shrew-hedgehog has four or five.

Most of the hedgehogs in tropical climates breed throughout the year, but those in desert or semidesert (long-eared and desert hedgehogs) breed only once between July and September. In the more temperate areas, where food is abundant but only seasonally available, hedgehogs may breed once or twice a year between May and September, depending on the weather. Litter sizes vary from 1–10 (usually 4–7) in woodland and long-eared hedgehogs and from 1–5 in desert hedgehogs.

In woodland hedgehogs, courtship occurs practically whenever a male encounters a female. The female will stand still, with partly erect spines. The male moves slowly around her, usually brushing against her, and frequently reversing direction. The female also turns so that she faces toward the male and, if unreceptive, will erect the spines on her forehead and butt at the male's flank. The female, and sometimes the male, make loud snorting noises throughout. Continued butts from an unreceptive female do not deter the male from circling her, often for hours.

Contrary to one old wives' tale, hedgehogs do not mate face to face. The female's vaginal opening is placed far back, immediately in front of the anus, while the male's penis is very long and located a long way forward. The female stands with spines flat and back depressed while the male mounts. Because the flattened spines on the female's back are very slippery, the male holds himself in position by grasping the spines on her shoulder in his teeth. Copulation may occur several times in succession before the two animals part company. There is no pair-bond formed and the male shows no paternal behavior.

During gestation, the female prepares a nest in which to give birth. The young are born naked with eyes and ears closed. Although spines are present at birth, they lie just beneath the skin, which is engorged with large amounts of fluid. This prevents the spines from piercing the skin and damaging the mother's birth canal. The fluid beneath the skin is rapidly resorbed after birth, allowing the skin to contract, which then forces the 150 or so white spines through the skin. Within 36 hours these are supplemented by the sprouting of additional, darkly pigmented spines. Young European hedgehogs grow quite rapidly; at 14 days their hair has started to grow, the eyes are beginning to open, and the animal

can partially roll up. At 21 days the first teeth have appeared and the young start to leave the nest with the mother in order to learn to fend for themselves. Weaning occurs at 6–7 weeks of age, after which the young either leave the nest or are driven off by the mother. The development of the young of desert hedgehogs is similar to that of woodland hedgehogs. Long-eared hedgehogs, however, appear to produce smaller young—2–2.4in (5–6cm) long, 0.1–0.14oz (3–4g), as opposed to 2.4–4in (6–10cm), 0.4–0.9oz (12–25g) in European hedgehogs—which mature much faster than the other two genera. The eyes are reputedly open at 1 week and by 2–3 weeks the young can eat solid food.

In the European hedgehogs, from mating to weaning takes about 12–13 weeks and so, if the food supply is adequate and breeding has occurred early enough in the year, a second litter is possible. The young of first litters have an advantage over those of

▲ **A spineless hedgehog.** Hedgehogs are born with the spines beneath the skin, to avoid damaging the mother's birth canal.

▷ **The Hedgehog family.** OVERLEAF The European hedgehog has litters of usually 4–7 young. At three weeks old the young accompany the mother and at 6–7 weeks they are weaned.

Spines and Curling in Hedgehogs

The most distinctive feature of hedgehogs is their spines. An average adult carries about 5,000, each about 1in (2–3cm) long, with a needle-sharp point. Each creamy white spine usually has a subterminal band of black or brown. Spines are actually modified hair, and along the animal's sides where spines give way to true hair, thin spines or thick stiff hairs can often be found which may show the transition from one to the other. To minimize weight without losing strength, each spine is filled with many small air-filled chambers separated by thin plates. Towards its base, each spine narrows to a thin angled flexible neck and then widens again into a small ball which is embedded in the skin. This arrangement transforms any pressure exerted along the spine (from a blow, or from falling and landing on the spines, for example) into a bending of the thin flexible part rather than driving the base of the spine into the hedgehog's body. Connected to the base of each spine is a small muscle which is used to pull the spine erect. Normally, the muscles are relaxed and the spines laid flat along the back. If threatened, a hedgehog will often not immediately roll up but will first simply erect the spines and wait for the danger to pass. When erected, the spines stick out at a variety of different angles, criss-crossing over one another and supporting each other to create a virtually impenetrable barrier.

Hedgehogs are additionally protected by their ability to curl up into a ball. This is achieved by the presence of a rather larger skin than is necessary to cover the body, beneath which lies a powerful muscle (the *panniculus carnosus*) covering the back. The skin musculature is more strongly developed

around its edges than at the center (where it forms a circular band, the *orbicularis* muscle) and is only very loosely connected to the body beneath. When the *orbicularis* contracts, it acts like the drawstring around the opening of a bag, forcing the contents deeper into the bag as the string is drawn tighter. When a hedgehog starts to curl up, two small muscles first pull the skin and underlying circular muscle forward over the head and down over the rump. Then the circular *orbicularis* muscle contracts, the head and hindquarters are forced together, and the spine-covered skin of the back and sides is drawn tightly over the unprotected underparts. So effective is this that on a fully curled hedgehog the spines that formerly covered its flanks and the top of the head are brought together to block the small hole (smaller than the width of a finger) which corresponds to the now-closed opening of the bag. As the skin is pulled tightly over the body, the small muscles which erect the spines are automatically stretched, and the spines erected, so that the tighter the hedgehog curls the spinier it becomes.

the second, in an additional 12–13 weeks preparation for winter and hibernation. The young of a second litter have only a month or two (when food supplies are already dwindling) in which to build up a store of fat. Up to 75 percent of the animals born in a summer may die due to an inability to prepare for winter.

The Greater moonrat is probably nocturnal, resting during the day among the roots of trees, under logs, or in empty holes. It is usually found near water. Both the Lesser moonrat and the shrew-hedgehog are also nocturnal.

Long-eared hedgehogs and desert hedgehogs both dig and live in burrows. These are 16–20in (40–50cm) deep and each is occupied by a single individual throughout the year (except when females have their young with them). This restriction to a single nest-site suggests that they may be territorial.

Woodland hedgehogs do not burrow but usually build nests of grass and dead leaves in tangled undergrowth. Such nests can be built quickly (compared to digging a burrow), and a single individual may occupy a given nest for only a few days and then move on and either build a new nest or find an abandoned one. For this reason, in open habitats (the only ones that have been studied) the home range of the Western European hedgehog is large for its bodyweight—50–87 acres (20–35ha) for males and 22–37 acres (9–15ha) for females. The males move further and faster than females—up to 1.9mi (3km) per night versus 0.6mi (1km) per night—probably because they need to look for females as well as for food.

All hedgehogs are capable of undergoing periods of dormancy (hibernation) during which their body temperature is allowed to drop to a level close to that of the surrounding air (heterothermy). This reduces the hedgehog's energy needs to a very low level (oxygen requirement declines from about 550ml/kg/h to about 10ml/kg/h) and allows it to survive periods of up to several months when food is scarce. Tropical hedgehogs do not hibernate, since food availability is not seasonal, but the two desert genera and the more temperate species usually hibernate during the winter (in northern Europe, October or November until March or April). Hibernation is dictated by the conditions and is not a species trait—tropical hedgehogs will hibernate if exposed to cold and low food levels, while European hedgehogs do not hibernate if food is available throughout the year. Hedgehogs intro-

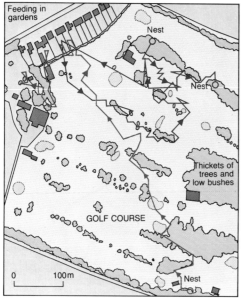

▲ **Hedgehogs and food bowls.** TOP Many people in Europe put out bowls of food in their garden for hedgehogs to visit at night. The animals do so, often with great regularity. This supplementary food may play an important role in achieving the weight needed to survive hibernation. Householders assume that "their" hedgehogs nest nearby and travel no further to reach the food than necessary. In fact, the animals may nest several hundred yards away, and although they move their daytime resting site frequently in summer, they make no attempt to live nearer to regular sources of supplementary food. Nor do they necessarily visit food bowls every night, even if available. Not all hedgehogs that could do so actually visit the food bowls. All this suggests that provision of large amounts of supplementary food does not significantly distort hedgehog behavior. One male (BLUE) was observed to travel over a 0.6mi (1km) round trip each night from its golf-course nest to a series of gardens to feed. It was blind. That it could find its way regularly and so easily indicates that sight was not a crucial sense. A female (RED) was tracked for 5¼ hours, during which she traveled 0.9mi (1.4km), foraging extensively both on the golf course and in the gardens.

duced into New Zealand from Europe hibernate only for very short periods during the southern winter or may not hibernate at all in the warmer areas.

Small supplies of energy are required to keep the body "ticking over" during hibernation and to provide the boost needed to bring the body temperature back up to normal when waking up. Most hibernators do not "sleep" continuously but will arouse periodically, once every two weeks for instance, stay awake for a day or so and then go back into hibernation again. The source of this energy is fat laid down during the summer. Thus European hedgehogs may almost double their weight during the summertime, mostly by laying down a thick layer of fat. Besides providing an energy store, the fat acts as an insulating layer. A specially built, well-insulated hibernation nest also helps to keep the animal warm, even when the external temperature is below freezing point.

Being largely solitary animals, hedgehogs and moonrats do not need an elaborate communication system. Visual signals are apparently absent and, although their hearing is acute, auditory signals are not widely used. Hedgehogs make snuffling and snorting noises while courting, and may hiss when angry or upset. Young hedgehogs separated from their mother make a twittering whistle. Probably the most important mode of communication is by odor. All hedgehogs and moonrats have a well-developed sense of smell and all appear to use odors in one way or another to obtain information about other members of their species. All also undoubtedly find their food largely by sense of smell.

Little is known about the moonrats. Both the Greater and Lesser moonrats have well-developed anal scent glands whose secretions smell to humans like rotten garlic or onions, noticeable from several feet. Captive animals use these glands to scent mark around the entrance to their nests. Hedgehogs also have anal scent glands, but they are not well developed and are not used in any overt way to leave marks. They do, however, leave trails of scent behind them as they walk along—probably just a generalized body scent, although it may contain information about the sex of the animal. Male hedgehogs have been observed to cross such a trail left by a female and immediately turn and follow it for 165ft (50m) or more until catching up with her and initiating courtship.

An unusual behavior of hedgehogs is self-anointing. The hedgehog suddenly pro-

duces copious foamy saliva which it smears all over the spines on its back and flanks. One opinion is that this behavior is elicited by strong-tasting substances—in experiments, it is elicited by cigarette ends, bookbinder's glue, toadskin, leather, creosote and cat food. The function of self-anointing is unknown but suggestions include: 1) it may produce strong odors which act as a sexual attractant; 2) it may reduce parasites on the skin; 3) it may be an attempt to clean the spines; 4) it may make the spines distasteful and thus deter predators.

Unlike the shy moonrats, hedgehogs rely on their spines for protection and so wander where there is no protective cover; if disturbed, most hedgehogs simply erect their spines and freeze until the disturbing factor has gone. Throughout Europe, the hedgehog has capitalized on an amicable relationship with people, and colonized urban areas. Gardens are a good habitat for a hedgehog, providing a mosaic of foraging places—lawns, flower beds, vegetable patches, and compost heaps, together with places in which to nest—hedges, rubbish or junk piles, or under garden sheds.

Hedgehogs play a small role in controlling insect pests. They carry large numbers of parasites among their spines, particularly fleas, ticks and ringworm (a fungus), but these all tend to be species which specialize on hedgehogs and are not easily transmitted to man or other animals. Throughout Europe, large numbers of hedgehogs are killed on the roads every year, but there is no evidence that this adversely affects their population size.

▲ **Hedgehog and hen's egg.** This European hedgehog seems to be making a not particularly urgent assault on a hen's egg. They do take birds' eggs and young when available.

◄ **Self-anointing.** This European hedgehog is coating its spines with saliva; this is flicked onto them by its long tongue, a strange, unexplained piece of behavior.

Hedgehogs figure prominently in folklore: over 2,000 years ago, the Roman author Pliny recorded that hedgehogs carry fruit impaled on their spines rather than in their mouths, and this story has been handed down through the ages. The Chinese tell the same tale. Undoubtedly, the spines of hedgehogs do occasionally catch and pick up things (usually dead leaves or twigs) and it is possible to impale soft fruit such as apples or grapes on the spines. However, European hedgehogs usually eat their food where they find it and do not normally carry it off somewhere else. Nor, in fact, would it be easy for them either to impale the fruit themselves or to remove it once it was attached. Other common folk tales are that hedgehogs suck milk from sleeping cows (possible, but unlikely—they may lap up milk that has oozed from a full udder), and that they are immune to snake bites (they may have some resistance, but in most cases a snake striking at the spine-covered back is

more likely to hurt itself than the hedgehog).

Future prospects are mixed for the hedgehog family. Those species which have formed benign relationships with man are not under any threat. Among the others, the Mindanao moonrat is already very rare and may be threatened with extinction because of forest clearance in the Philippines. The Hainan moonrat may be similarly affected but no reports on its status have been made since it was first discovered in 1959. The other moonrat species have much less restricted ranges but all live in forested areas in countries where increasing population and economic pressures have resulted in clearing the jungle for lumber and to provide agricultural land. As their habitat disappears, all three species of moonrat are likely to become rarer. The tropical hedgehogs may soon be similarly affected, but at the moment no hedgehog species is considered to be in danger of extinction.

AW

SHREWS

Family: Soricidae
Two hundred and forty-six species in 22 genera.
Distribution: Eurasia, Africa, North America, northern South America.

Habitat: forest, woodland, grassland, desert; terrestrial, but some species partially aquatic.

Size: head-to-tail length from 1.3–2.0in (3.5–4.8cm) in the Pygmy white-toothed shrew, the smallest living terrestrial mammal, to 10.5–11.5in (26.5–29cm) in the African forest shrew; weight from 0.07oz (2g) in the Pygmy white-toothed shrew to 1.2oz (35g) in the African forest shrew.

Gestation: 13–24 days.

Longevity: probably 12–18 months.

▶ **Refection.** Some shrews, like this Eurasian pygmy shrew, obtain certain nutrients by licking the rectum, which during the process projects from the anus. It is thought that some nutrients that would be lost in normal digestion are obtained in this way.

▼ **The smallest living terrestrial mammal** is the Pygmy white-toothed shrew. Its large ears are prominent here.

"It is a ravening beast, feigning itself gentle and tame, but being touched it biteth deep, and poisoneth deadly. It beareth a cruel mind, desiring to hurt anything, neither is there any creature it loveth." So wrote Edward Topsell of the European common shrew in his *History of Four-footed Beasts* published in 1607. His characterization highlights the curiously ironical place of shrews in popular folklore. There can be few mammal groups which are less of an imposition on man yet few which have been attributed with such an unfavorable disposition—the words "shrewd," "shrewish" and "shrew" were coined originally to describe a rascally or villainous character, although their meaning has changed somewhat over the centuries. Shrews have been seen as poisoners of horses, scavengers of raven flesh, a cause of lameness in livestock, a certain cure (when burned, powdered and mingled with goose grease) for swelling and as talismans against their own and other evils.

In reality, shrews are small, secretive mammals superficially rather mouse-like but with characteristically long, pointed noses. They are typically terrestrial, foraging in and under the litter in woods, and the vegetation mat beneath herbage. Some, however, are aquatic. Ecologically, they are important in breaking down animal tissue and returning raw materials to the soil. The eyes are small, sometimes hidden in the fur, and vision appears to be poor. Hearing and smell, however, are acute. Even so, the external ears are reduced and difficult to discern in some species. The foot is not specialized except in the species which regularly enter water. The Tibetan water shrew is the only species with webbed feet. Other "aquatic" species, like the European water shrew, have feet, toes, fingers and tail fringed with stiff hairs. These hairs increase the surface area, aid in propulsion and trap air bubbles so the shrew can "run" on the surface of the water. In most genera, the genital and urinary systems have a common external opening, but in long-tailed shrews the openings are separate. In mouse-shrews an intermediate situation exists.

The first set of teeth are shed or resorbed during embryonic development so that shrews are born with their final set. One cause of death, at least in the European common shrew, is starvation due to wearing down of the teeth. The fact that teeth are not replaced makes tooth wear a useful index of age. Analyses of tooth wear in the American short-tailed shrew, water shrew and the European common shrew, water shrew and pygmy shrew have shown that there are usually two generations present during the summer and one during the winter.

A skeletal feature unique to shrews and found only in the Armored shrew, an African species, is the possession of interlocking lateral, dorsal and ventral spines on the vertebrae. Along with the large number of facets for articulation, the spines create an exceptionally sturdy vertebral column. There are reliable reports of the Armored shrew surviving the pressure of a full-grown man standing on it.

Although they mainly use touch, shrews do communicate vocally. The most conspicuous vocalizations are the characteristically high-pitched screams and twitterings used in disputes with members of their own species. Shrews are habitually solitary and many species defend feeding territories from which they oust intruders. There is some evidence in the European common shrew that the pitch and intensity of these vocalizations transmit information about the competitive ability of residents and intruders, and help in settling disputes quickly and without injury. In addition, some species, at least of the genera *Sorex* and *Blarina*, may use ultrasound, which seems to be generated in the larynx and could provide a crude means of echolocation.

Shrews are widely distributed geographically, but genera vary enormously in their distribution and ecology. Some genera, like *Sorex*, *Neomys*, *Blarina*, *Cryptotis* and *Suncus*, are distributed on a continental scale, while others, like *Podihik*, *Anourosorex*, *Feroculus* and *Diplomesodon*, are so restricted that they occur only on particular islands or in certain, often unique, mainland habitats. Ten genera comprise only a single species each and the Sri Lanka shrew and the African forest shrew are known from only two and three specimens respectively.

While shrews are known from the Eocene (54 million years ago) onwards, knowledge of the evolutionary lineages of present forms is extremely thin. Part of the reason is undoubtedly the small size of the bones and teeth, which are easily overlooked. Shrews are found from the Oligocene (38 million years ago) onwards in North America, from the Eocene (54 million years ago) onwards in Europe, from the Pliocene (7 million years ago) onwards in Asia, and from the Miocene (26 million years ago) onwards in Africa. The best records seem to be for the existing European species. The European pygmy shrew has the oldest fossil record, extending back to the beginning of the Pleistocene (2 million years ago). At least two main lines of shrews died out in Europe towards the end of this period, possibly as a result of the arrival of more *Crocidura* species from North Africa and Asia. The presence of five co-existing species of *Sorex* in Finland suggests that, in the absence of *Crocidura*, abundance and diversity of shrews may be greater.

At the end of the Pliocene, at least four species of shrew were present in western Europe and probably also in the British Isles: the European pygmy shrew, which has remained virtually unchanged to the present day, *Sorex magaritodon*, *S. runtonensis* and *S. kennardi*. From the fossil evidence, it seems that the White-toothed or Musk shrew has only recently invaded from the east, as has the Lesser white-toothed shrew from the eastern Mediterranean region. An intriguing subspecies of the latter, the Scilly shrew, is restricted in its distribution to the Scilly Isles. Studies suggest that the Scilly landmass was close to a tongue of ice derived from the Irish and Welsh ice sheets during the last glacial maximum. One possibility is that it was introduced by Iron-age or earlier traders from France and northern Spain who came to Cornwall in search of the tin that was mined there.

In general, it appears that the gross form of shrews has changed very little since the early Tertiary. The only overall change seems to have been a slight reduction in size. The European common shrew and the Pygmy shrew, for instance, were slightly larger in the Pleistocene than they are today. In this sense, shrews represent a primitive stage in mammalian evolution. However, the existing species exhibit many non-primitive specializations and so cannot

▲ **A shrew's delight** is a long, juicy earthworm. Their reputation for voracity stems from their small size and active life with consequent high metabolic rate.

▶ **Plastered with air bubbles,** a European water shrew forages underwater. These shrews feed on small fishes, aquatic invertebrates and small frogs.

The 22 Genera of Shrews

Genus *Sorex*
Fifty-two species in N Eurasia, N America, including **American water shrew** (*S. palustris*), **European common shrew** (*S. araneus*), **European pygmy shrew** (*S. minutus*), **Masked shrew** (*S. cinereus*), **Trowbridge's shrew** (*S. trowbridgii*); tundra, grassland, woodland.

Genus *Microsorex*
Two species: **American pygmy shrews**; N America; forest.

Genus *Soriculus*
Nine species: **mountain shrews**; Himalayas, China; montane forest.

Genus *Neomys*
Three species in N Eurasia, including **Eurasian water shrew** (*N. fodiens*); forest, woodland, grassland, streams, marshes.

Genus *Blarina*
Three species in eastern N America, including **American short-tailed shrew** (*B. brevicauda*); forest grassland.

Genus *Blarinella*
One species: **Chinese short-tailed shrew** (*B. quadraticauda*); S China; montane forest.

Genus *Cryptotis*
Thirteen species in E USA, Ecuador, Surinam, including **Lesser short-tailed shrew** (*C. parva*); forest, grassland.

Genus *Notiosorex*
Two species in SW USA and Mexico, including **Desert shrew** (*N. crawfordi*); semidesert scrub, montane.

Genus *Megasorex*
One species: **Giant Mexican shrew** (*M. gigas*); SW Mexico; forest.

Genus *Crocidura*
One hundred and seventeen species in Eurasia and Africa, including **African forest shrew** (*C. odorata*); forest to semidesert.

Genus *Suncus*
Fifteen species in Africa, including **Pygmy white-toothed shrew** (*S. etruscus*); forest, scrub, savanna.

Genus *Podihik*
(considered by some to be synonymous with *Suncus*) One species: **Sri Lanka shrew** (*P. kura*); north-central Sri Lanka; possibly aquatic.

Genus *Feroculus*
One species: **Kelaart's long-clawed shrew** (*F. feroculus*); Sri Lanka; montane forest.

Genus *Solisorex*
One species: **Pearson's long-clawed shrew** (*S. pearsoni*); Sri Lanka; montane.

Genus *Paracrocidura*
One species: *P. schoutedeni*; Cameroun.

Genus *Sylvisorex*
Seven species: Africa; forest, grassland.

Genus *Myosorex*
Ten species: **mouse shrews**; C and S Africa; forest.

Genus *Diplomesodon*
One species: **Piebald shrew** (*D. pulchellum*); Russian Turkestan; desert.

Genus *Anourosorex*
One species: **mole-shrew** (*A. squamipes*); S China to N Thailand, Taiwan; montane, forest.

Genus *Chimarrogale*
Three species: **oriental water shrews**; E Asia; montane streams.

Genus *Nectogale*
One species: **Tibetan water shrew** (*N. elegans*); Sikkim to Shenshi; montane streams.

Genus *Scutisorex*
One species: **Armored shrew** (*S. somereni*); C Africa; forest.

themselves be regarded as primitive mammals.

A feature, at least of the European common shrew, which has interesting evolutionary implications is variations in the chromosome complement. Mammalian cells usually have a constant number of chromosomes which are typical of the species. In the European common shrew the number varies from 21–27 in males and 20–25 in females, due to the fusion of certain small chromosomes (so-called Robertsonian chromosome mutations). There are also multiple sex chromosomes: males are generally XYY and females, as in other mammals, XX. This variation makes possible 27 different chromosomal arrangements of which 19 have so far been found. While variation in chromosome numbers is known in invertebrates, the European common shrew is the first example among mammals.

Shrews are very active and consume large amounts of food for their size. Studies of several species have shown that their metabolic rate is higher than that of rodents of comparable size. Shrews cope with increased demands for food and water primarily by living in habitats where these are abundant. However, their generally small size enables them to utilize thermally protected microhabitats. At least one species, the Desert shrew, has mastered the physiological problems of living in a hot, arid climate by lowering its metabolic rate in a similar way to other desert-dwelling mammals. Several species, mainly from the subfamily Crocidurinae, but including the Desert shrew, are capable of lowering their body temperature in response to food deprivation. However, similar adaptations are found in "higher" placental mammals and any differences appear to be in degree rather than in kind—a function of the shrews' small size rather than their "primitive" place in the mammal hierarchy. Interestingly, the subfamily Soricinae ("hot shrews") have higher metabolic rates than subfamily Crocidurinae ("cold shrews"). This difference may be related to their different origins, northern and tropical respectively. Digestion in shrews is fairly rapid and the gut may be emptied in three hours. Since they carry available reserves for only an hour or two, frequent feeding is imperative. For this reason, shrews are active throughout the day and night. Adult specimens of the European common shrew are often encountered dead in the open during the fall. These are generally old individuals that have bred the previous summer and whose teeth are worn.

The apparent cause of death is starvation, and the carcasses remain uneaten owing to the presence (in common with other species) of skin glands whose secretion renders shrews unpalatable to most carnivores.

Those species whose foraging behavior and dietary habits have been studied have turned out to be opportunists with little specialization. They are mainly insectivorous and carnivorous (also taking carrion), but some also eat seeds, nuts and other plant material. The mode of foraging used by shrews depends on their habits. They may use runways, particularly those created by voles or other small mammals, or hunt on the vegetation surface. The direction taken during foraging appears to be arbitrary, and shrews tend to scurry about haphazardly until they come across prey. Shrews can detect a very wide size range of prey, from 4in earthworms to $\frac{1}{16}-\frac{1}{8}$in nematodes. Even small mites and the animal's own external parasites are not exempt. When prey are buried (as are some insect larvae and pupae), foraging involves digging or furrowing. Shrews excavate holes using the nose and forefeet and then lift the head with prey seized in the jaws. Where the ground is soft, the nose may be pushed into it and the body propelled forward by the hindfeet.

The bite of some shrews is venomous. The salivary glands of the American short-tailed shrew, for instance, produce enough poison to kill by intravenous injection about 200 mice. The poison acts to kill or paralyze before ingestion, and may be particularly important in helping to subdue large prey like fish and newts which water shrews are known to take.

Some shrew species, and possibly all, show refection. In the European common shrew the animal curls up and begins to lick the anus, sometimes gripping the hindlimbs with the forefeet to maintain position. After a few seconds, abdominal contractions cause the rectum to extrude and the end is then nibbled and licked for some minutes before being withdrawn. It appears that refection does not start until the intestine is free of feces. If the shrew is killed, the stomach and first few inches of the intestine can be seen to be filled with a milky fluid containing fat globules and partially digested food. It may be that shrews obtain trace elements and vitamins B and K in this way. Food-caching is known to occur in the European common shrew, the European water shrew and the American short-tailed shrew, and appears to be a means of securing short-term food supplies when competition is fierce or food is temporarily very abundant.

From the species studied, ovulation in shrews appears to be induced by copulation and females are receptive for only a matter of hours during each cycle. The European common shrew does not usually breed until the year after birth and only females have been recorded breeding in their first year. This is more common when the population density is high (up to 35 percent of individuals) than when it is low (around 2 percent of individuals). It is also common generally in the American short-tailed shrew. The breeding season is usually from March to November in northern temperate species, but throughout the year in the Tropics. The number of litters varies between one and 10 a year and the newborn are naked and blind. In the European common shrew some females mate one day after birth and are pregnant and lactating at the same time, suggesting that lactation and gestation are of similar duration (otherwise the second litter might be born before the first is weaned). The mammary glands begin to regress some days before the birth of the second litter. The milk supply is therefore adjusted to demand. The main determinant of weaning appears to be food-shortage. Pregnancy and suckling last for 13–19 days in the European common shrew and up to 21–24 days in the European water shrew. A peculiar feature of parent/offspring relationships in the genera *Crocidura* and *Suncus* is so-called "caravanning." When mature enough to leave the nest, the young form a line. Each animal grips the rump of the one in front and the foremost grips that of the mother. The grip is quite tenacious and the whole caravan can be lifted off the ground intact by picking up the mother.

Observations of mating in the European common shrew have shown that the male tends to approach the female warily, usually in a jerky series of approaches and retreats.

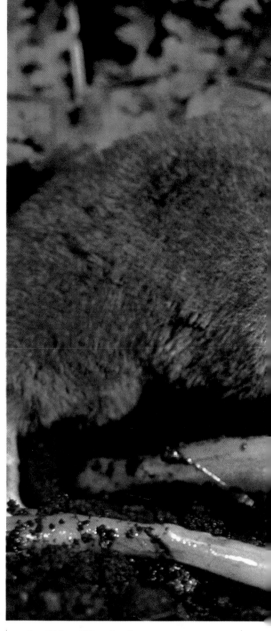

▲ **An efficient killer,** thanks to its venomous salivary glands, this American short-tailed shrew is killing a frog.

▶ **Territorial confrontation** between two American short-tailed shrews. This species, like several of the shrews, digs tunnel systems which form the basis of defended territories.

▼ **Caravanning in shrews.** Young shrews get a guided tour of their terrain by holding onto each other, led by their mother. They continue to hang on even if the mother is picked up.

Non-receptive females are very aggressive and emit high-pitched vocalizations. On the final approach, the male sniffs and licks the female's genitals and sometimes seizes the female and drags her into cover. He may attempt mating before the female goes into the mating posture and the penis is sometimes extruded on unsuccessful mounting attempts. When the female lifts her hindquarters, the male seizes the scruff of her neck and copulates. Penetration normally lasts for about 10 seconds.

Several species dig tunnel systems and these may be the focal point of defended territories. The American short-tailed shrew, the Lesser short-tailed shrew, the European common shrew and the European water shrew have been observed digging. Observations in captivity of the Smoky shrew, the Masked shrew, Trowbridge's shrew and the European pygmy shrew suggest that they do not burrow. In the European water shrew, the tunnel system is important in squeezing water from the fur and it also seems to be important in maintaining fur condition in the European common shrew. In captivity, European common shrews often cache food in their tunnels. Tunnel systems may also be important in avoiding predators and usually have more than one entrance/exit. Nests of grass and other plant material are usually built in a chamber off the tunnel system and shrews spend most of their sleeping and resting time there.

In the European common shrew, intruders onto feeding territories are attacked and driven off, and experiments have shown that the resident has a strong advantage. However, the resident advantage is greater when intruders have lower fighting ability and when food availability is low. When there is little food, the cost of intrusion to the resident is likely to be high and residents fight more vigorously. When two animals are tricked, in an experiment, into thinking they are both owners of a territory, the winner is the one who experiences the lower food availability. Winner and loser can therefore be alternated according to feeding experience. Although all shrew species appear to be solitary except at mating, there is evidence that the European water shrew may sometimes move about in small groups, probably families, and there is at least one account of an apparent mass migration by this species involving many hundreds of animals. The American least shrew is known to be colonial and there are reports of individuals cooperating in the digging of tunnels.   CJB

GOLDEN MOLES

Family: Chrysochloridae
Eighteen species in 7 genera.
Distribution: Africa south of the Sahara.

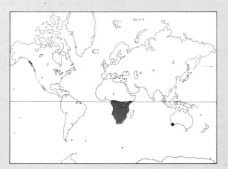

Size: ranges from head-body length 2.7–3.3in (70–85mm) in Grant's desert golden mole to head-body length 7.8–9in (198–235mm) in the Giant golden mole.

Habitat: almost exclusively burrowing in grassveld forest, river-banks, swampy areas, mountains, desert and semidesert.

Gestation and longevity: unknown.

Genus *Chrysospalax*
Two species, including **Giant golden mole** (*C. trevelyani*) ℝ. Distribution: forests in E Cape Province, Transkei, Ciskei. Coat: dark reddish brown, long, coarse and less glossy than other genera.

Genus *Cryptochloris*
Two species: **De Winton's golden mole** (*C. wintoni*), with pale fawn fur; **Van Zyl's golden mole** (*C. zyli*), with darker brown fur. Distribution: sandy arid regions in SW Cape and Little Namaqualand.

Genus *Chrysochloris*
Three species, including **Stuhlmann's golden mole** (*C. stuhlmanni*). Distribution: mountains in C and E Africa. Coat: dark gray-brown, more golden on belly.

Genus *Eremitalpa*
Grant's desert golden mole (*E. granti*). Distribution: sandy desert and semidesert of SW Cape, Little Namaqualand and Namib desert. Coat: silky grayish yellow, seasonally variable length.

Genus *Amblysomus*
Four species, including **Hottentot golden mole** (*A. hottentotus*). Distribution: S and E Cape, Natal, Swaziland, N and E Orange Free State, SE and E Transvaal. Coat: dark brown to rich reddish brown, more golden on belly.

Genus *Chlorotalpa*
Five species, including **Sclater's golden mole** (*C. sclateri*). Distribution: Cameroun to Cape Province.

Genus *Calcochloris*
Yellow golden mole (*C. obtusirostris*). Distribution: Zululand to Mozambique and SE Zimbabwe.

ℝ Rare.

THE iridescent sheen of coppery green, blue, purple or bronze on the fur of most golden moles and the silvery yellow fur of Grant's desert golden mole probably gave the family its common name. Golden moles are known as far back as the Lower Miocene (about 25 million years ago); climatic modifications may be responsible for their present discontinuous distribution, but they have special adaptations for a burrowing mode of life in a wide geographic range of terrestrial habitats.

Golden moles are solitary burrowing insectivores with compact streamlined bodies, short limbs and no visible tail. The backward-set fur is moisture repellent, remaining sleek and dry in muddy situations, and a dense woolly undercoat provides insulation. The skin is thick and tough, particularly on the head. The eyes have been almost lost and are covered with hairy skin; the ear openings are covered by fur and the nostrils are protected by a leathery pad which assists with soil excavations. A muscular head and shoulders push and pack the soil and the strong forelimbs are equipped with digging claws. Of the four claws, the second and third are elongated, and the third claw is extremely powerful. The first and fourth are usually rudimentary, but the sand burrowers *Crysochloris* and *Eremitalpa* have the first claw almost as long as the second, and *Eremitalpa* also has a well-developed fourth claw.

The sense of touch in golden moles is mainly used for detecting food, but smell is used during occasional exploratory forages on the surface in search of food, new burrow systems, or females for breeding. The ear ossicles are disproportionately large, giving great sensitivity to vibrations, which trigger rapid locomotion unerringly towards an open burrow entrance when on the surface or a bolt-hole when underground. Golden moles have an ability to orientate and when parts of burrow systems are damaged by flooding or other mechanical means they are joined together again by new tunnels constructed in the same places, linking up with the new burrow entrances.

Golden moles burrow just beneath the surface, forming soil ridges; desert-dwelling species "swim" through the sand just below the surface leaving U-shaped ridges. Stuhlmann's golden mole makes shallow burrows in sphagnum overlying peaty, swampy areas, or in rich humus and among dense roots. Similar damp mossy, peaty areas occur for the Hottentot golden moles in the Drakensberg mountains. Giant golden moles also use swampy areas and

▶ **A golden mole,** foraging on the surface. Golden moles spend more time burrowing in search of food than in any other activity. Food, consisting mainly of earthworms, insect larvae, slugs, snails, crickets and spiders, is eaten in the burrows immediately or carried along tunnels some distance from the site of capture before being eaten, but it is not cached. Desert golden moles seize legless lizards on the surface and drag them into the sand before eating them. Golden moles themselves are prey to snakes, owls and other birds of prey, otters, genets, mongooses and jackals.

▼ **Burrowing in the Hottentot golden mole.** A burrow system may extend to 37in (95cm) in depth and contain 800ft (240m) of burrows. Construction and occupation is influenced mainly by rainfall. Surface foraging for soil invertebrates amounts to 72 percent of total activity in the summer when rainfall is high. With hindfeet braced hard against tunnel walls, the mole loosens the soil with alternate or synchronized forward and downward pick-like strokes of the front claws. Displaced soil is tightly packed against the burrow walls and pushed up with the snout, head and shoulders to form ridges on the surface. To produce mole-hills, loose soil in deep tunnels is kicked behind with the hindfeet, swept into heaps with the snout, pushed along the tunnel and out onto the surface with thrusts of the head and shoulders. The burrow entrance is sealed with a compacted soil plug. Walls of the cylindrical burrows—1.5–2.4in (4–6cm) in diameter—are smoothed and compacted by the mole "waddling" back and forth with back arched against the ceiling, head down, stamping the floor with its hindfeet and snout. Bolt-holes are used by the moles when alarmed or as sleeping sites. While they are small, young golden moles live in a spherical nest of grass or leaves. The nest chamber may be a modified bolt-hole or sleeping site.

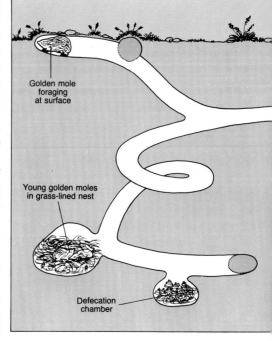

Golden mole foraging at surface

Young golden moles in grass-lined nest

Defecation chamber

scrutiny of tunnel walls by smell. Fighting occurs between individuals of the same sex and sometimes between male and female. Hottentot golden moles tolerate herbivorous mole-rats in the same burrow systems, and in the Drakensberg mountains golden mole burrows open into burrows of the ice-rat.

Courtship in Hottentot golden moles involves much chirruping vocalization, head-bobbing and foot stamping in the male, and grasshopper-like rasping and prolonged squeals with mouth wide open in the female. Both sexes have a single external urogenital opening. There appears to be no distinct breeding season. Testes are abdominal and sexually mature males may have enlarged or regressed testes throughout the year. Whether this is cyclic or what triggers breeding condition is not known. Females have two teats on the abdomen and two in the groin region. Pregnancy, lactation and the birth of 1–3 naked young—with a head-body length 1.9in (47mm); weight 0.16oz (4.5g)—also occurs throughout the year. Eviction from the maternal burrow system occurs when the young moles are 1.2–1.6oz (35–45g) in weight.

Species of *Amblysomus* inhabit areas where soil temperatures range from 33°F (0.8°C) in the Drakensberg mountains to 90°F (32°C) on the Natal coast. They are physiologically adapted to withstand unfavorable environmental conditions of extremes of temperature and scarcity of food. Although thermoregulation is poor because of low body temperature 92°F (33.5°C), a metabolic rate of 2 percent higher than expected for their size (probably due to their carnivorous diet), and a high rate of heat loss from the body at the thermoneutral range of 73–91°F (23–33°C), *Amblysomus* can vary their body temperature between 80° and 99.5°F (27° and 37.5°C) in normal situations, or reduce it to that of their surroundings and become torpid, thereby conserving energy. At higher altitudes, *Amblysomus* tend to be heavier and have lower metabolic rates than those nearer the coast.

The versatility of body mass and metabolism, and a thermoneutral range wider than is usual for small mammals, may largely account for the ability of the golden moles to survive in a wide climatic range of habitats, hence their long evolutionary history. But, sadly, the Giant golden mole, which has a more restricted distribution, is now in grave danger of extinction. Its forest range is split into isolated localities, with large parts in the Transkei and Ciskei being destroyed by domestic livestock or converted for economic development.　　MAK

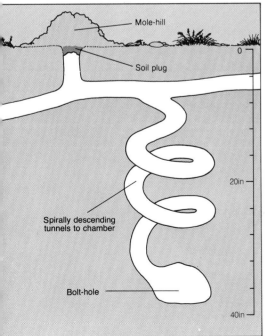

concentrate their burrows round the bases of bushes and trees. All except desert moles also excavate deeper burrows in which soil is deposited on the surface as molehills or in disused tunnels. This usually occurs when the surface becomes hard and dry. Hottentot golden moles may burrow 41ft (72m) on average every 24 hours. Average sustained burrowing lasts about 44 minutes, separated by inactive periods lasting about 2.6 hours. Grant's desert golden mole may leave 3mi (4.8km) of surface tracks in one night.

Food supply influences territorial behavior. Hottentot golden mole burrow systems are more numerous in the summer when food is more abundant, and a certain amount of home range overlap is tolerated. Burrow systems are larger and more aggressively defended in less fertile areas. A neighboring burrow system may be taken over by an individual as an extension of its home range. Occupancy is detected by

MOLES AND DESMANS

Habitat: Moles largely subterranean, usually under forests and grasslands but also under heaths. Desmans aquatic in lakes and rivers. Shrew moles construct true tunnels but forage in the litter layer.

Size: ranges from head-body length 1–3in (24–75mm), tail length 1–3in (24–75mm), weight under 0.4oz (12g) in the shrew moles to head-body length 7–8.5in (180–215mm), tail length 6.5–8.5in (170–215mm), weight about 19.5oz (550g) in the Russian desman.

Coat: desman fur is two-layered with short, dense waterproof underfur and oily guard hairs; stiff hairs enlarge the paws and tail for swimming. Moles have short fur of uniform length which will lie in any direction during tunneling. Shrew moles have guard hairs and underfur directed backwards. Moles are usually uniformly brownish black or gray, desmans brown or reddish on the back, merging to gray below.

Gestation: unknown in shrew moles (but greater than 15 days) and desmans; 30 days in European and 42 days in Eastern American mole.

Longevity: largely unknown. Up to 3 years in European and 4–5 years in Hairy-tailed mole.

Species include: **European mole** (*Talpa europaea*), **Mediterranean mole** (*Talpa caeca*), **Pyrenean desman** (*Galemys pyrenaicus*) v, **Russian desman** (*Desmana moschata*) v, **Star-nosed mole** (*Condylura cristata*), **Townsend mole** (*Scapanus townsendi*).

v Vulnerable.

IN 1702 William of Orange, the King of England and Scotland, was out riding when his horse tripped on a mole-hill, throwing and killing its regal rider. This was to the delight of the Jacobites who henceforth drank a toast: "The little gentleman in black velvet."

Most people in Europe and North America have seen mole-hills, but very few have seen the gentleman in question or his relatives. Their subterranean way of life makes moles very difficult to study and it is only in the last three decades that detailed information on their biology has been gathered. The other major group within the family, the desmans, have a way of life as different as it is possible to imagine—they are aquatic. Again, little is known about many aspects of their biology, due to their relative inaccessibility in the mountain streams of the Pyrenees and in the vastness of Russia.

Moles and desmans have elongated and cylindrical bodies. The muzzle is long, tubular and naked, apart from sensory whiskers. It is highly mobile and extends beyond the lower lip. In the Star-nosed mole the nose is divided at the end into a naked fringe of 22 mobile and fleshy tentacles. The penis is directed to the rear and there is no scrotum.

The eyes are minute but structurally complete. They are hidden within the coat and in some species, including the Mediterranean mole, they are covered by skin. The eyes are sensitive to changes in light level but provide little visual acuity. There are no external ears except in the Asiatic shrew-moles. Both moles and desmans rely to a

Territorial Behavior in the European Mole

European moles spend almost their whole lives underground, in their tunnels, which makes detailed study of their social behavior very difficult. However recent radio-tracking studies have shown that although several neighboring moles each inhabit their own tunnel systems, territories do overlap to a small extent. It is not known, as yet, whether tunnels in the area of overlap are shared or whether they remain separate, running between each other in the soil column. There is much evidence, however, that moles are well aware of the presence and activities of their neighbors. For example, during any particular activity period, neighbors forage in non-adjacent parts of their territories, avoiding contact. It is a testimony to the efficiency of this system of avoidance that conflict between established neighbors has not been recorded.

When a mole dies, or is trapped and removed from its territory, neighboring animals very quickly detect its absence and invade the vacated area, sometimes within two hours. For example, after several weeks of observation one radio-tagged animal was trapped and removed; within 12 hours a neighboring mole was spending his morning activity period foraging in the vacated territory, and his afternoon shift in his own territory. This continued for several days until a third male invaded the area and forced the second back to his former territorial limits. Clearly, within mole populations not all individuals are equal.

In other cases, a vacated territory may be shared among several neighbors. Such was the case with a group of four moles who occupied neighboring territories until one was removed. Within a matter of hours, the others had enlarged their territories to incorporate the vacated area. These enlarged territories were retained for at least several weeks.

Moles probably advertise their presence and tenure of an area by scent marking. Both sexes possess preputial glands which produce a highly odorous secretion that accumulates on the fur of the abdomen and which is deposited on the floor of the tunnels, as well as at latrines. The scent is highly volatile and must be renewed regularly if the mole is to maintain its claim to ownership of the territory. In the absence of scent the territory is quickly invaded.

▲ **Species of moles and desmans.**
(1) European mole (*Talpa europaea*). (2) American shrew-mole (*Neurotrichus gibbsi*). (3) Lesser Japanese shrew-mole (*Urotrichus pilirostris*). (4) Star-nosed mole (*Condylura cristata*). (5) Pyrenean desman (*Galemys pyrenaicus*).

great extent on touch. The muzzle is richly endowed with projections called Eimer's organs, which are probably sensitive to touch. Various parts of the body, including the muzzle and tail, and the legs of desmans, are supplied with sensory whiskers.

Desmans are adapted for swimming. The tail is long, flattened and broadened by a fringe of stiff hairs. The legs and feet are proportionally long and powerful. The toes are webbed, the fingers half-webbed, and both are fringed with stiff hairs. The nostrils and ears are opened and closed by valves. The fur is waterproof. When swimming, the hindlegs provide the main propulsive force.

In moles, the forelimbs are adapted for digging. The hands are turned permanently outwards, like a pair of oars. They are large, almost circular and equipped with five large and strong claws. The teeth are un-

specialized and typical of the Insectivora.

The moles and desmans probably originated in Europe and spread from there to North America and more recently to Asia. Moles are found in North America, Europe and Asia, shrew-moles in North America and Asia and desmans in Europe only. The distribution map is accurate for North America and Europe but grossly incomplete for Asia, where it simply reflects collecting effort. Some species were formerly much more widely distributed, for example fossils of the Russian desman are to be found throughout Europe and in Britain.

Moles dig permanent tunnels and obtain most of their food from soil animals which fall into them. When digging new deep tunnels they brace themselves with their hindfeet and then dig with the forefeet which are alternately thrust into the soil and moved sideways and backwards. Periodically, they dig a vertical shaft to the surface and push up the soil to make the familiar mole-hill. These tunnels range in depth from a few inches to 40in (100cm). Probably 90 percent of the diet is foraged from the permanent tunnels, the rest from casual digging. The diet of moles consists largely of earthworms, beetle and fly larvae and, when available, slugs. The European mole, which consumes 1.4–1.8oz (40–50g) of earthworms per day, stores earthworms with their heads bitten off, near to its nest in October and November.

Desmans obtain nearly all their food from water, particularly aquatic insects such as stone-fly and caddis-fly larvae, fresh water gammarid shrimps and snails. The Russian desman also takes larger prey such as fish and amphibians.

Desmans are largely nocturnal but they often have a short active period during the day. In contrast, most of the moles are active both day and night. Until recently it was thought that European moles always had three active periods per day, alternating with periods of rest in the nest. Recent studies with moles fitted with radio-transmitters reveal a rather more complex picture. In the winter, both males and females show three activity periods, each of about four hours, separated by a rest of about four hours in the nest. At this time they almost always leave the nest at sunrise. Females maintain this pattern for the rest of the year except for a period in summer when they are lactating. Then they return to the nest much more frequently in order to feed their young.

Males are more complex. In spring they start to seek out receptive females and remain away from the nest for days at a time, snatching cat-naps in their tunnels. In the summer they return to their winter routine but in September they display just two activity periods per day.

Details of the life cycle are known only for a few species, in particular the European mole. Little is known about the desmans and shrew-moles. In general, moles have a short breeding season, and produce a single litter of 2–7 young each year. Lactation lasts for about a month. The males take no part in the care of the young, and the young normally breed in the year following their birth.

In Britain, European moles mate in March to May and the young are born in May or June. The time of breeding varies with the latitude: the same species is pregnant in mid-February in northern Italy, in March in southern England and not till May or June in northeast Scotland. This suggests that length of daylight controls breeding, which may seem strange for a subterranean animal. However, moles do come to the surface, for example to collect grass and

other materials for their nests (one nest, near to a licenced hotel, was made entirely of potato chip bags!).

The average litter size in Britain is 3.7 but it can be higher in continental Europe—an average of 5.7 has been reported for Russia. One litter per year is the norm, but there are records of pregnant animals in September in England and in October in Germany. Sperm production lasts for only two months but sufficient spermatozoa may be stored to allow the insemination of females coming into this late or second period of heat.

The young are born in the nest. They are naked at birth, have fur at 14 days and open their eyes at 22 days. Lactation lasts for 4–5 weeks and the young leave the nest weighing 2oz (60g) or more some 35 days after birth.

After leaving the nest, the young leave their mother's territory and move overground to seek an unoccupied area. At this time many of them are killed by predators and by cars. With an average litter size of about four the numbers of animals present in May must be reduced by 66 percent by death or emigration if the population is to remain stable.

Little is known about the population density and social organization of desmans beyond the following snippets. Pyrenean desmans appear to be solitary and to inhabit small permanent home ranges which they

territory sizes in the European mole vary between the sexes, from habitat to habitat, and from season to season. The habitat and sex differences reflect differences in food supply and the greater energy demands of the larger male.

Female territory sizes remain similar throughout the year but in the spring males increase theirs dramatically as they seek out receptive partners.

Normally, moles remain within their territories for their whole lives. However radio-tracking has revealed that during hot, dry weather some moles leave their range and travel as far as 0.6mi (1km) to drink at streams. This necessitates crossing the territories of up to 10 other moles!

The Russian desman is widely trapped for its lustrous fur, and most of the skins in Western museums have come from the fur trade. To increase production the species was introduced to the river Dnepr.

All moles, particularly those in North America and Europe, are regarded as pests by farmers, gardeners and, above all, by golf-course green-keepers! Moles disturb the roots of young plants, causing them to wilt and die, soil from mole hills contaminates silage, and the stones they bring to the surface cause damage to cutting machinery. On the positive side, they have on occasion brought worked flints and Roman tesserae to the surface.

Nowadays, moles are usually controlled by poisoning. In Britain the most widely used is strychnine, but it has the disadvantage of being unacceptably cruel and endangers other animals besides moles: although available only by government permit, a disturbing amount is diverted to killing other forms of "vermin," including birds of prey.

In the past, moles were trapped on a massive scale in Britain, by professional trappers and agricultural workers who sold the skins to be made into breeches, waistcoats and ladies' coats. After World War I the market collapsed due to changes in fashion and imports from Russia. There was a similar trade in mole-skins in North America, particularly from the Townsend mole.

The two extant species of desmans are both endangered species: the Russian desman because of overhunting for its fur, the Pyrenean desman from over-zealous scientific collecting and from habitat destruction, particularly the damming of mountain streams. The formulation of management plans is severely hampered by a lack of knowledge of both species' basic biology.

scent mark with latrines. There is some evidence that Russian desmans are at times nomadic as a result of unpredictable water levels. They may be social, since as many as eight adults have been found together in one burrow.

There is much more information on the moles, although most comes from the European mole. Populations of European moles have a sex ratio of 1 : 1. Unlike those of small rodents, populations appear to be relatively stable.

Most mole species are solitary and territorial, with individuals defending all or the greater part of their home range. The Star-nosed mole is exceptional in that during the winter a male and female may live together. In other species, males and females meet only briefly, to mate.

Population densities vary from species to species and from habitat to habitat. Average numbers per acre are 2–10 for the European mole (5–25 per hectare), 2–5 for the Eastern American mole (5–12 per ha), 2–10 for the Star-nosed mole (5–25 per ha) and 2–11 for the Hairy-tailed mole (5–28 per ha).

Radio-tracking studies have shown that

MLG

EDENTATES

ORDERS: EDENTATA AND PHOLIDOTA
Five families: 14 genera: 36 species.

Anteaters
Family: Myrmecophagidae
Order: Edentata.
Four species in 3 genera.

Sloths
Families: Megalonychidae and Bradypodidae
Order: Edentata.
Five species in 2 genera.

Armadillos
Family: Dasypodidae
Order: Edentata.
Twenty species in 8 genera.

Pangolins
Family: Manidae
Order: Pholidota.
Seven species of the genus *Manis*.

"EDENTATE" means "without teeth," but only the anteaters are strictly toothless: sloths and armadillos have very simple, rootless molars which grow throughout life. In the 18th century, pangolins were also included in the Edentata on the grounds that they lack teeth, but they are now considered to belong to a separate order: the Pholidota. The diet of edentates ranges from an almost exclusive reliance on ants and termites in the anteaters, through a wide range of insects, fungi, tubers and carrion in the armadillos, to plants in the sloths.

By the early Tertiary, 60 million years ago (the beginning of the "Age of Mammals"), the ancestral edentates had already diverged into two quite distinct lines. The first, comprising small, armorless animals of the suborder Palaeanodonta, rapidly became extinct. But the other, the suborder Xenarthra, was on the brink of a spectacular radiation that was later to produce some of the most distinctive and bizarre of all the New World mammals. The four families, 13 genera and 29 species of living edentates are descended from the early xenarthrans and, although highly specialized, they retain many common ancestral features.

The living and recently extinct edentates are distinguished from all other mammals (including the pangolins) by additional articulations between the lumbar vertebrae, which are termed xenarthrales. These bony elements provide lumbar reinforcement for digging, and are especially important for the armadillos. The living edentates also differ from most mammals in having rather simple skulls, with no canines, incisors or premolars, and in having a double posterior vena cava vein (single in other mammals), which returns blood to the heart from the hindquarters of the body. Females have a primitive divided womb only a step removed from the double womb of marsupials, and a common urinary and genital duct, while males have internal testes, and a small penis with no glans.

Despite these unifying characteristics, the extinct edentates differed greatly in size and appearance from their modern relatives and, in terms of numbers of genera, were ten times as diverse. The rise and fall of these early forms is closely linked to the fact that throughout the Tertiary, from 65 million years ago, South America was a huge, isolated island. At the beginning of this epoch, ancestral edentates shared the continent only with early marsupials and other primitive mammals, and flourished in the virtual absence of competition. By the early Oligocene (38 million years ago), three families of giant ground sloths had emerged, with some species growing to the size of modern elephants. In their heyday during the late Miocene, 30 million years later, ground sloths appeared in the West Indies and southern North America, apparently having rafted across the sea barriers as waif immigrants. Four families of armored, armadillo-like edentates were contemporary with the ground sloths for much of the Oligocene. The largest species, *Glyptodon*, achieved a length of 16.5ft (5m) and carried a rigid 10ft (3m) shell on its back, while the related *Doedicurus* had a massive tail with the tip armored like a medieval mace. Although *Glyptodon* and the giant ground sloths survived until historical times—and are spoken of in the legends of the Tehuelche and Araucan Indians of Patagonia—only the smaller tree sloths, anteaters and armadillos persisted to the present day.

The extinct edentates are believed to have been ponderous, unspecialized herbivores that inhabited scrubby savannas. They were probably outcompeted and preyed upon by the new and sophisticated northern invaders. In contrast, the success of the living edentates was due to their occupation of relatively narrow niches, which allowed little space for the less specialized newcomers. The anteaters and leaf-eating sloths, for example, have very specialized diets. To cope with the low energy contents

▶ **Prehistoric edentates.** The edentates produced three major groups: "shelled" forms (Loricata), including the extinct glyptodons and living armadillos; "hairy" forms (Pilosa), including the extinct Giant ground sloth and living tree sloths; and the anteaters (Vermilingua). (1) The Giant ground sloth (*Megatherium*), from the Pleistocene of South America, was up to 20ft (6m) long. (2) *Eomanis waldi*, a small armored pangolin from the Eocene of Germany. (3) *Glyptodon panochthus*, a giant shelled form from the Pleistocene of South America. (4) Giant anteater (*Scelidotherium*), from the Pleistocene of South America.

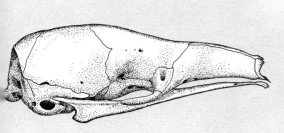

Southern tamandua 5in

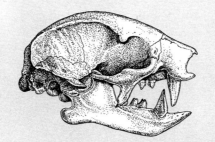

Linné's two-toed sloth 5in

Skulls of edentates

Although Edentata means "without teeth", only the anteaters, such as the Southern tamandua, are completely toothless. Both sloths and armadillos are equipped with a series of uniform peg-shaped cheek or grinding teeth (premolars and molars). These lack an enamel covering and have a single so-called "open root" which allows continuous growth. True incisor and canine teeth are absent in all edentates, but sloths have enlarged canine-like premolars.

of their foods, both groups evolved metabolic rates that are only 33–60 percent of those expected for their body-weights, and variable but low—91–95°F (32.7–35°C)—body temperatures that burn fewer calories. Armadillos eat a wide range of foods, but are specialized for a partly subterranean way of life; they also have low body temperatures—91.5–96°F (33–35.5°C) — and rates of metabolism (29–57 percent of expected) to avoid overheating in their closed burrows. Lacking similarly sluggish metabolisms, the invading mammals were not able fully to exploit these habitats, and competition with the edentates was probably minimal.

As consequences of specializing and slowing their metabolisms, the sloths and anteaters use energy frugally, and generally move slowly over small home ranges. Females attain sexual maturity at 2–3 years of age and breed only once a year thereafter. They produce small precocious litters (usually one young), and invest much time and energy in weaning and post-weaning care. Defense against predators is passive, and primarily dependent on cryptic camouflage. While anteaters, and occasionally sloths,

may try to flee from an assailant, they more often stand their ground and strike out with their claws. Sloths are reputedly able to survive the most severe injuries: bite wounds and deep scars rarely become infected, and heal completely within weeks. Armadillos show similar trends towards economizing their use of energy, but these are not as marked as in their ant- and plant-eating relatives. The armadillos are less constrained because of their more varied and energy-rich diets, and the ability (of some species) to store fat and enter torpor.

The social lives of edentates are probably dominated by the sense of smell. All species produce odoriferous secretions from anal glands, which are used to mark paths, trees or conspicuous objects; these probably advertise the presence, status and possibly the sexual condition of the marking individual. Scent marks may also serve as territorial markers, and allow individuals priority of access to scarce resources, such as food.

With their lack of teeth, long, sticky tongues, and taste for ants, the pangolins exploit a niche equivalent to that occupied by the South American anteaters. These similarities suggest that selection for the ant-eating habit has acted in parallel in both the Old and New World. CRD

3

4

ANTEATERS

Family: Myrmecophagidae
Four species in 3 genera.
Order: Edentata.
Distribution: southern Mexico, C America
south to Paraguay and northern Argentina;
Trinidad.
Habitat: savanna, parkland, thorn scrub, steppe;
deciduous, montane and tropical rain forest.

Size: from head-body length 6–9in (16–22cm),
tail length 6–10in (16–25cm) and weight
10.6–17.6oz (300–500g) in the Silky anteater
to head-body length 39–47in (100–120cm),
tail length 27.5–35.5in (70–90cm) and weight
44–86lb (20–39kg) in the Giant anteater. Male
anteaters are 10–20 percent heavier than
females.

Coat: coarse, stiff, dense; gray with black and
white shoulder stripe (Giant anteater) or light
fawn-dark brown with variable patches of black
or reddish-brown from shoulders to rump
(tamanduas); soft, silky gray-yellowish-orange
with darker mid-dorsal stripe (Silky anteater).

Gestation: 130–150 days (tamanduas); 190
days (Giant anteater).

Longevity: Unknown in the wild; 26 years
(captive Giant anteater); at least 9½ years
(captive Northern tamandua).

Species: **Giant anteater** (*Myrmecophaga
tridactyla*) v *, **Northern tamandua**
(*Tamandua mexicana*), **Southern tamandua**
(*Tamandua tetradactyla*) *, **Silky anteater**
(*Cyclopes didactylus*).

v Vulnerable. * CITES listed.

▶ **Piggy-back anteaters.** ABOVE The young of
the Giant anteater may ride on its mother's
back for up to a year, although weaning takes
place at six months. The coloration of the
young is so similar to that of its mother that the
two animals appear to merge.

▶ **A Giant anteater** investigating a termite
mound.

WITH its long, elongated snout, diagonal
black and white shoulder stripe and
long, bushy tail, the Giant anteater differs
strikingly in appearance from all other New
World mammals. The three smaller species
of anteaters have prehensile tails, naked on
the undersides, with shorter snouts than
their larger relative, but all lack teeth and
specialize in eating ants and termites.

The anteaters have characteristically
long, narrow tongues with minute,
backward-pointing spines, which are
covered in sticky saliva when the animals
are feeding. All have five fingers and four or
five toes, although the fifth finger of the
Giant anteater and the first, fourth and fifth
fingers of the Silky, or Two-toed anteater are
much reduced and not visible externally.
The three middle fingers of tamanduas and
the second and third fingers of the Giant and
Silky anteaters bear sharp, powerful claws,
1.5–4in (4–10cm) long, which are used in
defense and for opening the nests of ants and
termites. To protect these claws, anteaters
walk on their knuckles and the sides of their
hands with the claws tucked inwards; this
produces an awkward limping gait.

The Giant anteater is distributed widely in
Central America and South America east of
the Andes, extending as far south as
Uruguay and northwestern Argentina. This
species specializes in eating large ground-
dwelling ants, such as carpenter ants in the
Venezuelan *llanos*, and usually ignores termites, leaf-eating ants, army ants and other
species with large jaws. Prey colonies are
located by scent, opened but not demolished
by the powerful claws and cropped on
average for about a minute; as few as 140
ants (0.5–1 percent of the daily requirement) may be taken from a single colony on
any day. Since a Giant anteater travels at
some 46ft (14m) a minute it can revisit
many prey colonies within its home range at
regular intervals, and so avoid overexploit-
ation of its food. Detection by smell of its
preferred prey is probably excellent: experiments have shown that captive animals can
discriminate an odor for which they have
been positively conditioned, even when it
exists at four thousandths of the concentration of a neutral odor. The tongue of
the Giant anteater can be pushed out a remarkable 24in (60cm) up to 150 times a
minute to obtain its prey, and the sheath
containing the tongue and tongue-
retracting muscles is anchored on the
breast-bone. The salivary glands secrete
enormous quantities of viscous saliva onto
the tongue, and trapped ants are drawn
back and masticated first by horny papillae

on the roof of the mouth and sides of the
cheeks, then by the muscular stomach. This
species evidently obtains most of its water
from ants, although the tongue may be used
on occasion to lap up free water, and juicy
fruits and larvae are sometimes picked up by
the lips.

The abundance of the Giant anteater
varies with habitat and perhaps corresponds
with the distribution of its preferred prey. In
tropical forest on Barro Colorado Island,
Panama, and in the undisturbed grasslands
of the southeastern highlands of Brazil,
populations may attain densities of 5–10
animals per sq mi (1–2 per sq km); in the
mixed deciduous forests and semi-arid *llanos*
of Venezuela, populations may be ten times
as sparse, with individuals occupying correspondingly large home ranges of 6,200
acres (2,500ha).

In the southern part of its geographical
range, the Giant anteater is believed to breed

in the fall (March–May), but in captivity individuals also mate in spring (August–October). Courtship has not been described in this species; however, since adults are normally solitary, breeding individuals probably come together just before copulation and part shortly afterwards. The female gives birth standing upright, using her tail as the third leg of a tripod, and licks the precocious youngster after it has crawled up through the fur onto her back. Females usually bear only one young and suckle it for some six months.

Although they are capable of a slow, galloping movement at the age of just one month, the young emit short, shrill whistles if left on their own, and they do not feed independently of the mother until fully grown at the age of two years. Adults are normally silent, but bellow if provoked. Both sexes respond to the smell of their own saliva and can produce secretions from an anal gland; these odors are perhaps used in communication.

Giant anteaters have relatively slow rates of metabolism and one of the lowest recorded body temperatures—91°F (32.7°C)—of any terrestrial mammal. Although they do not burrow, they dig out shallow depressions with their claws and lie asleep in these for 14–15 hours a day; they are covered by their great fanlike tail and warned of predators, such as pumas and jaguars, by their keen hearing. Normally docile, threatened anteaters swiftly rear up on their hindlegs and slash at an adversary with their curved claws. An embrace in the immensely strong forearms of an anteater is as fearsome as its claws, and dogs, large cats, and even humans have succumbed.

The two species of tamanduas, or collared anteaters, are rather less than half the size of the Giant anteater, with distributions that generally overlap that of the larger species.

Both tamanduas are clothed in dense, bristly hair and, in marked contrast to the Giant anteater, have naked prehensile tails which assist in climbing. The ears of tamanduas are relatively large and point out from the head, suggesting a keen sense of hearing, but as in their large relative the eyes are small and their vision is probably poor. In both species the mouth opening is only the diameter of a pencil—half that of the Giant anteater—but the rounded tongue can be extended some 16in (40cm).

Although the background color of the tamanduas is fawn or brown, the northern species always has a black area that runs along the back, developing into a collar in front of the shoulders and a second, wider, band around the middle of the body. This "vest" is also present in the Southern tamandua, but only in individuals in the southern part of the range, remote from the northern species, southeast of the Amazon basin. The vest is absent in Southern tamanduas inhabiting northern Brazil and Venezuela across to a line west of the Andes; here the geographical distributions of the two species abut and the differences in their coat colors are most striking. Uniform gold, brown, black and partially vested Southern tamanduas occur throughout the Amazon basin. This confusing variation has contributed to this species being split into some 13 subspecies, in contrast to the more constant Northern tamandua with five subspecies and the Giant anteater with only three.

Tamanduas inhabit savanna, thorn scrub and a wide range of wet and dry forest habitats, where their mottled coloration provides effective camouflage. Northern tamanduas spend about half their time in trees in the tropical forest of Barro Colorado Island, whereas the Southern tamandua, in various habitats in Venezuela, has been estimated to spend 13–64 percent of its time aloft. Both species are nocturnal and may use tree hollows as sleeping quarters during the daylight hours. The tamanduas move in a clumsy, stiff-legged fashion on the ground, and are unable to gallop like their giant relative.

Because of their small size and arboreal habits, Northern tamanduas on Barro Colorado Island occupy home ranges of only 125–345 acres (50–140ha), less than one-sixth the size of those used by the terrestrial Giant anteater. However, in the more open *llanos* of Venezuela, Southern tamanduas may occupy larger ranges of 845–990 acres (350–400ha), with densities of perhaps 7.5 animals per sq mi (3 per sq km).

Tamanduas specialize in eating termites and ants and detect them by scent; however, they are repelled by leaf-eating ants, army ants and other species capable of marshalling chemical defenses. The Northern tamandua can detect and avoid soldiers of the Niggerhead termite, but will readily feed on the vulnerable workers and reproductive castes of the same species. The tamanduas feed to a larger extent on termites, especially arboreal termites, than the Giant anteater, although the methods of feeding and processing of prey are similar in all three species. Both tamanduas are also reputed to eat bees and their honey, and will take fruit and even meat in captivity.

Tamanduas probably mate in the fall and give birth to a single young in spring. Unlike the Giant anteaters, however, the offspring do not at first resemble the parents and vary in color from almost white to black. The mother carries the young on her back for an indeterminate time, setting it down only occasionally on the safety of a branch while she feeds. Tamanduas are normally solitary, but may communicate by hissing and by the release of a powerful and—to the human nose—unpleasant odor, evidently produced by the anal gland. This habit has earned them the nickname of "stinker of the forest."

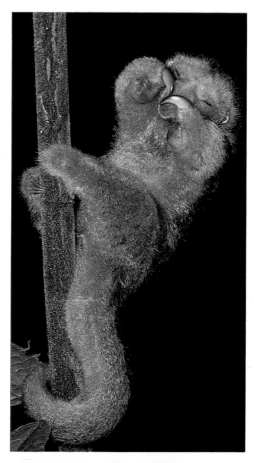

▲ **The gold, brown and white patterning** of the Southern tamandua is effective camouflage in its scrub and forest habitats.

◄ **Like a soft toy** with nylon fur, ABOVE a Silky anteater clings to a tree in a defensive posture, claws in front of its face.

◄ **Arboreal anteater.** The Northern tamandua is nocturnal and spends much of the daytime asleep in trees.

yellow, but it becomes progressively grayer, with a darker mid-dorsal stripe, in the south. Although the Silky anteater is restricted to tropical forest, it is said to favor certain kinds of trees such as the Silk cotton tree; this species produces seeds embedded in massive balls of soft, silverish fibers which resemble, and camouflage, the anteater from owls, Harpy eagles and other predators. The Silky anteater has small ears, but a larger mouth and eyes than its relatives. It uses a peculiar joint in the sole of its hindfoot, which allows the claws to be doubled back under the foot, and its strongly prehensile tail as aids in grasping branches.

The Silky anteater rarely eats termites, but specializes instead on ants which live in the stems of lianas and on tree branches. In captivity, it will also take beetles and fruits. In keeping with its low body temperature— 91.4°F (33°C)—and relatively low metabolic rate, the Silky anteater moves slowly and with deliberation; however, nightly bouts of activity last about four hours, and are punctuated by rests of only a few minutes. During the day, the animal sleeps curled up on a branch with its tail wrapped around its feet; usually no two days are spent in the same tree.

Nothing is known of mating and courtship in the Silky anteater but, some time after birth, the single young is fed on semi-digested insects that are regurgitated from the stomachs of the mother and father. Both parents carry the young for an indeterminate time although, as in the tamanduas, the young may occasionally be left alone in a leaf nest in a tree hollow while the mother feeds. Adults utter soft whistling sounds and have a cheek or facial gland, but it is not known if this has any function in communication.

Although some small use is made of tamandua skin in local leather industries, anteaters are of little commercial value and they are seldom used for food. Nevertheless, the spectacular Giant anteater is sought by trophy hunters and live animal dealers, and has been exterminated in many areas of Peru and Brazil. Large numbers of tamanduas die on roads in settled areas or are killed by locals and their dogs for "sport," while Silky anteaters are collected, at least in Peru, for the live animal trade. Unfortunately, because all anteaters have a very stable and predictable diet, the widespread and rampant destruction of habitat and associated prey species in many parts of South America may present a still greater threat to their survival than overhunting.

Although tamanduas defend themselves in much the same way as the Giant anteater, they are more likely to flee or hiss at an assailant than their larger relative. The attitude of the vested tamandua hugging its adversary has led to the further nickname "Dominus vobiscum" because of its supposed likeness to a priest at the altar.

Because of its nocturnal and strongly arboreal habits, the squirrel-sized Silky anteater is seen more rarely than its three larger relatives. Yet, it is distributed widely as seven subspecies from southern Mexico through Central America to northern Peru on the western slopes of the Andes, and east of the cordillera throughout most of the Amazon basin. In the northern part of this range, the short silky fur is a uniform golden

CRD

SLOTHS

Families: Megalonychidae (two-toed sloths), and **Bradypodidae** (three-toed sloths)
Five species in 2 genera.
Order: Edentata.
Distribution: Nicaragua through Colombia, Venezuela and the Guianas to north-central Brazil and nothern Peru (two-toed sloths); Honduras through Colombia, Venezuela and the Guianas to Bolivia, Paraguay and northern Argentina; on the west to coastal Ecuador (three-toed sloths).

Habitat: lowland and upland tropical forest; montane forest to 7,000ft (2,100m) (Hoffmann's two-toed sloth only).

Size: from head-body length 18–24in (56–60cm), tail length 2.4–2.8in (6–7cm) and weight 7.7–9.4lb (3.5–4.5kg) in the three-toed sloths to head-body length 23–28in (58–70cm), tail absent and weight 8.8–17.6lb (4–8kg) in the two-toed sloths.

Coat: Stiff, coarse, grayish-brown to beige, with a greenish cast provided by growth of blue-green algae on hairs. Two-toed sloths with darker face and hair to 6in (15cm); three-toed sloths with darker face and hair to 2.4in (6cm), light fur on shoulders; Maned sloth with dark hair on head and neck.

Gestation: 6 months (Linné's two-toed sloth, three-toed sloths); 11.5 months (Hoffmann's two-toed sloth).

Longevity: 12 years (at least 31 in captivity).

Two-toed sloths
Two species of genus *Choloepus*: **Hoffmann's two-toed sloth** (*Choloepus hoffmanni*) [*], **Linné's two-toed sloth** (*Choloepus didactylus*).

Three-toed sloths
Three species of genus *Bradypus*: **Brown-throated three-toed sloth** (*Bradypus variegatus*) [*], **Pale-throated three-toed sloth** (*Bradypus tridactylus*), **Maned sloth** (*Bradypus torquatus*) [E].

[E] Endangered. [*] CITES listed.

ALTHOUGH sloths are renowned for their almost glacial slowness of movement, they are the most spectacularly successful large mammals in Central and tropical South America. On Barro Colorado Island, Panama, two species—the Brown-throated three-toed sloth and Hoffmann's two-toed sloth—account for two-thirds of the biomass and half of the energy consumption of all terrestrial mammals, while in Surinam they comprise at least a quarter of the total mammalian biomass. Success has come from specializing in an arboreal, leaf-eating way of life to such a remarkable extent that the effects of competitors and predators are scarcely perceptible.

The sloths have rounded heads and flattened faces, with small ears hidden in the fur; they are distinguished from other tree-dwelling mammals by their simple teeth (five upper molars, four lower), and their highly modified hands and feet which terminate in long—3–4in (8–10cm)—curved claws. Sloths have short, fine underfur and an overcoat of longer and coarser hairs which, in moist conditions, is suffused with green. This color derives from the presence of two species of blue-green algae that grow in longitudinal grooves in the hairs, and help to camouflage animals in the tree canopy. All species have extremely large many-compartmental stomachs, which contain cellulose-digesting bacteria. A full stomach may account for almost a third of the body-weight of a sloth, and meals may

be digested there for more than a month before passing completely into the relatively short intestine. Feces and urine are passed only once a week, at habitual sites at the bases of trees.

The sloths are grouped into two distinct genera and families, which can be distinguished most easily by the numbers of fingers: those of genus *Choloepus* have two fingers and those of genus *Bradypus* have three. Unfortunately, despite the fact that both genera have three toes, the two-

▲ **Gathering moss,** or rather algae, a Brown-throated three-toed sloth clings to a tree in the rain forest of Panama. The algal growth on the hair seems appropriate in view of the extreme sluggishness of the animals. In fact the algae serves as camouflage.

◀ **Tree hanger.** ABOVE A Brown-throated three-toed sloth sunbathing in Panamanian rain forest.

◀ **Wet-look sloth.** Hoffman's two-toed sloth in the rain forest of Central America.

▷ **Cradled by its mother,** OVERLEAF a young Brown-throated three-toed sloth peers through the foliage. Young are carried for up to nine months and feed from this position.

fingered forms are known as two-toed and the three-fingered forms as three-toed sloths.

While representatives of both families occur together in tropical forests through-out much of Central and South America, sloths within the same genus occupy more or less exclusive geographical ranges. These closely related species differ little (10 per-cent) in body-weight and have such similar habits that they are apparently unable to coexist.

Where two-toed and three-toed sloths occur together, the two-toed form is 25 percent heavier than its relative and it uses the forest in different ways. In lowland tropical forest on Barro Colorado Island, the Brown-throated three-toed sloth achieves a density of 3.5 animals per acre (8.5 per ha),

over three times that of the larger Hoffmann's two-toed sloth. The smaller species is sporadically active for over 10 hours out of 24, compared with 7.6 hours for the two-toed sloth and, unlike its noc-turnal relative, it is active both day and night. Three-toed sloths maintain overlap-ping home ranges of 16.3 acres (6.6ha), three times those of the larger species. Despite their apparent alacrity, however, only 11 percent of three-toed sloths travel further than 125ft (38m) in a day, and some 40 percent remain in the same tree on two consecutive nights; the three-toed sloths, by contrast, change trees four times as often.

Both two-toed and three-toed sloths maintain low but variable body temp-eratures—86–93°F (30–34°C)—which fall during the cooler hours of the night, during wet weather and when the animals are inactive. Such labile body temperatures help to conserve energy: sloths have metabolic rates that are only 40–45 percent of those expected for their body-weights as well as reduced muscles (about half the relative weight for most terrestrial mammals), and so cannot afford to keep warm by shivering. Both species frequent trees with exposed crowns and regulate their body temperatures by moving in and out of the sun.

Sloths are believed to breed throughout the year, but in Guyana births of the Pale-throated three-toed sloth occur only after the rainy season, between July and September. The single young, weighing 10.5–14oz (300–400g), is born above ground and is helped to a teat by the mother. The young of all species cease nursing at about a month, but may begin to take leaves even earlier. They are carried by the mother alone for six to nine months and feed on leaves they can reach from this position; they utter bleats or pure-toned whistles if separated. After weaning, the young inherit a portion of the home range left vacant by the mother, as well as her taste for leaves. A consequence of "inheriting" preferences for different tree species is that several sloths can occupy a similar home range without competing for food or space; this will tend to maximize their numbers at the expense of howler monkeys and other leaf-eating rivals in the forest canopy. Two-toed sloths may not reach sexual maturity until the age of three years (females) or 4–5 years (males).

Adult sloths are usually solitary, and patterns of communication are poorly known. However, males are thought to advertise their presence by wiping secretions from an anal gland onto branches, and the pungent-smelling dung middens conceivably act as trysting places. Three-toed sloths produce shrill "ai-ai" whistles through the nostrils, while two-toed sloths hiss if disturbed.

Oviedo y Valdés, one of the first Spanish chroniclers of the Central American region in the 16th century, wrote that he had never seen an uglier or more useless creature than the sloth. Fortunately, little commercial value has since been attached to these animals, although large numbers, especially of two-toed sloths, are hunted locally for their meat in many parts of South America. The Maned sloth of southeastern Brazil is considered rare due to the destruction of its coastal rain-forest habitat, and the fortunes of all five species depend on the future of the tropical forests.   CRD

ARMADILLOS

Family: Dasypodidae
Twenty species in 8 genera.
Order: Edentata.
Distribution: Florida, Georgia and South
Carolina west to Kansas; eastern Mexico, C and
S America to Strait of Magellan; Trinidad and
Tobago, Grenada, Margarita.
Habitat: savanna, pampas, arid desert, thorn
scrub; deciduous, cloud and rain forest.

Size: from head-body length 5–6in (12.5–15cm),
tail length 1–1.2in (2.5–3cm) and weight
2.8–3.5oz (80–100g) in the Lesser fairy armadillo,
to head-body length 30–39in (75–100cm),
tail length 18–20in (45–50cm) and weight
99–132lb (45–60kg) in the Giant armadillo.

Coat: broad shield of pale pink or yellowish
dark brown armor (scute plates) over shoulders
and pelvis, with varying numbers of flexible
half rings over middle of back; some species
with white-dark brown hairs between the scute
plates.
Gestation: 60–65 days (hairy and Yellow
armadillos) to 120 days (prolonged by delayed
implantation) (Common long-nosed armadillo).
Longevity: 12–15 years (to 19 in captivity).

Long-nosed armadillos
Six species of genus *Dasypus*, including
Common long-nosed armadillo
(*D. novemcinctus*), **Southern lesser long-nosed
armadillo** (*D. hybridus*) **Brazilian lesser long-
nosed armadillo** (*D. septemcinctus*).

Naked-tailed armadillos
Four species of genus *Cabassous*, including
Southern naked-tailed armadillo
(*C. unicinctus*).

Hairy armadillos
Three species of genus *Chaetophractus*, including
Andean hairy armadillo (*C. nationi*),
Screaming hairy armadillo (*C. vellerosus*),
Larger hairy armadillo (*C. villosus*).

Three-banded armadillos
Two species of genus *Tolypeutes*, including
Southern three-banded armadillo (*T. matacus*).

Fairy armadillos
Two species of genus *Chlamyphorus*, including
Greater fairy armadillo (*C. retusus*).
Other species: **Yellow armadillo** (*Euphractus
sexcinctus*), **pichi** (*Zaedyus pichiy*), **Giant
armadillo** (*Priodontes maximus*) [V] [*].

[V] Vulnerable. [*] CITES listed.

CLAD in a suit of hard and bony body
plates, the Giant armadillo is the most
heavily armored of modern mammals.
Though itself a dwarf when compared with
some of its enormous ancestors—whose
10ft (3m) long body shells were used as
roofs or tombs by the early South American Indians—it is the most conspicuous
of the twenty species in the armadillo
family, which includes the frequently encountered Common long-nosed armadillo
as well as the rare Andean hairy species.

Armadillo armor develops from the skin
and is composed of strong bony plates, or
scutes, overlaid by horn. There are usually
broad and rigid shields over the shoulders
and hips, with varying numbers of bands
over the middle of the back which are
connected to the flexible underlying skin.
The tail, top of the head and outer surfaces of
the limbs are also armored, but the under-
surface is covered only with soft, hairy skin.
To protect this vulnerable area, most species
are able to withdraw the limbs under the hip
and shoulder shields and sit tightly on the
ground, while some, such as the three-
banded armadillos, can roll up into a ball.
Armadillos have rather flattened heads with
a long extendable tongue, and small but
upright ears. Most species have 14–18 teeth
in each jaw, but the Giant armadillo, with a
total of 80–100 small and vestigial teeth,
has more than almost any other mammal.
While the hindlimbs always bear five clawed
digits, the forelimbs are powerful and terminate in three, four or five curved claws
which are used for digging. Armadillos often
excavate labyrinthine burrow systems, but
also dig to obtain food and evade predators.
All species are nocturnal.

The most widespread species is the Common long-nosed or Nine-banded armadillo,
which occurs in six slightly different subspecific forms from the southern United
States through Central America to Uruguay
and Argentina. The population density of
this species varies throughout its range from
only 0.94 animals per sq mi (0.36 per sq km)
in the dry *cerrado* of Brazil, to about 130 per
sq mi (50 per sq km) in the coastal prairies
of Texas; it may be more abundant still in
the tropical forests of Panama.

The success of the Common long-nosed
armadillo is probably due to its flexible diet
and reproductive behavior, which allow it to
exploit all but the most arid habitats.
Although possessing relatively weak dentition and jaws, this species detects small
vertebrates and insects with its keen sense of
smell, and digs them from the soil and litter
with manic speed. To keep the scent of the

prey while digging, the animal places its
nose flush to the soil, and holds its breath for
up to six minutes to avoid inhaling the dust.
When digging, the armadillo loosens the soil
with its nose and forefeet and piles it up
underneath the body. Then, pausing mom-
entarily to balance on its forefeet and tail, it
kicks reflexively with the hindfeet to scatter
the soil behind it. This armadillo also takes a
wide range of fungi, tubers, fallen fruits and
carrion when available, but in the southern
part of its range it has developed a taste for
termites and ants. Using its long, sticky
tongues to extract these prey from their nests,
it may eat up to 40,000 ants at a sitting.

No less flexible in its reproductive
behavior, the Common long-nosed armadillo mates in July and August (summer) in
the United States, but from November to
January (summer) in South America. However, implantation is delayed for about 14
weeks, so that after the four-month gestation period, the young—usually single-sex
quadruplets—are born in time for the spring

◄ **Full frontal.** The pichi, a small armadillo of the pampas of Argentina and Patagonia, displays the beautiful radial patterns on its armored carapace.

▼ **The Larger hairy armadillo, feeding.** They often obtain maggots from beneath carcasses and sometimes burrow into the carcasses themselves.

flush in invertebrate food. At birth, the young are covered in a soft, leathery skin which hardens within a few weeks.

Unlike their common relative, the five other species of long-nosed armadillos are more specialized in their habits and have restricted geographical ranges which show no subspecific variation. The large Greater long-nosed armadillo, for example, occurs only in the rain forests of the Orinoco and Amazon basins, while the smaller Brazilian, Northern and Southern lesser long-nosed are restricted to savanna, forest edges and thorn scrub in parts of northern and central South America. The rare Hairy long-nosed armadillo occupies a still smaller range on the high Andean slopes of Peru at altitudes of 7,900–10,500ft (2,400–3,200m). These species seem to be less omnivorous than the Common long-nosed armadillo, and feed largely on termites and ants. Except for the Southern lesser long-nosed armadillo, which bears 8 or even 12 young, all long-nosed armadillos have litters of four. However, young of the Common long-nosed armadillo are weaned in only a few weeks and reach sexual maturity at the age of six months to a year (twice as long in all the other species).

While the long-nosed armadillos are most often seen alone, adult females show the strongest tendency to maintain exclusive home-range areas. In contrast, the home ranges of male Common long-nosed armadillos overlap freely and may encompass the ranges of several females; male ranges are 50 percent larger than those of females and range in size from 4.4 acres (1.8ha) on the coastal prairies of Texas to 26.6 acres (10.8ha) in Florida. The home ranges of both sexes include up to twelve different den sites (the average is 4.5 per animal on sandy soil, and 8.5 per animal on coastal prairie), which are usually used by a single individual on different nights. The burrows are 24–180in (0.6–4.6m) long, 7in (18cm) wide and up to 79in (2m) deep with two or more entrances. Grass, weeds and debris are raked in to line the one or two nest chambers, and often clog and hide the burrow entrances from view. Records of four or more animals in a nest are usually of mothers and their young or of newly independent all-brother or all-sister groups.

The spacing behavior of armadillos, especially of adult females, is probably regulated by olfactory communication and aggression, and to a lesser extent by the more poorly developed senses of sight and hearing. The long-nosed armadillos have glands on the ears, eye-lids and soles of the feet, as well as a bean-shaped pair of anal glands which produce a yellow nauseous secretion. Adults often sniff each other's anal regions on meeting, and it is likely that this strong odor advertises the presence of an individual to others; spacing behavior may be reinforced by the deposition of droppings and urine along paths or on prominent objects. The secretion may also deter predators, although it cannot be squirted, as in pangolins or skunks. Armadillos sometimes resolve territorial disputes by kicking, chasing and fighting but, except for a high-pitched squealing, the grunts and buzzes uttered during these squabbles differ little from the sounds made while foraging.

Along with the closely related Giant armadillo, the four smaller species of naked-tailed armadillos range widely from Central America to northern Argentina and Uruguay. These species have 10–13 movable bands across the back, short snouts and five long, powerful claws on the forefeet; that on the third digit is especially large. Although the geographical ranges of naked-tailed armadillos generally do not overlap, individuals are often found in savanna, thorn forest and tropical forest habitats with the Giant armadillo and other more distantly related species. Never abundant, the maximum density estimated for the Southern naked-tailed armadillo is only 3.1 per sq mi (1.2 per sq km) in the Venezuelan *llanos*; but the Giant armadillo in optimum lowland forest habitat in Surinam is only half as abundant as this. Using their long claws, the naked-tailed armadillos dig more efficiently than their long-nosed relatives, but run less swiftly on the surface of the ground. Their burrows are often near or underneath termite hills, and sparse observations of feeding suggest that these insects form 90–98 percent of the diet. They appear to breed at any time in captivity, and give birth to one or two blind, helpless young weighing 3.5–4oz (100–115g).

The armor of the three hairy armadillos is broader and flatter than in most other species, and is sparsely covered by brownish hairs 1.2–1.6in (3–4cm), which grow between the bony scute plates. Until recently, they were classified with the more modestly haired Yellow armadillo and pichi as six-banded armadillos (the actual number of bands varies from six to eight), from which they differ principally in size. The hairy armadillos occur in desert, temperate grassland and forest in southern South America, and can tolerate cool and very dry conditions; indeed, the rare Andean Hairy armadillo occurs only in the high, bleak *puna* of

An Armored Invader

Although primarily an inhabitant of the tropical forests and warm, moist grasslands of South America, the Common long-nosed armadillo has extended its range south to the cooler regions of Uruguay and Argentina, and north into the southern United States. Formerly, this armadillo occurred no further north than Mexico, but in 1880 it crossed the Rio Grande and entered Texas. As the armadillo gradually advanced northwards, its taste for insect pests was noticed and it was successfully introduced to several southern crop-growing states. In Florida, several armadillos escaped from zoos or private owners in the 1920s, and these also established wild populations. By 1939, specimens were being reported from all southeastern states, and today the species extends as far north as central Oklahoma and possibly New Mexico.

The opportunistic feeding and reproductive habits of the Common long-nosed armadillo have no doubt assisted the advance, but its ability to excavate deep burrows in the most compacted soils has also been important. Unlike other armadillos, the Common long-nosed armadillo is able to swim across water barriers, inflating its stomach and intestine with air for bouyancy. Since the breath can be held for several minutes, this species is also able to trot across shorter river crossings.

The southward advance of the Common long-nosed armadillos is probably limited by competition from the Three-banded and Hairy armadillos, and by its inability to tolerate aridity.

In the United States, cold has slowed the northward advance. Unlike the more cold-adapted forms, the body temperature can be dropped only 4.5°F (2.5°C) (from 94.1°F; 34.5°C) to reduce the losses, while frosts reduce the abundance of insect food which is needed to make up the deficit. Like its giant ancestors, the armadillo may have to evolve a larger body with more insulating fat if it is to advance further north.

Bolivia. The small pichi, half the size of the hairy armadillos, occupies open pampas country in Patagonia, south to the Strait of Magellan, while the Yellow armadillo, evidently the most abundant of the six-banded forms, occurs in Brazilian savanna and forest at densities of up to 7.5 per sq mi (2.9 per sq km).

The hairy armadillos conserve heat and moisture in their dry, harsh environments by maintaining low but variable body temperatures—for example, 75.2–95.3°F (24.0–35.2°C)—in the pichi—and by spending the coldest times of day underground. Alone among armadillos, the pichi is able to

▲ **A Brazilian lesser long-nosed armadillo,** resting in a surface burrow.

◄ **The soft, pink leathery skin** of this young Common long-nosed armadillo will soon harden into a tough carapace.

◄ **Like a puzzle ball,** the Southern three-banded armadillo leaves no chinks for predators when it curls up.

enter torpor in winter, but all of the hairy species can shiver to produce heat and shift their daily activity cycle to forage, as required, in the warm midday sun or in the cool, moist evenings. In the northern Monte Desert of Argentina, where annual rainfall is only 5in (13cm), the Screaming hairy armadillo obtains moisture in summer from a broad diet of insects (45 percent), plants and tubers (29 percent) and rodents and lizards (26 percent), foraging over an area of 8.4 acres (3.4ha). Hairy armadillos are believed to produce up to two litters of two young each year.

Sharing the geographical ranges of the hairy armadillos, but differing in its preference for ants and termites, the Southern three-banded armadillo has adapted to dry forest and savanna habitats by evolving very thick armor. Air trapped beneath the shell reduces heat loss so effectively that the animal is often active on the coldest of winter days and nights. Unlike the hairy armadillos, it seldom digs burrows, and sleeps under bushes; in southern Brazil it may reach densities of eighteen animals per sq mi (7 per sq km). It has the ability,

unique among armadillos, to roll into a complete ball, presenting only its thick armor to would-be predators. The single young are born between October and January and, although blind, they are able to walk and close their shells within hours.

Fairy armadillos are the smallest members of the armadillo family, and are known only from the sandy soil regions of southern South America. They have very flexible body armor, and five powerfully clawed digits for digging. Largely subterranean, these species are believed to surface once a day to feed on insects.

The long-nosed, six-banded and Southern three-banded armadillos are hunted for meat throughout Central and South America but, except for the very rare and geographically restricted forms such as the Brazilian three-banded armadillo, they do not appear to be seriously declining. However, the Giant armadillo has disappeared from much of its former range in Brazil, Peru and elsewhere, and is currently considered endangered, while loss of habitat may reduce populations of the rare and vulnerable fairy armadillos.   CRD

PANGOLINS

Family: Manidae
Seven species of genus *Manis*.
Order: Pholidota.
Distribution: Senegal to Uganda, Angola,
western Kenya; south to Zambia and northern
Mozambique; Sudan, Chad, Ethiopia to
Namibia and South Africa. Peninsular India,
Sri Lanka, Nepal and southern China to Taiwan
and Hainan; south through Thailand, Burma,
Laos, Peninsular Malaysia, Java, Sumatra,
Kalimantan and offshore islands.

Habitat: forest to open savanna.

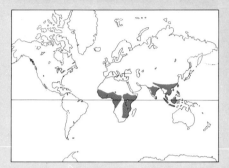

Size: from head-body length 12–14in
(30–35cm), tail length 22–26in (55–65cm)
and weight 2.6–4.4lb (1.2–2.0kg) in the Long-
tailed pangolin, to head-body length 30–33in
(75–85cm), tail length 25–31in (65–80cm)
and weight 55–73lb (25–33kg) in the Giant
pangolin. Males 10–50 percent heavier than
females in most species, up to 90 percent
heavier in Indian pangolin.

Coat: Horny, overlapping scales on head, body,
outer surfaces of limbs, and tail, varying in
color from light yellowish-brown through olive
to dark brown. Scales of young Chinese
pangolin purple-brown. Undersurface hairs
white to dark brown.

Gestation: 139 days (Cape pangolin).
Longevity: at least 13 years (captive Indian
pangolin).

Four African species: **Giant pangolin**
(*M. gigantea*), **Cape pangolin** (*M. temmincki*),
Small-scaled tree pangolin (*M. tricuspis*),
Long-tailed pangolin (*M. tetradactyla*); Three
Asian species: **Indian pangolin**
(*M. crassicaudata*), **Chinese pangolin**
(*M. pentadactyla*), **Malayan pangolin**
(*M. javanica*).

▶ **Overlapping brown scales,** ABOVE, give the
pangolins a unique, animal-artichoke
appearance. This is the Small-scaled tree
pangolin, an African species.

▶ **A Cape pangolin** drinking at Etosha
National Park, Namibia. Cape pangolins sleep
by day in burrows up to 20ft (6m) deep. They
feed mostly on four genera of termites but when
in competition with other termite-eaters such
as the aardwolf and aardvark, they may take
ants.

THE pangolins are distinguished from all
other Old World mammals by their
unique covering of horny body scales,
which overlap like shingles on a roof. The
scales, which grow from the thick underlying skin, protect every part of the body
except the underside and inner surfaces of
the limbs, and are shed and replaced
periodically. With the body curled tightly
into a ball, the scales form a shield that is
impregnable to all but the larger cats and
hyenas, with their bone-crunching jaws.

Pangolins specialize in eating ants and
termites and, like their South American
counterparts, they probe the nests of their
prey with a long, narrow tongue. In the
largest species, the Giant pangolin, the
strap-like tongue can be pushed out
14–16in (36–40cm), although it is 27.5in
(70cm) in total length, and is housed in a
sheath that extends to an attachment point
on the pelvis. Viscous saliva is secreted onto
the tongue by an enormous salivary
gland—22–24.5cu in (360–400cu cm)—
which sits in a recess in the chest. The simple
skull lacks teeth and chewing muscles;
captured ants are ground up in the specialized, horny stomach. Pangolins have a
small, conical head with a reduced or absent
outer ear, and an elongate body that tapers
to a stout tail. Thick lids protect their eyes
from the bites of ants, and special muscles
close the nostrils during feeding. The limbs
are short but powerful and terminate in five
clawed digits; the three middle claws on the
forefoot are 2.2–2.9in (55–75mm) long and
curved.

In Africa, two of the four species of
pangolins are principally arboreal, and inhabit the rain-forest belt from Senegal to the
Great Rift Valley. While the common Small-
scaled tree pangolin occupies home ranges
of 49–74 acres (20–30ha) in the lower
strata of the forest, the smaller Long-tailed
pangolin is more restricted to the forest
canopy. Here, moving often by day to avoid
its relative, the smaller species seeks the soft,
hanging nests of ants and termites (prefer-
ring arboreal species), or attacks the
columns that move among the leaves. Both
species have a slender but strongly prehensile tail (the 46 or 47 tail vertebrae of the
Long-tailed pangolin are a mammalian
record), with a short, bare patch at the tip
which contains a sensory pad. They are able
to scale vertical tree trunks by gaining a
purchase with the fore-claws and then
drawing up the hindfeet just behind them;
the jagged edges of the tail-scales provide
additional support. These arboreal pangolins sleep aloft, curled up among

epiphytes (plants growing on trees) or in the
fork of a branch.

The terrestrial African pangolins are larger than their tree-dwelling relatives, and
occur in a spectrum of habitats from forest to
open savanna. They use their powerful
claws to demolish the nests of ground
termites and ants. The Giant pangolin, with
a stomach capacity of 3.5 pints, may take
200,000 ants a night, weighing over 25oz
(700g).

To protect their digging claws, the terrestrial pangolins walk slowly on the outer
edges of their forefeet with the claws tucked
up underneath; the curious, shuffling gait
this produces has been likened to that of a
"perambulating artichoke." However, all
species can move more swiftly—up to 3mph
(5km/h)—by rearing up and running on
their hindlegs, using the tail as a brace.

The three Asian species of pangolins are
less well known than their African counterparts, and can be distinguished from them

by the presence of hair at the bases of the body-scales. Intermediate in size between the African species, the Asian pangolins are nocturnal and usually terrestrial, but can climb with great agility. They inhabit grasslands, subtropical thorn forest, rain forest and barren hilly areas almost devoid of vegetation, but are nowhere abundant. The geographical range of the Chinese pangolin is said to approximate that of its preferred prey species, the subterranean termites.

Although pangolins are usually solitary, their social life is dominated by the sense of smell. Individuals advertise their presence by scattering feces along the tracks of their home ranges, and by marking trees with urine and a pungent secretion from an anal gland. These odors may communicate dominance and sexual status, and possibly facilitate individual recognition. The vocal expressions of pangolins are limited to puffs and hisses; however, these probably serve no social function.

Pangolins usually bear one young weighing 7–18oz (200–500g), although two and even three young have been reported in the Asian species. In the arboreal species, the young clings to the mother's tail soon after birth, and may be carried in this fashion until weaned at the age of three months. Young of the terrestrial species are born underground with small, soft scales, and are first carried outside on the mother's tail at the age of 2–4 weeks. In all species, births usually occur between November and March; sexual maturity is at two years.

In Africa, large numbers of pangolins are killed for their meat and scales by the native peoples, and the future of one species, the Cape pangolin, is seriously endangered. In Asia, powdered scales are believed to have medicinal and aphrodisiac qualities, and the animals are hunted indiscriminately. Unless controlled, the population densities and ranges of the three Asian pangolins will continue to dwindle.   CRD

BATS

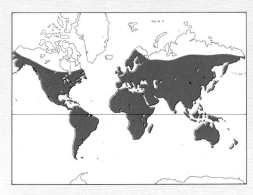

ORDER: CHIROPTERA

Nineteen families; 187 genera; 951 species.
Distribution: worldwide except Arctic,
Antarctic and highest mountains.
Habitat: highly diverse.

Size: weight and wingspan range from 0.05oz
and 6in in Kitti's hog-nosed bat to 3.3lb and
6.5ft in flying foxes (*Pteropus* species).

Coat: variable, but mostly browns, grays,
yellows, reds and blacks.
Gestation: variable, and with delayed
implantation can range from 3 to 10 months in
a single species.
Longevity: maximum 30 years but average 4–5
years.

Suborder Megachiroptera

Flying foxes
Family Pteropopidae
Forty-four genera and 173* species in Old
World including: **Straw-colored flying fox**
(*Eidolon helvum*); **rousettes** (*Rousettus* species);
Rodriguez flying fox (*Pteropus rodricensis*);
Samoan flying fox (*P. samoensis*); **Hammer-
headed bat** (*Hypsignathus monstrosus*);
Franquet's flying fox (*Epomops franqueti*);
Dawn bat (*Eonycteris spelaea*); **long-tongued
fruit bats** (*Macroglossus* species).

Suborder Microchiroptera

Mouse-tailed bats
Family Rhinopomatidae
One genus and 3 species in Old World
including: **Greater mouse-tailed bat**
(*Rhinopoma microphyllum*).

Sheath-tailed bats
Family Emballonuridae
Thirteen genera and 50* species in Old and
New Worlds including: **Sac-winged bat**
(*Saccopteryx bilineata*).

Hog-nosed bat
Family Craseonycteridae
One species in Old World: **Kitti's hog-nosed bat**
(*Craseonycteris thonglongyai*).

Slit-faced bats
Family Nycteridae
One genus (*Nycteris*) and 11* species in Old
World.

False vampire bats
Family Megadermatidae
Four genera and 5 species in Old World
including: **Greater false vampire** (*Megaderma
lyra*). (Note: the New World False vampire bat
belongs to the family Phyllostomatidae.)

Horseshoe bats
Family Rhinolophidae
One genus and 69* species in Old World
including: **Greater horseshoe bat** (*Rhinolophus
ferrumequinum*).

Leaf-nosed bats
Family Hipposideridae
Nine genera and 61* species in Old World.

Leaf-chinned bats
Family Mormoopidae
Two genera (*Pteronotus* and *Mormoops*) and 8 species in New World.

Bulldog bats
Family Noctilionidae
One genus (*Noctilio*) and 2 species in New World.

Short-tailed bats
Family Mystacinidae
One genus (*Mystacina*) and 2 species in Old World.

Spear-nosed bats
Family Phyllostomatidae
Forty-seven genera and 140* species in New World including: **Greater spear-nosed bat** (*Phyllostomus hastatus*); **Fringe-lipped bat** (*Trachops cirrhosus*); **False vampire** (*Vampyrum spectrum*) (note: not to be confused with the Old World false vampires, family Megadermatidae); **Pallas' long-tongued bat** (*Glossophaga soricina*); **Mexican long-nosed bat** (*Leptonycteris nivalis*); **Geoffroy's long-nosed bat** (*Anoura geoffroyi*); **Great stripe-faced bat** (*Vampyrodes caraccioloi*); **Great fruit-eating bat** (*Artibeus lituratus*).

Vampire bats
Family Desmodontidae
Three genera and 3 species in New World including: **Common vampire** (*Desmodus rotundus*).

Funnel-eared bats
Family Natalidae
One genus (*Natalus*) and 8 species in New World.

Thumbless bats
Family Furipteridae
Two genera and 2 species (*Furipteus horrens* and *Amorphochilus schnabli*) in New World.

Disk-winged bats
Family Thyropteridae
One genus (*Thyroptera*) and 2 species in New World.

Sucker-footed bat
Family Myzopodidae
One species (*Myzopoda aurita*) in Old World.

Common or vesper bats
Family Vespertilionidae
Forty-two genera and 319* species in Old and New Worlds including: **Gray bat** (*Myotis grisescens*); **Little brown bat** (*M. lucifugus*); **Large mouse-eared bat** (*M. myotis*); **Natterer's bat** (*M. nattereri*); **Yuma myotis** (*M. yumanensis*); **Fish-eating bat** (*Pizonyx vivesi*); **Common pipistrelle** (*Pipistrellus pipistrellus*); **Eastern pipistrelle** (*P. subflavus*); **Leisler's bat** (*Nyctalus leisleri*); **Noctule bat** (*N. noctula*); **Big brown bat** (*Eptesicus fuscus*); **Bamboo bat** (*Tylonycteris pachypus*); **Hoary bat** (*Lasiurus cinereus*); **Red bat** (*L. borealis*); **Brown long-eared bat** (*Plecotus auritus*); **Schreiber's bent-winged bat** (*Miniopterus schreibersi*); **Painted bat** (*Kerivoula picta*).

Free-tailed bats
Family Molossidae
Twelve genera and 91* species in Old and New Worlds including: **Mexican free-tailed bat** (*Tadarida brasilensis*); **Wrinkle-lipped bat** (*T. plicata*); **Naked bat** (*Cheiromeles torquatus*).

* Number of species changing as research continues.

NEARLY one quarter of mammalian species are bats. Apart from birds, they are the only other vertebrates capable of sustained flight. They have exploited all major land habitats with the exception of the polar regions, highest mountains, and some remote islands, particularly in the eastern Pacific. On New Zealand, Hawaii, the Azores and many oceanic islands, bats are the only indigenous mammals and, like birds, their mobility allows them readily to investigate and colonize new areas if roosts and food are available.

In Europe, the Leisler's bat long ago reached the Azores in the north Atlantic, and the Hoary bat from the Americas similarly colonized the Hawaiian Islands with minimum distances from the mainland of 930 and 2300mi (1,500 and 3,700km) respectively. Both species are narrow-winged, fast-flying bats that are migratory over at least part of their current ranges. Most bats are only active at night, but island species in the absence of birds of prey are often also active by day, and a few bats of most species will occasionally fly during daytime.

Flying, especially at night, poses problems of obstacle avoidance and navigation, but facilitates finding food which may be patchily distributed in space and time. In general, birds solved this problem by evolving superb eyesight, but their hearing is average and sense of smell very poor. Although some bats, such as Old World flying foxes, have excellent sight, most rely upon highly acute hearing which, with often complex sound production, enables bats to navigate, feed and locate roosts by echolocation. Many bats, particularly the fruit-eating species, have a keen sense of smell. The light-gathering capability of megachiropterans' eyes is enhanced by numerous projections from the rods (monochrome receptors).

Bats (order Chiroptera) are separated into the suborders Megachiroptera and Microchiroptera. The megachiropterans comprise a single family, the flying foxes, and live in the Old World tropics and subtropics from

◀ ▼ **Bat heads.** Bats exhibit a wide variety of head shapes. LEFT. The fruit-eating flying foxes, such as the Common long-tongued fruit bat (*Macroglossus minimus*), have a dog-like face and generally small simple ears, and characteristically large eyes which are the primary sense in navigation.

BELOW At the other extreme many insect-eating species, such as the Narrow-eared leaf-nosed bat (*Hipposideros stenotis*), have extraordinary, even grotesque, faces, often with huge ears and with elaborate growths (nose leaves) around nostrils or mouths, associated with echolocation.

THE BAT BODY PLAN

▶ **Body plan** of a typical bat with a simple nose.

▼ **Bat tails.** Major variations in tail shape of bats; (**a**) free tail (free-tailed bat—*Tadarida*); (**b**) mouse tail (mouse-tailed bat—*Rhinopoma*); (**c**) full membrane (mouse-eared bat—*Myotos*); (**d**) sheath tail (Old World sheath-tailed bat—*Emballonura*); (**e**) short tail (tube-nosed fruit bat—*Nyctimene*); (**f**) tail lacking (flying fox—*Pteropus*).

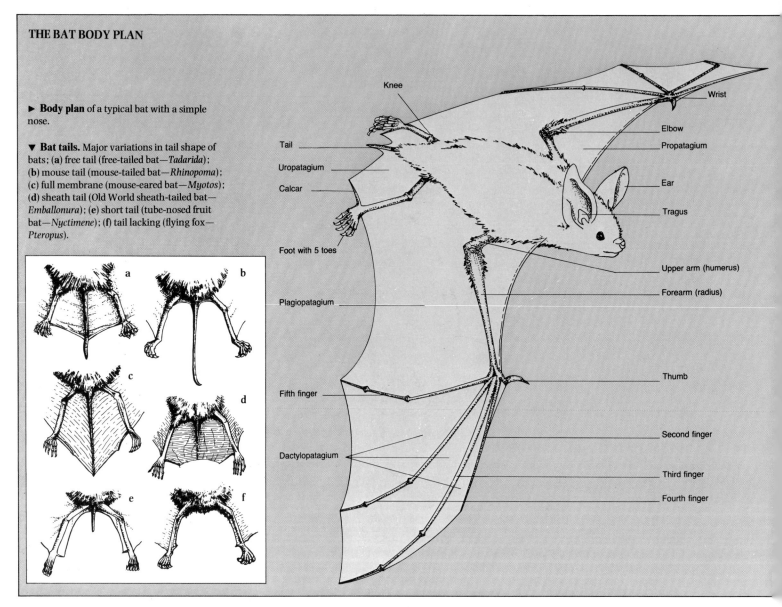

Africa to the Cook Islands in the Pacific. They include the largest bats, for example the Samoan flying fox with a reported wingspan of 6.6ft (2m) and weight 3lb (1.5kg), but some are tiny, such as the long-tongued fruit bats (*Macroglossus* species) (wingspan 12in/30cm, weight 0.5oz/15g). Microchiropterans occur throughout the world and are grouped into 18 families. They include the smallest bat (and mammal), Kitti's hog-nosed bat (wingspan 6in/15cm, weight as little as 0.05oz/1.5g), and species as large as the New World False vampire bat (wingspan up to 3.3ft/1m, weight 7oz/200g).

Bats have wings that flap, a character which separates them from all other mammals. Even so-called flying mammals such as flying squirrels and colugos which possess expanded flaps of skin are not able to undertake powered flight—they just glide. The membrane (or patagium) consists in bats of skin, sandwiching bundles of elastic tissue and muscle fiber, and is supported by the finger bones, arms and legs. The muscle fibers keep the wing tensioned in flight and gather it up while at rest. Holes heal within a few weeks—even broken finger bones mend quickly.

The wing pattern is essentially similar in all bat species, but differences in shape reflect the variety of ecological niches and feeding behavior exhibited by bats. The upper arm (humerus), is shorter than the forearm (radius) and the second forearm bone, the ulna, is more or less reduced to a sliver of bone. All bats have a clawed thumb, although in two species of smoky bats the thumbs are functionless. Bats mostly use thumbs for moving around roosts but some, especially the fruit-eating bats, hold and manipulate food with them. Flying foxes of the genus *Pteropus* have particularly large thumbs and claws which are also used for

▶ **Evolution of bats.** Evolution chart showing the relationships between present-day families and their grouping into superfamilies and orders. The fossil record of bats is exceptionally poor with only 30 fossil genera discovered. There are no known early flying foxes (Megachiroptera), so it is not known whether the two suborders evolved independently or from a common ancestor.

Bats have some similarity with both insectivores and primates, and it is often stated that bats probably evolved from an ancestral shrew-like insectivore. In the absence of any evidence such speculation is pointless and may be misleading.

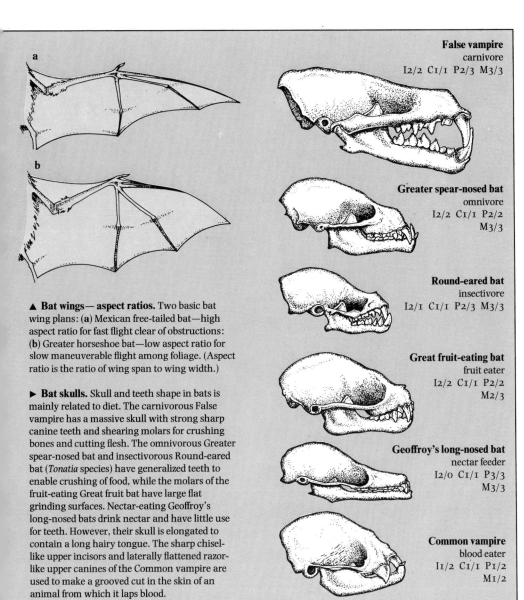

▲ **Bat wings— aspect ratios.** Two basic bat wing plans: (a) Mexican free-tailed bat—high aspect ratio for fast flight clear of obstructions: (b) Greater horseshoe bat—low aspect ratio for slow maneuverable flight among foliage. (Aspect ratio is the ratio of wing span to wing width.)

► **Bat skulls.** Skull and teeth shape in bats is mainly related to diet. The carnivorous False vampire has a massive skull with strong sharp canine teeth and shearing molars for crushing bones and cutting flesh. The omnivorous Greater spear-nosed bat and insectivorous Round-eared bat (*Tonatia* species) have generalized teeth to enable crushing of food, while the molars of the fruit-eating Great fruit bat have large flat grinding surfaces. Nectar-eating Geoffroy's long-nosed bats drink nectar and have little use for teeth. However, their skull is elongated to contain a long hairy tongue. The sharp chisel-like upper incisors and laterally flattened razor-like upper canines of the Common vampire are used to make a grooved cut in the skin of an animal from which it laps blood.

False vampire
carnivore
I2/2 C1/1 P2/3 M3/3

Greater spear-nosed bat
omnivore
I2/2 C1/1 P2/2
M3/3

Round-eared bat
insectivore
I2/1 C1/1 P2/3 M3/3

Great fruit-eating bat
fruit eater
I2/2 C1/1 P2/2
M2/3

Geoffroy's long-nosed bat
nectar feeder
I2/0 C1/1 P3/3
M3/3

Common vampire
blood eater
I1/2 C1/1 P1/2
M1/2

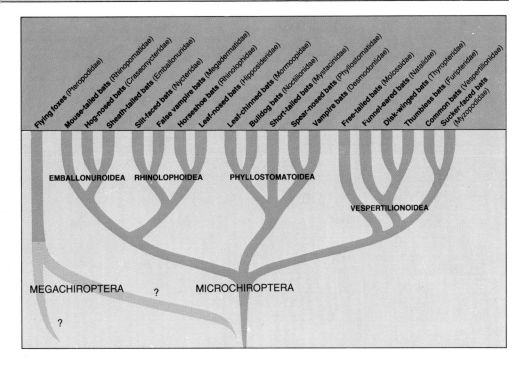

fighting. The thumb serves as an attachment for the propatagium (that part of the wing membrane in front of the forearm), which can be broad, especially in some of the flying foxes and slow-flying bats.

In all bats the second digit is relatively short, and for most flying foxes it terminates in a small claw, but this is absent in the Microchiroptera. The third digit is the longest and extends to the wing tip; the ratio of its length relative to the fifth digit, which is a measure of the wing width, characterizes the flight pattern (see diagram). Bats with the third digit about $1\frac{1}{3}$ times longer than the fifth have short, broad wings, low aspect ratios and are generally slow flyers. (Aspect ratios are the ratio of wing span to average wing width). Bats with the third digit about twice as long as the fifth have long thin wings, high aspect ratios and fly rapidly. Most free-tailed bats that have high aspect ratios such as *Tadarida*, generally roost well above the ground so that when they take off they can fall 6.6–10ft (2–3m) to gain enough speed to fly. They fly faster than most other species (22.5–34mph or 36–55km/h) but they are not very maneuverable and normally fly clear of trees or other obstructions. By contrast, the horseshoe bats are mostly slow-flying, with low aspect ratios. They are highly maneuverable and may even hover or turn in a space no larger than the wing span. These bats generally fly less than ·16mph (26km/h).

Some of the long-winged bats fold the wing tips when at rest. Most extreme in this respect is the Naked bat of Southeast Asia, heaviest of all microchiropterans, which, after folding its wings, tucks the ends into pouches beneath the wings that join in the middle of the back. In this way, the large 24in (60cm) wingspan presents no encumbrance while moving around the roost.

Tails in bats are extremely variable, in size ranging from absent, as in some flying foxes and Kitti's hog-nosed bat, to long and thin in mouse-tailed bats (*Rhinopoma* species). The tail membrane (or uropatagium) is absent in some bats, such as flying foxes of the genus *Pteropus*, or very small, as in the mouse-tailed bats, but can be large and supported by the tail as in the slit-faced bats (*Nycteris* species). The latter are unique among mammals in having a T-shaped bone at the tail tip, the function of which is unknown.

The tail membrane may be used to aid maneuverability, as it is a conspicuous feature of most insectivorous species. In some species, eg the Natterer's bat, insects are caught in the tail before transfer to the mouth. The bats that catch insects with the wing may transfer the prey to the tail which serves as a holding pouch until the bat lands at a perch to devour the food.

The legs, which support the uropatagium that extends between them as well as the plagiopatagium (the main part of the membrane between the body and fifth finger), are generally weak. They project sideways and backward and the knee bends back rather than forward as in other mammals. Together with the feet with their five clawed toes of equal length, the hind limbs function as "clothes hanger hooks." Some bats, such as the large flying foxes and horseshoe bats, cannot walk on all fours (quadrupedally), but others, such as many of the common bats, can scurry very rapidly around their roosts, or while chasing prey on the ground. Most agile is the Common vampire, which has especially strong legs and long thumbs enabling it to run and leap very quickly. The two short-tailed bats (*Mystacina* species) also run freely, climb with agility, and excavate burrows, aided by wings that roll up out of the way and by talons on the claws of thumbs and toes.

Bats spend much of their time at roosts washing and grooming, often hanging by one foot while the other vigorously combs all parts of the body. Although the feet show very little variation, fishing bats, such as *Noctilio* species, have long laterally flattened claws and toes. These are drawn through water to gaff fish which are lifted to the mouth prior to the bat landing to eat.

Evolution

Bats were originally tropical animals, though some have now adapted to living in temperate climates. Unlike other mammalian orders the fossil record of bats is poor. About 30 fossil genera have been described compared with 187 current genera, and excepting five genera they are attributable to at least 10 of the 19 current families. The five oldest fossils are not referrable to modern families but nevertheless do not vary significantly from the variety of body forms living today. The earliest fossil is of a virtually complete skeleton recovered from what was a lake bed in Wyoming about 50 million years ago in the Eocene epoch of the Tertiary period. This species, named *Icaronycteris index*, was so well preserved that membranes were visible and remains were found in the area of its stomach indicating that it was probably insectivorous. This fossil indicates that bats were fully developed early in the Eocene epoch (54–38 million years ago) and were

◀ ▶ **Representatives of 11 families of microchiropteran bats.** (Species from other families are shown as photographs in this section). (**1**) Lesser mouse-tailed bat (*Rhinopoma hardwickei*—family Rhinopomatidae); (**2**) Bate's slit-faced bat (*Nycteris arge*—family Nycteridae); (**3**) Kitti's hog-nosed bat (*Craseonycteris thonglongyai*—family Craseonycteridae); (**4**) Diadem leaf-nosed bat (*Hipposideros diadema*—family Hipposideridae); (**5**) New Zealand short-tailed bat (*Mystacina tuberculata*—family Mystacinidae); (**6**) Yellow-winged bat (*Lavia frons*—family Megadermatidae); (**7**) Mexican funnel-eared bat (*Natalus stramineus*—family Natalidae); (**8**) Smoky bat (*Furipterus horrens*—family Furipteridae); (**9**) Davy's naked-backed bat (*Pteronotus davyi*—family Mormoopidae); (**10**) Honduran disk-winged bat (*Thyroptera discifera*—family Thyropteridae); (**11**) Sucker-footed bat (*Myzopoda aurita*—family Myzopodidae). Not to scale.

contemporary with other mammals, including rodents, insectivores and primates.

Classification

Modern classification of bats suffers primarily from the lack of adequate data. About 100 species have been caught less than 20 times and about 20 species are recognized on the basis of a single specimen. New species are constantly being found and described as collecting techniques improve. At least eight species are known to have become recently extinct, some probably as a direct result of man's recent influence on habitats. Even in western Europe, three new species have been described in the last 25 years and others are suspected. As recently as 1974 a new family was erected to contain the newly discovered Kitti's hog-nosed bat from Thailand. Existing taxonomy is based mainly on external form (morphology) but results of modern biochemical techniques are beginning to demand reassessment. Ecological research is also providing clues to separate sibling species that were previously overlooked. Some species are clearly related while others may have characters intermediate between two presently recognized groups. As information improves some regrouping is necessary. For example, the rare short-tailed bats of New Zealand have recently been separated into two species, *Mystacina tuberculata* and *M. robusta*.

The variety of body forms that is the basis of our current classification reflects the adaptations each species has made in response to the ecological niche in which it has evolved and helped to differentiate. Only three of the 19 bat families have representatives in both the Old and New Worlds, although there are bats occupying similar niches in both areas. Those families that have representatives throughout the world are the sheath-tailed bats, common bats and free-tailed bats. These include about half of all bats and are almost exclusively insectivorous.

In the Old World, the fruit-eating niche is occupied mostly by one family, the flying foxes, whereas in the New World the niche is occupied by the spear-nosed bats. This family is the most diverse of all, embracing fruit-eaters, carnivores and insectivores, with the closely related vampires being blood-eaters (see pp84–85).

About 250 species of spear-nosed bats and flying foxes are important to over 130 genera of plants because they pollinate and/or disperse their seeds. In the New World alone over 500 plant species are pollinated by bats (see pp86–87). Bat-adapted plants often have large white flowers that show up in the dark, or smell strongly so as to attract bats, and all produce copious quantities of nectar and pollen. Nectar flow is synchronized with bat activity, in some plants, such as bananas, beginning at dusk and continuing for over half the night, while in a Passion flower nectar flow begins after midnight and stops shortly after dawn.

Over 650 species eat insects, representing members of all families except the flying foxes, and even a few of these take some insects, but perhaps only accidentally while eating ripe fruit.

The three species of vampires consume blood. Probably about 10 bats in the fisherman and common bat families catch fish, but none exclusively, as they also take various Arthropoda (insects etc). Similarly, about 15 bats, mainly of the false vampire and spear-nosed families, are carnivores, but some of these species also take insects and even fruit. There are no truly herbivorous species, nor marine species, although the two bulldog or fisherman bats roost and feed along shorelines.

Echolocation

For 150 years biologists have marveled at the ability of bats to fly and catch insects in the darkness, even if deliberately blinded. It was an Italian, Lazzaro Spallanzani, who in 1793 first discovered that bats were disoriented when they could not hear but that blinded bats could still avoid obstacles. In 1920 the English physiologist Hartridge suggested that bats navigated, and located and captured prey, using their sense of hearing. In the late 1930s the invention of a microphone sensitive to high frequencies enabled Donald Griffin in the United States to discover in 1938 that bats produce ultrasonic sounds. The term "ultra-sonic" means sounds of higher frequency than is audible to humans.

Before describing what sounds bats produce and how they use them, it is important to understand the descriptive terminology. When an object vibrates it causes pressure changes in the surrounding air. The ear may intercept these pressure changes and, through the eardrum and middle ear, transfer them to the inner ear or cochlea. This has sensitive cells that selectively respond by sending signals to the brain, which interprets them as sound. The number of vibrations per second is termed "frequency" and is measured in hertz (Hz). Humans can perceive sounds from 20Hz to 20,000Hz, while bats' sensitivity ranges from less than

▶ **Echolocating prey.** Sonograms showing search, approach and terminal phases of the hunt in two species of bat.

(a) The North American Big brown bat, produces frequency modulated (FM) calls (see text) steeply sweeping from 70–30kHz. While foraging the bat emits 5–6 pulses per second, each of about 10 milliseconds (msec) duration until an insect is located. Immediately the pulse rate increases, duration shortens, with the frequency sweep starting at a lower frequency. As an insect is caught (or just missed) the repetition rate peaks at 200 per second, with each pulse lasting about 1msec.

(b) Hunting horseshoe bats produce their long (average 50msec) constant frequency (CF) calls (see text) at a rate of 10 per second. They often feed among dense foliage. A problem facing a bat is how to distinguish fluttering insect wings from leaves and twigs oscillating in the wind. While foliage produces a random background scatter of echoes the insect with a relatively constant rapid wing-beat frequency will appear like a flashing light to a bat using a CF component. As the bat closes on the insect the CF component of each pulse is suppressed in amplitude and reduced to under 10msec while the amplified terminal FM sweep is used for critical location and capture of the prey.

▶ **Sonar hunt**—a Greater horseshoe swoops on a moth. Such a battle is not necessarily one-sided. Some months have evolved listening membranes that detect the bat's sonar pulses, giving the moth opportunity to escape. To counter this some tropical bats only send out signals at wavelengths that cannot be detected by the moths. In the last resort moths may dive away from the bat at the very last moment.

▼ **Sound collectors**—the external ears of bats using ultrasound to navigate and hunt prey as with this Lesser long-eared bat (*Nyctophilus geoffroyi*), are enlarged and folded into complex shapes. The separate lobe seen inside the front of the ear is known as a tragus.

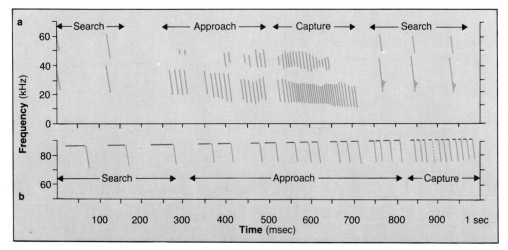

100Hz to 200,000Hz (normally written as 200kHz).

Sound vibrations travel through air in pressure "waves" and the distances between successive peaks, termed the wavelength, is measured in meters. The higher the frequency, the shorter the wavelength. Also sounds vary in intensity (from loud or quiet), and this reflects the energy or "amplitude" of each wave. The intensity of sound is usually recorded in decibels (dB).

Most animals produce simultaneous sounds comprising a number of frequencies and of differing amplitudes. Some sounds are "harmonics" of particular frequencies, that is, they are double, treble or quadruple etc, the lowest frequency. This latter is termed the fundamental (or base) frequency, with others being called the second, third or fourth etc harmonic.

Probably all microchiropterans use ultrasound which they produce with their larynxes. A single species, such as the high, fast-flying Noctule bat in Europe, produces different emissions while migrating, cruising looking for food, chasing and catching food, and when flying or feeding in close company with other bats. During high migrating flight loud low-frequency pulses at one-second intervals are used, presumably to keep it in contact with the ground. If prey is detected pulses lasting under 5 milliseconds (msec) are produced sweeping down through a frequency range of over 40kHz and up to 200 per second in the terminal phase of the chase. Individuals flying in a group alter their frequencies slightly so that they can more easily detect their own echoes.

Sounds are emitted through the open mouth or nostrils depending on species. Those bats with elaborate noses, including horseshoes, leaf-nosed, slit-faced, false vampires and spear-nosed bats, and some common bats like the long-eared *Plecotus*, emit sounds through the nose. The nose-leaf, acting as a transducer, may modify, direct and focus the sound, producing a more concentrated beam. In order to scan an area the head is moved from side to side. The shape of the nose-leaf is constantly modified to accommodate the changing needs.

Most species use pulses that sweep down through a range of frequencies—so-called frequency-modulated (FM) calls. They can be produced as a shallow sweep of long duration, or a steep sweep of short duration. It is believed the steep FM pulses improve object discrimination and that this can be further refined by producing harmonics. Some bats, eg *Nyctalus* species, suppress the fundamental while accentuating a harmonic.

Leaf-nosed and horseshoe bats, as well as at least one of the leaf-chinned bats, are known to emit pure constant frequency (CF) pulses, terminating in a short FM sweep. Bats of other microchiropteran families also produce a CF pulse, usually while traveling at high altitude well away from obstructions. (See diagram and caption for how bats find prey by echolocation.)

At sea level sound travels at 1,115ft per second. A stationary observer listening to a passing train perceives higher frequencies as it approaches and lower frequencies when it is moving away – the so-called Doppler effect. It results because the number of sound waves arriving per second increases with oncoming vehicles and decreases as they go away. A bat emitting sounds and the prey reflecting echoes are moving independently, therefore the echo will be heard by the bat at a different frequency from the emission. Bats primarily using FM already listen to a wide range of frequencies but for species using pure-tone CF the echo may return at a frequency to which their ears are less sensitive. To compensate for this Doppler shift, bats like the Greater horseshoe lower the frequency of their CF emission so that the returning echoes arrive at their maximum hearing acuity of 83kHz.

Members of only one megachiropteran genus, *Rousettus*, produce echolocation sounds. Most flying foxes roost in trees and navigate only by sight. However, rousette bats usually roost in caves and their echolocation enables them to navigate out of the cave, and thereafter they rely on sight. Unlike other echolocation bats, rousettes produce sound pulses with their tongues.

The unsophisticated sounds embrace a wide band (5–100kHz), but include mostly high-amplitude long wavelengths (low frequencies) which are best for long-range orientation. The sounds are audible to humans as metallic clicks.

Reproduction

Reproductive behavior is known in detail for only a few bat species but even so a variety of systems are found. For many, particularly temperate bat species, food availability varies over the year. Because of the high energy demands of producing milk (lactation) to feed the young it is crucial that birth coincides with a period of consistently abundant food. Migration and hibernation also limit the optimum mating season. Probably most bats produce one offspring per litter and one litter per year, but a number have twins and the Red bat in North America averages three. In northern Europe, pipistrelles produce a single offspring, but in more southerly areas twins are common. Since among recorded births twins are more frequent in well-fed captive bats than in the same species in the wild, twinning is probably related to better nutrition.

Sexual maturity is usually attained within 12 months from birth. For example, many pipistrelles and the Little brown bat give birth at the end of their first year although in the latter species males do not breed until their second. At the edge of their range in Britain male Greater horseshoe bats mostly mature in their second year; however, females are normally four years old before their first pregnancy (exceptionally seven or more years) and some do not breed each year for the first few years after

▲ **Crowded crèche.** Masses of newly-born, naked Schreiber's bent-winged bats in the roof of a nursery cave. Such nurseries can contain up to 280 young per square foot (about 3,000/square meter) which are nursed and reared to independence by their mothers. In Australia young are born in December and disperse, sometimes over hundreds of miles, during February and March. Nursery caves are selected for their high temperature and humidity, and have been used for thousands of years.

▶ **Blind as a bat**—but only until their eyes open. A female flying fox and newly born young. Most bats have only one young at a time.

◀ **Dawn bat roost in Indonesian cave.** Anything from a few dozen to tens of thousands of Dawn bats roost in such limestone caves. These bats breed throughout the year and at any time more than 50 percent of the females are either pregnant or nursing young.

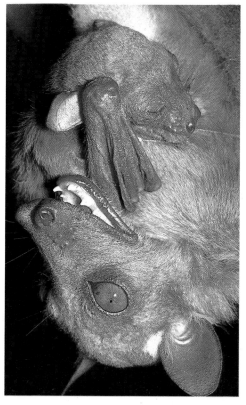

maturity. Almost certainly the poor breeding success of this insectivorous species is due to Britain's fickle climate, which greatly affects insect abundance. Greater horseshoe bats that go into hibernation with a relatively low body weight usually fail to breed. Also cold, wet, windy weather can result in insects becoming unavailable, and during lactation females need a continuous food supply if the baby is to survive. Lack of insects for several days will cause mothers to abandon their young.

In equatorial forests food supply is often relatively constant throughout the year, but bats still breed once a year, although not necessarily all at the same time. Some tropical species come into heat (estrus) several times a year, often with an estrus immediately after birth, which can result in two or even three litters per year. Such is the case with some insectivorous common bats (*Myotis* species) and the nectar-eating Pallas' long-tongued bat.

As far as is known, most bats are not selective in mate choice, are promiscuous and do not form pair bonds. A few species,

such as the Hammer-headed bat in Africa (see pp88–89), form leks where the adult males gather in an area and advertise themselves by calling to attract females, who then select their mate. Male European Noctule bats, and the related Leisler's bat, occupy and probably defend a roost site throughout the fall, from which they repeatedly fly out during the night, calling loudly for a few minutes before returning to the roost, until a female is attracted. Up to 18 mature females may be with an individual male at any one time but no harem structure exists. Male Greater spear-nosed bats hold harems of females (see pp68–69).

In cool temperate species the female's receptive period begins in the fall and continues during hibernation. The male sperm is formed in summer and mating begins in the fall shortly after lactation and weaning of the season's young. Mating takes place at roosts and may occur at times throughout hibernation, with some females inseminated several times. During hibernation, some aroused males fly along cave passages, landing beside torpid females, which they awaken and copulate with, to the accompaniment of loud vocalizations.

Both males and inseminated females store viable sperm for up to seven months. This facility is unique amongst mammals and is mostly found in the common and horseshoe bats, occuring in both tropical and temperate species. It appears to ensure that females in temperate areas can be ready for ovulation and fertilization as soon as conditions become favorable in spring.

Delayed implantation of the fertilized ovum has been recorded in at least two genera. In the Straw-colored flying fox of Africa, blastocyst implantation is delayed three months so that births coincide with the onset of the wettest season when the maximum amount of fruit is available.

Some populations of the widely distributed insectivorous Schreiber's bent-winged bat also exhibit delayed implantation. In tropical areas, development may proceed without delay after mating and fertilization. With increase in latitudes, implantation is delayed for an increasing period. In Europe, fertilization occurs in the fall but, because of hibernation, development does not begin until spring. Depending on how long the previous season's young are suckled, gestation in this species can vary from three to 10 months.

Among temperate bats with body temperatures that are variable, the length of gestation is variable, depending on the weather and availability of food. During cold weather when insects cannot be caught, the bats enter torpor and fetal development ceases. As a result these bats can time births precisely to coincide with maximum food availability. Fetal growth rates in bats are slower than any other mammalian order, although those of some primates are similar. Gestation, which may last 40 to 240 days, has a low metabolic cost for the pregnant bat.

Most temperate species form maternity or nursery colonies which consist almost exclusively of adult females. Such clustering reduces heat loss and hence energy costs to each individual. Males usually roost some distance away, so avoiding competition for food.

In some species the young are born with the mother hanging upside down, but in others the mother turns head uppermost and catches the baby in the interfemoral membrane. Suckling may begin within a few minutes of birth. Most species, and especially the insectivorous bats which require maximum maneuverability, leave

their offspring at roost while feeding. When young are carried it is usually only when changing roosts. The young of most small species develop very quickly and fly within about 20 days; however, it may be three months before the larger flying foxes take their first flights. Vampires are the slowest developers, being suckled for up to nine months. Although maximum body dimensions are achieved within a few weeks after weaning, maximum weight may be reached only after several years.

Greater horseshoe bats of northerly latitudes do not reach their maximum weight for nine years, by which time females tend to breed every year rather than in alternate years. This probably reflects the increasing skill of the individual in finding food and roost sites adjacent to the best feeding grounds. Hibernating bats from lower latitudes with longer summers have more time from the end of weaning to the beginning of hibernation in which to accumulate food reserves. Bats that have a relatively low weight in early winter often fail to produce young the following year.

Maximum longevity for the Little brown bat and probably many others is in excess of 30 years, but very few bats in any population will achieve that age. Average lifespan is often about 4–5 years.

Energy Conservation and Hibernation

Animals have differing ways of surviving seasons when food is sparse or absent. The herds of antelope on the African plains, for example, migrate hundreds of miles to find grass. Other species survive periods when food is scarce by laying in stores for the winter or by hibernating. Many bat species fall into this latter category.

Harem Life in Greater spear-nosed bats

In Trinidad in the West Indies, Greater spear-nosed bats roost by day within caves in clusters of 10–100 individuals. Each cluster is either a harem consisting of one adult male and many adult females (an average harem consists of about 18 females), or a group of "bachelor" males.

The membership of a harem and its roosting location are very stable. The same adult females roost together for many years, perhaps for life (10 years or longer) and harem males can retain a harem for over three years. Bachelor group membership is less stable than that of harems, due at least in part to the occasional replacement of a harem male by a bachelor. Females within a harem and males within a bachelor group appear amicable, but throughout the year harem males vigorously defend their females from intrusion by other harem males or bachelors.

The resident harem males father most, if not all, of the pups born into their harems. Because of the large size of harems and the potentially long tenure of harem males, some males father over 50 pups during their reproductive life-span, while many bachelor males father none. Clearly, the reproductive advantages to a male obtaining a harem are enormous.

Neither the membership nor the stability of female harem groups depends on the harem males. The basic social organization in Greater spear-nosed bats appears to result from a male attaching himself to an existing female group and attempting to exclude all other males from access to these females.

Stable associations of females are common in mammalian social systems, and in many cases, for example lions, African elephants, Black-tailed prairie dogs and Belding's ground squirrels, the females within a group are relatives. In Greater spear-nosed bats, females are not generally related because all juveniles

◄ **Up in the rafters,** a group of female Long-eared bats, with young that are left in the roost at night when mothers leave to forage.

▼ **Cluster of Greater spear-nosed bats** with nursing young. In Trinidad mating takes place in the day-roosting groups between October and December and each female gives birth to a single young; most bats are born within a few days of each other in early April. A male which resides with a harem during the previous mating season (October–December) fathers most bats born to his harem females. If this male is displaced between the mating season and the birth of young, the new harem male does not kill or interfere with the young. Since females give birth only once a year, such behavior would not hasten a female's ability to mate and reproduce with the new male. (See boxed feature.) (The colored rings were used to identify individuals.)

A number of physiological changes occur during hibernation which allow the body temperatures to be reduced and energy stores to be eked out. (A similar function is served by the daytime torpor of many temperate bats in summer—discussed towards the end of this section). Several groups of animals hibernate, for example bears (Carnivora), squirrels and dormice (Rodentia), hedgehogs (Insectivora), but none to the degree of many bats. The body temperatures of most mammal hibernators fall less than 18°F (10°C) from the normal active temperature, whereas the core body temperatures of some hibernating bats drop to slightly below 32°F (0°C). The lowest such temperature recorded is 23°F (−5°C) for the Red bat.

In the fall, temperate bats rapidly gain weight as they accumulate food reserves, mostly in the form of subcutaneous fat, which can account for up to one-third of the total body mass at the beginning of hibernation. The change from summer to winter habit is sudden and may be triggered by an inter-relationship of daylength, temperature and food availability, combined with the body mass an individual bat has achieved. Generally old adult females are first to begin hibernation, followed in succession by adult males and juveniles.

It is not known how bats choose their hibernation sites (hibernacula). Their individual choice is crucial to their eventual survival through to spring. The lower the body temperature they can tolerate the longer their energy stores will last. However, low temperatures may have disadvantages, such as increased susceptibility to disease. Each species has its preferred range of temperatures. For example, the Brown long-eared bat of Europe and the Red bat of North America hibernating in hollow trees survive variable temperatures down to slightly below 32°F (0°C) while the European Greater horseshoe bat prefers the warmer (45–54°F/7–12°C) and more stable temperatures found in caves and mines.

Tree-holes and similarly exposed and poorly insulated sites are chosen by Noctule bats and many other hibernating bats which often gather in large clusters. They must prevent themselves freezing and use energy to maintain a warmer temperature with minimal cost to each individual. In cold weather, single roosting bats under the same conditions would need to move to a better insulated or warmer site to maintain the same level of energy consumption. In areas with very cold winters, for example central and eastern Canada and northeastern Europe (where the January isotherm is below 23°F/−5°C), few bats hibernate in hollow trees but bats migrate south in the winter to places with less extreme climates where clusters of up to 1,000 bats are known in large trees.

Caves, mines and fortifications are used by many bats which prefer less variable temperatures. Some, like the Greater horseshoe bat, appear to select sites very precisely according not only to temperature but also to the quantity of their individual energy store. Old adult females weighing 0.9oz (26g) in November select temperatures of 52°F (11.5°C), while in April they are found in roosts of 47°F (8.5°C) and weighing 0.75oz (21g). Comparable figures for first year females are 0.8oz (22g) at 51°F (10.5°C) in November but 0.6oz (16g) and 43°F (6.0°C) in April.

disperse prior to their first birthdays. Young females born in different parental groups in the same cave and in different caves assemble to form new stable groups; rarely, young females may join established harems.

It is not certain why these stable groups of females form. Normally they travel alone and independently of one another to their foraging areas, but occasionally they "swarm" at a large patch of food, suggesting that cooperation may occur on the foraging grounds. This could involve sharing food or information about the location of food, or defending food from members of other groups. Whatever benefits these females obtain from living in groups, it is apparent that kin-selection plays no role in determining group membership or group stability.   GFM

It is important for all hibernating bats that humidity is high, usually over 90 percent, to prevent excess evaporative losses which would necessitate more frequent awakenings to drink. This is particularly important for species like horseshoe bats that hang in exposed sites wrapped in their wings. The other hibernating bats fold their wings at their sides and often seek crevices where evaporation will be negligible.

Individual bats, such as horseshoe bats, return to exactly the same roost each winter and for a given individual five or more precise sites are used in succession depending on the changing temperature needs throughout hibernation.

Bats do not hibernate continuously but periodically awake, sometimes actually flying to a new site, while others remain *in situ*. Why they wake is puzzling, but a simple explanation is that they need to eliminate surplus water and waste products, which are toxic to tissues. Biologists have long noted that bats urinate shortly after being disturbed and this is part of the process of reestablishing a physiological balance (homeostasis). Some bats awake approximately every ten days, while others may go as long as 90 days. However, in the wild one cannot be sure that a bat that appears to have not moved in 90 days has not woken, urinated and returned to torpor without moving. Periods of torpor tend to be longer early in hibernation when warmer sites are selected but as the winter progresses and food reserves become depleted cooler roosts are preferred. It might be expected that bats choosing cooler sites would awake less frequently than the same species occupying warmer roosts. However, while this may be so in early winter, many bats in cooler areas awake with increasing frequency towards the end of hibernation.

Some cave-roosting species characteristically hibernate singly, or occasionally in small groups. Other species, such as the Little brown and Gray bats of North America and the Large mouse-eared and Shreiber's bent-winged bats of Europe and Asia, form clusters numbering tens or hundreds of thousands of individuals. These aggregations may have bats packed in densities of over 270 per square foot (3,000 sq m). The purpose of these dense gatherings is not understood because the temperatures within the clusters are often similar to those of individuals of the same species which are roosting separately. However, these clustered animals are often heavier at the end of hibernation than comparable bats that have roosted singly.

▲ **Daytime camp** of Spectacled fruit bats. Only large fruit bats roost in such exposed sites, sometimes stripping away leaves to improve vision. These bats are at the mercy of the elements and wrap their wings tightly around themselves when cold or wet, or hang with flapping outstretched wings when hot.

◄ **In cold storage.** The dew covering of this hibernating Daubenton's bat (*Myotis daubentoni*) indicates that its body temperature has dropped to that of its very humid surroundings in a cold cave.

▼ **Not clustered for warmth,** a hibernating group of Little brown bats in a cave roof. The temperature within this cluster would be similar to that of a solitary bat, so the reason for hibernating together is not known.

In contrast to hibernation, many temperate bats enter periods of torpor in their day roosts during summer when there is no overriding need to maintain a higher rate of metabolism. Vesper or common bats, and horseshoe bats can tolerate by far the widest range of body temperatures. These insectivorous bats which do not attempt to maintain a more or less constant temperature when living in temperate climates are termed heterotherms as distinct from homeotherms. For example in man, a homeotherm, normal temperature fluctuation is within 3.6°F (2°C) of about 98.6°F (37°C). Bats that hibernate often have active temperatures around 100.4–104°F (38–40°C) and up to 107.6°F (42°C) in flight, but they can allow their temperature to drop about 86°F (30°C) during digestion (often taking less than one hour), and subsequently down to the temperature of their surroundings. Corresponding heartbeat rates range from over 1,000 per minute to less than 20.

This ability to lower temperatures, and hence save energy, is particularly important for bats that live in cool temperate climates and depend primarily on flying insects, because insect abundance, even in summer, is variable from night to night. On wet, windy, cool nights insects will not fly and hence some bats will not even attempt to leave their day roost. Males generally become torpid at any time during the year but adult females in late pregnancy do not do so as they need to maintain higher metabolic rates so that the fetal development continues, ensuring young are born at the time of year when food is most plentiful.

Bats that hibernate may become torpid at any time in summer, especially in cold weather when food is absent. However, torpor in summer is less extreme than torpor in hibernation. The physiological differences between summer and winter torpor are not clearly understood. Some species in the tropics may enter a period of summer torpor (or aestivation). Like hibernators, they put on food reserves when food is plentiful then enter a type of torpor when food is sparse. Often their body temperature is about 86°F (30°C), much higher than a true hibernator.

Ecology

Bats occupy niches in all habitats except polar or the highest alpine regions and the oceans. Most are insectivorous, but there is a wide range of diets: insects, caught in flight and at rest; other arthropods, including scorpions, woodlice and shrimps; vertebrates, including mice, other bats, lizards, amphibians (see pp82–83) and fish, and blood of mammals or birds, as well as fruits, flowers, pollen, nectar (see pp86–87) and some foliage. While most bats specialize on a relatively narrow diet range, with none more limited than the Common vampire, which feeds throughout its life on the blood of mostly one breed of cattle (see pp84–85), some, like the Greater spearnosed bat, are omnivorous, feeding on vertebrates, insects and fruit (see pp68–69).

Nearly all bats feed at night and roost during the day at a variety of sites depending on species. In cool temperate regions it is advantageous to select roosts large enough to contain a large number of bats, so that each bat minimizes heat and evaporative water losses. Fine tuning of requirements may be achieved by bats moving round the roost either throughout the day or seasonally and by spacing themselves at varying distances. For example, a Yuma myotis in California moves down from the warmer air at the top of the roost when temperatures reach about 100.4°F (38°C), then flies off if temperatures exceed 104°F (40°C).

There are three main types of roost (caves; holes or crevices; and the open) and each species tends to specialize in one type. Caves insulate against climatic changes, but are unevenly distributed, although generally large numbers of bats may be accommodated in a single site. Tree and other cavities are more widely distributed but can accommodate smaller numbers and are more exposed to climatic changes. Only the large flying foxes hang in exposed camps from tree branches which are often deliberately stripped of leaves so as to improve visual observation within the colony. These bats are at the mercy of the elements and wrap their wings tightly around themselves when cold or wet, or hang with flapping outstretched wings when hot.

Social organization in colonies is poorly known (but see pp68–69). Colonial roosts have the advantage of energy conservation, but at night the bats have to fly farther in search of food. For example, cave colonies of the insectivorous Mexican free-tailed bat in the southwestern United States can total about 50 million individuals, which consume at least 550,000lb (250,000kg) of insects nightly, collected from many hundreds of square miles. They fly to feeding areas in tens or hundreds and undertake group display flights similar to those of flocking birds like starlings. These are thought to attract other bats to good feeding areas.

For some unknown reason Natterer's bats roosting in bat boxes in Germany invariably emerge and return in a specific order, with the earliest bats out the last to return.

Colonies of the small, insectivorous, Sac-winged bat in Central America maintain annual home ranges that encompass a variety of habitats. Insect abundance is very patchy, occurring at any one time over those plants which are in flower. Thus the size of each bat colony's home range is correlated with the distribution of vegetation types. This species forms year-round harems which roost on the side of trees with large buttresses. Up to five harems may be found on one tree, with much movement of females between adjacent harems. Territorial adult males entice females by elaborate displays involving vocalizations and flashing of the species' wing-sacs. The complex vocalizations include audible (to humans) "songs" lasting 5–10 minutes with repeated phrases. Intruding males will be pursued and even attacked. The territorial males similarly defend dense patches of insects from other males but allow their harem of up to eight females to feed. Large patches of food may be divided amongst several males with their harems.

Some bats feed on plants, mostly trees and large cacti, for nectar, pollen or fruit and such plants appear to have two flowering and fruiting patterns. There are those that flower and fruit in short seasons ("big bang" types) and others that produce small quantities over many months ("steady state" types). "Big bang" types tend to be visited by a large range of generalist bat species, while "steady state" plant species often have a species of pollinating bat that is specific to them. "Big bang" plants produce huge quantities of flowers, an adaptation which compensates for the fact that visiting bats destroy many flowers, while "steady state" plants are far more efficiently pollinated

and produce smaller quantities of flowers.

A typical "big bang" tree is the durian (*Durio zibethinus*) of Southeast Asia, which is pollinated by the cave-roosting Dawn bat. Throughout the year this species of bat visits at least 31 flower species. Dawn bats forage over an area of at least 25mi (40km) radius in flocks whose members may benefit from collective scanning of a wide area.

A typical "steady-state" plant is the Passion flower (*Passiflora mucronata*), which produces flowers at a rate of one per branch per night over several months that are pollinated primarily by Pallas' long-tongued bat. In its search for the widely dispersed flowers, the bat flies to and fro along a beat sipping nectar several times each night from the same flower, effectively bringing about cross-pollination.

Among the large array of fruit-eating spear-nosed bats in Central and South America, competition between species for limited food resources appears to be reduced by adjustment of feeding times. Four species of spear-nosed fruit bats (three *Artibeus* and a *Vampyrodes*) visit the same species of fig tree at different times and this probably reduces conflict between bat species. Territorial defense of fruiting trees does not appear to occur, although there is often much squabbling over fruits when large numbers of bats of the same and different species are present. Flying foxes tend to land in trees and consume fruit *in situ*, while spear-nosed fruit bats usually pluck fruits and fly to a safe perch to eat them. Predators, such as snakes and carnivores, often gather in trees with ripening fruit, knowing that bats will come to feed.

Typically bats are gregarious at roosts, forming mixed-sex groups for much of the year, but adult females often segregate for birth and weaning. Many of the insectivorous species from temperate regions are in this category, such as the Eastern pipistrelle, Big brown bat and Little brown myotis in North America, and the Common pipistrelle, Large mouse-eared bat, Greater horseshoe bat and Schreiber's bent-winged bat in Europe. In some species both sexes remain separate in single-sex groups except when mating, the extreme examples of this being species that are solitary roosters, for example the flying fox *Epomops franqueti* in tropical Africa, and the small insectivorous Red bat in North America. Some bats form harems which may be more or less permanent throughout the year, for example the Sac-winged bat or Greater spear-nosed bat in the neotropics (see pp68–69), and bamboo bats (*Tylonycteris* species) in South-

► **A second to live**—a Greater False vampire bat (*Megaderma lyra*) swoops on an unsuspecting mouse. False vampires are truely carnivorous, feeding on rodents, birds, frogs, lizards, fish, and even other bats, as well as insects and spiders. They hunt among trees and undergrowth flying close to the ground. Captured prey is sometimes taken back to the roost—a hollow tree, cave or building—to be eaten.

▼ **Sipping nectar**—a Gray-headed flying fox (*Pteropus poliocephalus*) feeds from a eucalyptus flower.

The present figure of over 130 genera of plants, representing many hundreds of species, known to be bat-adapted will undoubtedly increase as research proceeds and many more bat/plant interactions are discovered. Since bats often form half the mammalian species in rain forests, their survival is vital to the ecology of these and to the well-being of other habitats. Even though some species form enormous colonies which tend to make people consider the species' numbers to be limitless, the number of colonies is normally small.

east Asia; others form harems just for mating, for example the Noctule bat in Europe. Others apparently occur in monogamous family units, for example the New World False vampire and the Painted bat from Asia.

Myths and Conservation

Europeans have long regarded bats with superstitious fear. Why some people fear bats is not known, but poorly understood animals are often feared. Bats are generally secretive by day and emerge at night, traditionally a time when the Devil is at work. In European medieval art the Devil is often depicted with bat wings. In more ancient civilizations, notably the Persians and Chinese, bats symbolized longevity and happiness and highly stylized bats decorate all kinds of objects from buildings to furniture, fabrics and porcelain. Superstitions like "blind as a bat" and "bats becoming inextricably stuck in a woman's hair" are now disappearing due to education programs, mostly in the popular press. Indeed bat conservation projects all contain a large element of education.

Bat populations are declining rapidly worldwide and several species have recently become extinct. Bats that form large colonies, especially in the tropics, provide valuable sources of high quality meat, and their guano (excrement) is used and traded as fertilizer.

In Africa, Southeast Asia and islands in the Indian and Pacific oceans, the large fruit-eating flying foxes of the family Pteropodidae have been caught in small numbers for their meat for hundreds of years. Recently an increase in accessibility to habitats and in numbers of firearms have resulted in over-exploitation and now many species are threatened with extinction. On the western Pacific island of Guam the flying fox, *Pteropus tokudae*, has become extinct and a larger relative, *Pteropus mariannus*, which formerly lived throughout the Mariana island chain, is very vulnerable. It is extinct on several islands but survives on uninhabited well-vegetated volcanic islands, although even here it is sought after by raiding hunters. Other flying foxes on Yap and Samoa are similarly close to extinction, and some of their meat is traded to Guam. Hunting is very inefficient because several bats may be hit by shot simultaneously, some injured bats flying away before dying, and hence only some of those hit are usually recovered.

Thirty years ago thousands of the endemic Rodriguez flying foxes occupied Rodrigues Island east of (and a dependency of)

Mauritius. Now only about 200 remain due to deforestation and consequent removal of roosting sites and food. The few remaining acres of forest are critically threatened by encroaching agriculture and collection of firewood. These bats have always suffered periodic natural disasters since Rodrigues is in the Indian Ocean cyclone belt and every three years or so a large proportion of bats die by being blown out to sea, or subsequently by starvation since all the food is stripped off the trees. A breeding colony has been established by the Jersey Wildlife Trust in the English Channel Islands and survival of the species seems assured.

► **Silent hunter of Australian nights,** the Australian ghost bat (*Macroderma gigas*) has two notable statistics to its name. Firstly it is the largest microchiropteran bat; and secondly it is listed as vulnerable to extinction in the Red Data Book due to habitat loss—the fate of many bats with restricted distribution.

► **Survival in question.** BELOW Island species such as this Seychelles fruit bat (*Pteropus seychellensis*) are very sensitive to habitat disturbance and hunting.

▼ **Whirlwind of bats** leaving a cave at dusk in Java. Cave-dwelling bats are particularly susceptible to destruction through blockage of, or trapping at, narrow entrances.

a single small entrance through which all bats must pass. In Thailand, the small insectivorous Wrinkle-lipped bat forms cave colonies of over one million animals, from which local people have been gathering guano weekly for over 200 years to sell to farmers as fertilizer. Hunters now set nets around the cave entrances to catch, for meat, the fruit bats that roost in the same cave, at the same time killing large numbers of Wrinkle-lipped bats which are discarded. In consequence, guano production has declined and a local livelihood is threatened, as well as the bats.

Similar population losses have occurred in many countries worldwide, for example of the Mexican free-tailed bat in the southwest United States. Colonies up to 50 million were formerly estimated and more that 100,000 tons of guano have been extracted from one cave alone, but in this species declines in numbers appear to be related to the use of agricultural pesticides rather than to hunting.

In the United States fear of bats has been deliberately generated by the multi-million dollar pest-control industry to attract business for the destruction of bats in buildings. In reality, the anti-coagulant pesticide used in houses to kill bats is a more serious health hazard to humans than the bats themselves. The bats do not present a significant health hazard unless people pick up sick bats. In temperate regions the major causes of population decline appear to be loss of habitat and deliberate and accidental killing. Bats that are disturbed regularly while in hibernation will die through starvation and many roost sites such as caves and hollow trees have been blocked or felled, and habitats have been severely modified mainly through changes in agricultural and forestry practice, resulting in a reduction in the size of insect populations. Remedial timber treatments in buildings used by bats are known to cause the deaths of such colonies. To counter the decline in bat populations worldwide, education programs are being conducted by Bat Conservation International, an organization which gathers information on the status, distribution and threats, and implements research surveys and education programs (see pp80–81).

Bats are now protected by legislation in all European and many other countries; some important roost sites and feeding habitats are being specially designated. In general there is a severe lack of detailed knowledge about the ecological requirements of most bat species, and hence it is difficult to plan appropriate conservation measures. RES

Because of their importance for pollination and seed dispersal, the decline of some flying foxes populations is having serious effects on crops, and tropical forest and savanna habitats. For example, in Malaysia, colonies of the cave-dwelling Dawn bat in the Batu caves, near Kuala Lumpur, are threatened with destruction because of limestone quarrying and by over-exploitation by hunters using fishing nets to catch them. Formerly these bats ranged up to 25mi (40km) to find nectar and pollen, particularly from durian, each acre of which produced $10,000-worth of fruit annually. Since the decline in bat numbers durian production is failing.

In West Africa the Straw-colored flying fox seasonally forms clusters of one million bats. In the past a few bats were speared for food but modern shotguns can kill up to 30 per shot. Agricultural departments in several countries have suggested that these bats are a pest and should be thinned out or killed completely. However, recent research has demonstrated that this species is the most important disperser of seed in rain forests and savannas. For example, it disperses seed of iroko, a hardwood tree in West Africa which is the basis of a $100m-a-year industry.

Cave-dwelling bats are particularly vulnerable to destruction because often there is

THE 19 FAMILIES OF BATS

Abbreviations: HBL = head-and-body length; TL = tail length; FL = forearm length; WS = wingspan; WT = weight.
[*] contains species CITES-listed; [E] contains species endangered.

Despite their abundance, bats have not been studied in as much detail as most other mammalian orders. In recent years, partly as a result of technological advances which facilitate the study of nocturnal animals, an upsurge in interest has begun rapidly to improve our knowledge. New species are being discovered and others reclassified. However, various authorities recognize differing numbers of families, genera and species, and substantial changes will continue. Undoubtedly there are many new species awaiting discovery, especially in tropical forests. Unfortunately, with the loss of forests, species may become extinct before discovery.

With such a diverse order of mammals it is difficult in a few words to give a true flavor of the variety of shapes, sizes and life-styles. Diagnostic characters for each family, together with their size range and ecological niche, are given.

Suborder Megachiroptera

Flying foxes [E]
Family Pteropodidae
Flying foxes or Old World fruit bats.

Over 173 species in 44 genera. Old World tropics and subtropics from Africa to E Asia and Australasia including many islands in the Indian and Pacific oceans east to the Cook Islands. A few species reach warmer temperate regions north to Turkey and Syria and to the extreme south of Africa and SE Australia.
Size ranges from small to the largest bats, having wingspans approaching 6ft: HBL 2–16in; tail absent; FL 1.5–9in; WS 12–79in; WT 0.5–53oz.
Most species with dog-like faces, large eyes and conspicuous widely separated simple ears. Most have a claw on the second digit in addition to the thumb and males are generally larger than females. The majority do not navigate by echolocation but instead use their excellent eyesight. Members of the widespread genus *Rousettus* use poorly developed echolocation emissions in addition to eyesight, especially to locate their roosts, which are often in caves.
Coat: drab brown but a few species are brightly colored, eg **Rodriguez flying fox** (*Pteropus rodricensis*) varies from black to silver, yellow, orange and red. **Tube-nosed bats** (genus *Nyctimene*) are brightly colored with speckled membranes and a dorsal stripe; cryptic coloration helps avoid predation while roosting among foliage.
A few species have secondary sexual characters which develop in males for use in attracting females, eg tufts of light-colored or white hair emanating from glandular patches on shoulders. Males attract females by singing loudly and flashing the hair tufts. Diet primarily plant material, chiefly soft ripe fruits but also flowers, nectar and pollen which are taken by some smaller species (eg *Macroglossus* species) by their long tongue bearing bristle-like papillae; some may eat insects. May eat leaves at times of extreme food shortage. Flying foxes are essential to the pollination of many plants and to dispersing seeds. Some of the medium-sized and larger fruit bats are highly gregarious, forming colonies which may exceed one million individuals. The very large **Common flying fox** (*Pteropus vampyrus*) of SE Asia and Indonesia and the **Indian flying fox** (*P. giganteus*) of the Indian subcontinent often roost in the same sites throughout the year, whereas an ecologically comparable species in Africa, the **Straw-colored flying fox** (*Eidolon helvum*), usually migrates seasonally. The largest colonies, formed by the cave-dwelling **rousette fruit bats** (*Rousettus* species), number several million; these bats, which feed primarily on nectar and pollen, must fly considerable distances nightly to find sufficient food for survival.

Suborder Microchiroptera

Mouse-tailed bats
Family Rhinopomatidae
Mouse-tailed, rat-tailed or long-tailed bats.

Three species in 1 genus (*Rhinopoma*). N Africa to the S Sudan, Middle East, India and SE Asia, Sumatra. Arid or savanna areas, also agricultural and disturbed habitats.
Size small: HBL 2–3in; TL 2¼in; FL 2–3in; WT 0.4–0.9oz.
Tail exceptional being about as long as the head and body length and entirely free of membrane. Ears connected across the forehead with a distinct but simple tragus. Small noseleaf looking like a pig's muzzle. Insectivorous. Roosts of many thousands known, normally in caves or rock crevices, but have been associated for several thousand years with the pyramids, temples, palaces and other man-made structures. Do not hibernate but accumulate large quantities of fat seasonally and become torpid during cold dry weather when insects unavailable.

Sheath-tailed bats
Family Emballonuridae
Sheath-tailed or sac-winged bats.

Fifty species in 13 genera. Worldwide including many islands in the Indian and Pacific Oceans. Include some of the world's smallest bats with others medium-sized: HBL 1–4in; TL 0.1–0.5in; FL 1–3in; WT 0.1–1.4oz.
Tails short, projecting on the upperside out of the tail membrane so that the tip is free but ensheathed. Many species have small glandular wing sacs (larger in males) found in the propatagium and open to the upper surface; purpose unknown, but may attract females. Other species have large throat glands whose secretions often smell strongly. Coat mostly drab brown or black, some white and a few have cryptic patterns and tufts of hair. One of the smallest bat species—the monotypic **Proboscis bat** (*Rynchonycteris naso*) of Latin America—has grizzled fur with two light curved lines on the back and tufts of hair on the forearms. Insectivorous. Roost in all kinds of sites from hollow trees to buildings and caves as well as in the open. Roost holding their wings at about 45° to the body, appearing like dead leaves. Some highly colonial, eg **tomb bats** (*Taphozous* species); others solitary. Most occur in the tropics but some in cooler areas where they become torpid and may hibernate.

Kitti's hog-nosed bat [*] [E]
Family Craseonycteridae
Hog-nosed or Butterfly bat.

Single species (*Craseonycteris thonglongyai*), first described in 1974. W Thailand. Bamboo forests and teak plantations (natural vegetation had been removed mostly by the 1950s). The world's smallest bat and mammal: HBL 1–1.3in; tail absent; FL 0.8–1in; WS 6–6.5in; WT 0.05–0.10oz.
Tailless, but interfemoral membrane stretched between its rather thin legs. Ears relatively large with a tragus (prominence in front of outer ear opening). Nose glandular and pig-like in appearance. Upperparts brown to reddish or gray, underside paler, wings darker. Insectivorous and colonial, forming small roosting groups in caves. Total world population is thought to be about 200 bats.

Slit-faced bats
Family Nycteridae
Slit-faced, hollow-faced or hispid bats.

Eleven species in one genus (*Nycteris*). Africa and adjacent Asia, E Mediterranean and Red Sea, *N. javanica* in Malaysia and Indonesia. Arid areas as well as rain forests.
Medium sized: HBL 1.5–3in; TL 1.5–3in; FL 1.3–2.3in; WT 0.3–1oz.
Complex nose-leaf divided by a groove containing nostrils towards the muzzle tip and a deep pit between the eyes. Ears large and tragus small; unique amongst mammals in having a tail that is T-shaped at tip.
Coat: long, usually rich brown to grayish.
Insectivorous, including arthropods such as scorpions and spiders. Roost in caves, rock cliffs and animal burrows as well as trees and buildings where they often roost singly. Sometimes small groups occur with other species. Have several periods of estrus (heat) and give birth twice per year.

False vampire bats [*] [E]
Family Megadermatidae
False vampire or yellow-winged bats.

Five species in 4 genera. Old World tropics from C Africa, through India and SE Asia to the Philippines and Australia. Among the larger microchiropteran bats with the **Australian ghost bat** (*Macroderma gigas*), the largest: HBL 2.5–5.5in; tail absent; FL 2–5in; WT 0.7–7oz.
Ears very large and erect joined over the forehead; tragus divided. Eyes large. Nose-leaf prominent, largest in the African **Yellow-winged bat** (*Lavia frons*).
Coat: drab but very variable, ranging from bluish-gray to brown and whitish. Yellow-winged bat very colorful with ears and wings yellowish-orange and the fur usually bluish-gray to olive-green.
Diet variable, including small vertebrates, bats, small mammals, birds, reptiles, amphibia and fish as well as insects and spiders; legs, feathers and wings often litter the ground beneath perches. Color linked to their favorite roost sites. Drab-colored species mostly roost in caves, some solitary and others in small colonies. The Yellow-winged bat hides among foliage in bushes or trees where it can watch for passing food, mostly insects which it will catch and eat by day or night. Hunt rather like flycatchers, returning to a favorite perch after each foray.

Horseshoe bats [E]
Family Rhinolophidae

About 69 species in one genus (*Rhinolophus*).
Old World especially in the tropics; a few species in temperate Europe, Asia and Japan.
Mostly small; HBL 1.3–4in; TL 1–2in; FL 1–2.7in; wt 0.1–1.4oz.
Vernacular name derives from the horseshoe-shaped front part of the complex nose-leaf. Nostrils open central to the horseshoe and a sella projects forward with a generally pointed lancet running lengthwise. Ears usually large, pointed and always without a tragus. Like the flying foxes, the heads of these bats face downwards (ventrally) whereas most bats look along their long axis. Hind limbs poorly developed, unable to walk quadrupedally. Broad wings make them among the most maneuverable of species in flight. Coat: very variable color, from yellow through red to dark brown, gray and black.
Insectivorous, catching their food close to or from the ground. Roost mainly in caves or mines but also hollow trees and buildings. At roost fold their wings around themselves. Some species solitary but most are gregarious, sometimes forming huge colonies of many thousands. Several species hibernate and some aestivate.

Leaf-nosed bats
Family Hipposideridae
Leaf-nosed or trident bats.

At least 61 species in 9 genera.
Old World tropics from Africa through SE Asia to the Philippines, Solomons and Australia.
Closely related to the horseshoe bats but their size-range much larger: HBL 1–5.5in; tail mostly absent but may be up to 2in; FL 1–4.5in; wt 0.1–4oz.
Nose-leaf lacks a well-defined horseshoe and the lancet is a transverse leaf often with three points; no sella arising from the center. Ears generally large and pointed with no tragus. Mostly drab grays and browns but a few species brightly colored, orange or yellowish-gold, occasionally with whitish fur patches.
Diet: insects and other arthropods, but larger species such as the **Great round-leaf bat** (*Hipposideros armiger*) may opportunistically take small vertebrates as they do readily in captivity.
Roost mainly in caves but use all

kinds of shelter, including animal burrows. A few species apparently roost singly but all may be colonial and some form huge colonies numbering hundreds of thousands and possibly millions in large caves. However, each bat usually roosts slightly apart, at wing-tip distance, rather than forming dense clusters like many other species. Some species regularly roost in mixed-species groups and are often associated with a number of species from different families.

Leaf-chinned bats
Family Mormoopidae
Leaf-chinned, naked-backed or ghost-faced bats.

Eight species in 2 genera.
Extreme SW USA through C America and Caribbean south to central S Brazil.
Small to medium sized: HBL 1.5–3in; TL 0.5–1.3in; FL 1.3–2.5in; wt 0.2–0.8oz.
Lack a nose-leaf but have leaf-like development of the lips so that a dish-shape can be created. Several species apparently have naked backs but this is due to the wing membranes joining at the upper midline. Ears small with a tragus. Tail projects slightly beyond the end of the interfemoral membrane. Fur short and dense, reddish-brown to brownish-gray.
Insectivorous, feeding low, near to, or over water. Primarily roost in caves where at least half a million may occur, often producing large quanitities of guano which is sometimes mined for fertilizer. Large colonies occur at over 11,000ft in the Andes. Do not hibernate.

Bulldog bats
Family Noctilionidae
Bulldog or fisherman bats.

Two species in one genus (*Noctilio*).
Latin America from Mexico to Argentina.
Fishing bulldog bat (*Noctilio leporinus*): HBL 4–5.5in; FL 3–4in; wt 2.4oz. **Southern bulldog bat** (*N. albiventris*); HBL 3in; FL 2–3in; wt 0.5–0.8oz.
Fishing bulldog bat has short orange or yellowish fur which sheds water readily. This species is highly adapted for catching and eating fish, the most characteristic feature being huge feet on long legs with incredibly sharp claws. The toes are highly flattened laterally so as to present minimal resistance when pulled through water while attempting to gaff fish. Fish quickly transferred to the mouth where a combination of long thin

canines and large jowl-like upper lips, which form internal pouches, secure the slippery fish. Fish are thought to be caught by the bat echolocating ripples as the fish break the surface. Fish up to 3in long are taken. Fishing is generally undertaken in pools, slow-flowing rivers or sheltered coastal lagoons, but bats have been seen over open water areas. They also take insects, especially if fish are difficult to find. The smaller species is primarily insectivorous.

Short-tailed bats [E]
Family Mystacinidae

Two species (*Mystacina tuberculata* and *M. robusta*). New Zealand and adjacent islands.
Small bats: HBL 2in; TL 0.7in; FL 1.4–2in; wt 0.2–1oz.
Thumb and toe claws have extra projection or talon, unique among bats, which may aid running, climbing, or burrowing for food or excavating roost sites. Fur mole-like, gray, dense and velvety. Wings with thick membranes, and fold or roll up to facilitate movement on ground and digging. Tail dorsally perforates the upperside of the interfemoral membrane, as in the Emballonuridae. Ears simple and separate, with a long tragus. The tongue is partly extensible with papillae at its tip. Omnivorous, eating fruit, nectar and pollen as well as insects and other arthropods. Scurry through leaf-litter looking for animal food but fly weakly in search of plant diet. Roost in caves, rock crevices, seabird burrows or specially excavated burrows in decaying trees. Colonial but little is known of ecology. These two species and a vespertillionid bat are the only indigenous mammals in New Zealand.

Spear-nosed bats
Family Phyllostomatidae
Spear-nosed or New World leaf-nosed bats.

About 140 species in 47 genera.
New World from extreme SW USA throughout C America and Caribbean south to N Argentina.
Generally robust animals with sizes ranging from small to the largest American bat, the **False vampire** (*Vampyrum spectrum*): HBL 1.5–5in; tail absent or 0.1–2in; FL 1–4in; wt 0.2–7oz. Wingspan up to 3.3ft in *Vampyrum*.
Most species have a spear-shaped nose-leaf but five have none, or a more complex shape. Ears usually simple but may be very large and a tragus is invariably present. Apart from one more or less white bat, the

Honduran white bat, (*Ectophylla alba*), others are brown, gray or black, occasionally with hair tufts which are red or white and associated with glands producing oily secretions. Several species have longitudinal whitish lines on the face and/or body. Diet mainly insects, but a few carnivorous or omnivorous, eating small bats and other mammals, birds, reptiles and amphibians; and many feed on fruit, pollen and nectar, aided by the presence of a long tongue bearing bristly papillae in many species, eg **Spear-nosed long-tongued bat** (*Glossophaga soricina*), **Geoffroy's long-nosed bat** (*Anoura geoffroyi*) and **Mexican long-nosed bat** (*Leptonycteris nivalis*).
Roost sites variable including caves, mines, culverts, tree-hollows, animal burrows, termite nests and among foliage. A few species of the genera *Uroderma* (**tent-building bats**) and *Artibeus* make shelters by biting through leaf-ribs and hence forming "tents." Generally form small aggregations but some live in colonies of many hundreds. None hibernate. One or two species in the USA and high in the Andes may aestivate.

Vampire bats
Family Desmodontidae

Three species in 3 genera.
Mexico to N Argentina.
Medium-sized bats: HBL 2.5–3.5in; FL 2–2.5in; wt 0.5–1.2oz.
External tail lacking. Muzzles appear swollen and glandular, giving the impression of a nose-leaf. Fur is grizzled, being shades of brown, and one species, the **White-winged vampire** (*Diaemus youngi*), has white wing-tips and edges. Teeth highly specialized. The **Common vampire** (*Desmodus rotundus*) has 22 teeth, of which only the 6 chisel-like incisors and 4 razor-like canines play any part in feeding. A small sliver of skin about 0.1–0.3in is removed, usually from an area devoid of hair or feathers. The blood that flows, aided by anticoagulants in the saliva, is lapped with the tongue which has two lateral grooves that narrow and widen during feeding. The Common vampire feeds on mammalian blood, mostly from domesticated species (see pp84–85); the other two much rarer species apparently prefer birds. Colonial, but groups tend to be small, usually much less than 100. Some authorities include this family in the Phyllostomatidae.

CONTINUED ▶

Funnel-eared bats
Family Natalidae
Funnel-eared or long-legged bats.

Eight species in one genus.
N Mexico through Colombia and Brazil, and including many E Caribbean islands.
Small and delicate: HBL 1.3–2in; TL 2–2.3in; FL 1–1.6in; wt 0.1–0.3oz.
Lightly built with long slender wings, legs, and with tails longer than the head and body. Ears funnel-shapèd and large with a short triangular tragus. Nose simple. Colors variable although rather drab from brown to reddish, yellowish and gray.
Little is known about these bats, but they occur in small groups or larger colonies mostly in caves, but also in hollow trees and elsewhere.
Apparently feed on tiny insects which are caught using the very high frequency ultra-sounds of up to 170kHz. There is some evidence that the bats aestivate but they do not hibernate.

Thumbless bats
Family Furipteridae
Thumbless or smoky bats.

Two species in 2 genera.
Tropical S America from Panama and Trinidad to Peru and Brazil.
Small bats: HBL 1.3–2.3in; TL 1–1.5in; FL 1.2–1.6in; wt 0.1–0.2oz.
Thumbs virtually absent (actually present but functionless). Ears funnel-shaped as in funnel-eared bats but broader, covering the eyes. Coat brown to gray. Virtually nothing is known of these bats but some have been found roosting in caves and they feed on small insects.

◄ **Tropical tent-makers.** These tent-building bats (*Uroderma bilobatum*) bite through the ribs and veins of leaves so that they bend over giving protection from sun, wind, rain and predators. The bitten spots also afford good footholds.

Disk-winged bats
Family Thyropteridae
Disk-winged or New World sucker-footed bats.

Two species in one genus (*Thryroptera*).
Hondurus to Peru and Brazil; tropical forest.
Small bats: HBL 1.3–2in; TL 1–1.3in; FL 1–1.5in; wt 0.1–0.2oz.
Wrists, ankles and functional thumb have disk suckers borne on short stalks; just one sucker able to support the weight of the bat roosting in smooth furled leaves such as those of *Heliconia* or bananas. Ears funnel-shaped with a tragus. Coat: drab reddish-browns or blackish, and whitish eventually. Diet: insects. Roost head upmost, singly or in small groups; little else known of their ecology.

Sucker-footed bat
Family Myzopodidae

One species (*Myzopoda aurita*). Madagascar. Very rare, in palm forests.
Small to medium sized: HBL 2–2.3in; TL 1.7–2in; FL 1.7–2in; wt?
Suction disks present on wrists and ankles (as in disk-winged bats) but they are not on stalks and do not appear to be as efficient in support. Fossils have been found in mainland Africa. Diet: assumed to be insects but nothing is known of its ecology.

Common or vesper bats
Family Vespertilionidae

At least 319 species in 42 genera. Worldwide except polar regions and remote islands; genus *Myotis*, containing over 60 species, probably more widely distributed than any mammalian genus except *Homo*. Mostly small but a few are medium to large: HBL 1–4in; TL 1–3in; FL 0.8–3in; wt 0.1–2oz.
Most have simple muzzles but about 10 species in 3 genera have a slight nose-leaf and 12 species in two genera have tubular nostrils. Tails substantial, extending to or slightly beyond the end of the interfemoral membrane. Ears normally separate and range from small to enormous, being most extreme in the **long-eared bats** (*Plecotus* species), where they approach the head-and-body length. Bats of five genera have wing and/or foot disks to aid grip on smooth leaves or bamboo. Coat mostly rather drab browns and grays but several genera bright yellow, red or orange, sometimes with white patches. The **Painted bat** (*Kerivoula picta*) has scarlet or orange fur, black

membranes and the finger bones picked out in orange. This cryptic coloration allows the bats to hide among flowers and foliage and is similar to the **butterfly bats** (*Glauconycteris* species), which have white spots and stripes in the cream to black fur with wings elaborately pigmented to look like dead leaves. Small clusters of *K. argentata* look like the hanging mud nests of wasps. Diet mainly insects and other arthropods, but a few species eg *Pizonyx vivesi* eat fish and others may be partially carnivorous. Roost sites include hollow trees and crevices in trees and rocks, amongst flowers and foliage, in bird nests and animal burrows. Majority cave-dwelling but have adapted to living in man-made structures including buildings, tunnels, wells, and culverts. Recently the **Northern serotine** (*Eptesicus nilssoni*) has been able to colonize treeless areas north of the Arctic circle in Lapland due to the building of permanent houses. Among the most adapted bats for exploiting a specialized roost are the tiny flat-headed sucker-footed **bamboo bats** (*Tylonycteris* species) of SE Asia, which gain access to bamboo stems through the small oval flight hole of a beetle whose larva has fed on the bamboo.
Some species roost singly or in small groups, while others form colonies which may total over one-million. Colonies generally occupy different roost sites seasonally and some species are known to migrate over 600mi either to find suitable sites for hibernation or to find adequate food. Species inhabiting temperate areas generally hibernate while some in the tropics and subtropics aestivate. Marked bats in the wild have lived over 30 years.

Free-tailed bats
Family Molossidae

At least 91 species in 12 genera. Warm or tropical areas from C USA, south to C Argentina; S Europe and Africa, east to Korea, the Solomons and Australasia.
Most are small- to medium-sized bats, with two large species, the naked bats of genus *Cheiromeles* of which *C. torquatus* is the heaviest microchiropteran: HBL 1.5–5in; TL 0.5–3in; FL 1–3.5in; wt 0.3–8oz.
Robust bats with a large proportion of the thick tail projecting beyond the tail membrane. Membranes leathery and wings long and narrow, facilitating fast flight. Ears with a tragus usually joined across the forehead and directed forward,

perhaps partly for streamlining. Fur usually short and sleek, drab brown, gray or black, but some are reddish with whitish patches, eg in *Xiphonycteris spurrelli*. The large naked bats have very thick black skin with wings joining at the mid-line of the back, and large skin pouches laterally into which the wing tips are tucked while at rest. Although essentially naked, they do have some short hairs, particularly associated with a throat sac, which many species possess, and the outer toe characteristically has short stiff bristles used in grooming. All *Molossus* species are insectivorous, catching their food in flight. Some members of several genera tend only to form small groups, others, especially of the genus *Tadarida* (about 40 species), form the largest colonies of any warm-blooded vertebrate. Nursery colonies of the **Mexican free-tailed bat** (*T. brasiliensis*) in SW USA have totalled about 50 million individuals and it is possible larger aggregations exist in tropical forest areas. The largest colonies occur in caves, but other species utilize all kinds of sites from rock clefts to hollow trees, among foliage and in buildings. Occasionally *Molossus* species appear to burrow and roost in rotten timber, and naked bats can be found in earth holes. Fly faster than members of any other family and may travel several hundred miles each night. Some species, eg *T. brasiliensis*, migrate over 800mi from summer to winter sites. None hibernate.

A Problem of Conservation

The Greater horseshoe bat

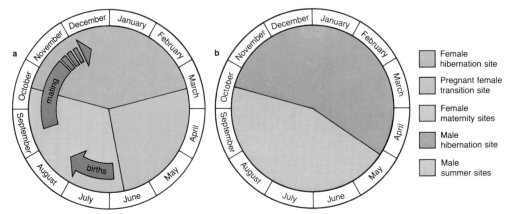

In the last hundred years the Greater horse-shoe bat has rapidly declined in abundance and distribution throughout its range in Europe and Asia from Britain to Japan. It is already extinct in northern parts of Europe and in some areas of the eastern Mediter-ranean. In Britain, colonies of several thousand were common a century ago; now the total population is only about 2,200. The causes of decline are many, but include vandalistic killing, destruction of roosts, disturbance of roosts by tourists visiting caves, and sport caving. Recently large colonies have been killed by insecticides used in timber treatments in buildings.

Recent research has been designed to ascertain the timing and rates of declines, identification and assessment of the likely causes, particularly giving emphasis to de-veloping a conservation strategy to prevent extinction. A major problem of working on such an endangered species is to avoid contributing to a further reduction—the Greater horseshoe (*Rhinolophus ferrume-quinum*) is a sensitive species whose behavior patterns easily change as a result of distur-bance. Two chief lines of research were followed relating to roosting and feeding behavior.

Greater horseshoe bats hibernate in sites with humidities close to saturation, so as to minimize water losses due to evaporation. Draught-free, dark, humid areas with slight seasonal temperature fluctuations are always used, each bat choosing the best temperatures according to its own body mass. In the fall, the heaviest bats occupy the warmest sites up to 54°F (12°C), while low-weight animals in the late winter selec-ted about 43°F (6°C). First-year, low-weight Greater horseshoes lose about 30 percent of their body mass while hibernating, while adults, which weigh 15–20 percent more, only lose 20 percent. It would be expected that older, and therefore experienced, animals would use less energy in hibern-ation than the young bats, but the older bats select the warmest sites where metabolic rates are higher. However, older animals, particularly females, awake from torpor less frequently than juveniles, resulting in con-siderable energy saving as consumption increases 100-fold during arousal.

Energy is also conserved in summer by clustering, especially after feeding, so that each bat spends less energy keeping warm during digestion. With the seasonally differ-ing environmental needs of Greater horse-shoes, a large number of roost sites are required by the colony, perhaps as many as 200. Individual bats will fly more than

37mi (60km) between roosts, even in very cold weather, to find hibernation sites.

In summer, pregnant females gather, often with non-breeding adults and imma-ture individuals (including a few males), in a maternity roost. These sites traditionally were in caves but since the 98 percent-plus decline in population over the last 10 years in Britain, maternity roosts are now sited in buildings. This change is due to the advan-tage of using a roost whose temperature is warmer than a cave. In southern Britain, cave temperatures are typically about 50°F (10°C), whereas roofs heated by the sun exceed 86°F (30°C). Originally cave matern-ity colonies were in the apex of dome-shaped areas where the large cluster comprising many thousands of bats collectively raised the temperature to about 82–86°F (28–30°C) so as to ensure continual development of the fetus at minimal cost to the mother. With the declining size of clusters each bat uses more energy to keep warm and even-tually none remains for reproduction.

▲ **Year in the life of horseshoe bats.** Adult males and females generally lead separate lives apart from mating. Then, it is thought, females visit a male at his traditional roost, although males are known occasionally to visit females at the maternity roost for unknown reasons. Juveniles and immatures tend to associate more with mature females than males.

(a) Females. On leaving hibernation sites (at which the oldest females tend to be solitary) pregnant females gather in increasing numbers at transition roosts before moving to maternity sites where birth and mating occur. Most juveniles remain in the maternity roost during the summer.

(b) Males tend to occupy the same traditional site both during winter hibernation and during the summer.

▶ **Wrapped against the cold,** a Greater horseshoe hangs from a cave roof with its wings closed around it. This prevents excess water loss. By changing the degree of wrapping the bats are able to critically adjust their immediate surroundings.

▼ **A rare sight,** Greater horseshoes clustered in a cave roof.

Adult males, often with immature males, usually occupy traditional roosts for most of the year spaced out in all areas of the colony's annual range, which varies from 270–965sq mi (700–2,500sq km). Periodically these males fly to the maternity roost but do not stay. The purpose of this is unknown, but perhaps they are trying to attract females for mating when they are ready. By remaining dispersed from the maternity roost the males avoid competition for food. Sperm formation occurs in summer and by September only one male remains in each roost site. It is assumed that other males are driven off, because the same male remains often for many years. It is not definitely known where mating occurs but it is likely that females visit the males in these traditional sites as soon as they are in heat.

Analysis of fecal pellets, collection of insects at feeding sites and radio-tracking techniques have been used to study food and feeding behavior. In spring, when nights tend to be cold and windy, bats immediately enter woodland and feed preferentially on large (0.04oz/1g) cockchafer beetles. After a hot day in summer the bats fly direct to woodland, then, seemingly realizing that more insects would be available over pasture, return and forage close to the ground. If the weather turns cold again the bats first fly over pasture, covering a large area field by field, presumably in search of and remembering the previous night's dense patches of food, but finding none return quickly to woodland. Because of the high energy cost of flying, it is important that adequate food is found quickly. Sometimes bats will either fail to leave the roost or return quickly when insects are absent.

In midsummer, lactating females forage over permanent pasture which has the highest density of insects. Large noctuid moths form the major prey, but prior to hibernation the large Dor beetle becomes the dominant food.

Radio tracking has revealed many previously unsuspected facets of the behavior and roost selection of Greater horseshoes. Further work is required, but it appears that woodland and adjacent old pasture are the two key habitats for this species and both these habitats have disappeared rapidly in the last 50 years. For the Greater horseshoe bats to survive, a large number of different undisturbed roosts are required adjacent to large tracts of woodland interspersed with permanent pasture. This survival recipe will be difficult to realize, and it appears that further population declines are inevitable.

RES

To Eat or be Eaten

Predatory habits of a frog-eating bat

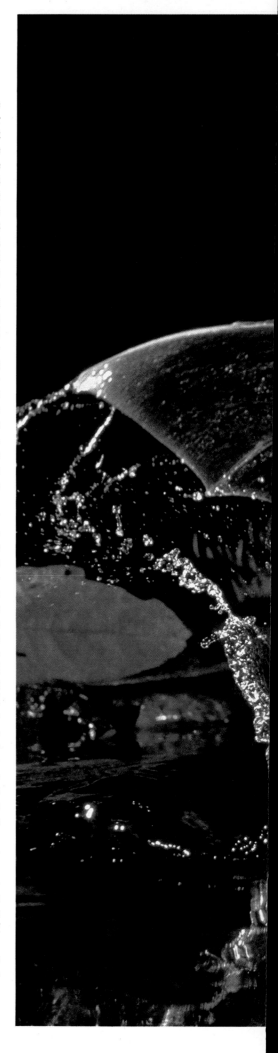

The Fringe-lipped bat lives in lowland tropical forests throughout most of Latin America. It feeds upon a variety of prey ranging from insects to lizards, but prefers frogs. Specialized hearing adaptations permit these bats to locate and identify the calls of courting male frogs.

Some of the most elaborate and striking displays by animals are those employed by males to attract and court females. Familiar examples include the elaborate plumes of male peacocks, the huge antlers of the extinct Irish elk, and the brilliant flashing of fireflies. According to the theory of sexual selection which Darwin first proposed in *On the Origin of Species* and developed more fully in *The Descent of Man, and Selection in relation to Sex*, these displays have evolved under the influence of female choice—the more elaborate the male's display the more likely it is to attract a female. But Darwin and others realized that there was a limit to which these displays could evolve because of their "costs," which include increased energy expenditure and greater risk of predation: a male peacock, for example, with a longer tail might attract more females but even if he had the energy necessary for growth, a tail which was too cumbersome for flight would make him an easy victim for predators.

Despite the importance of this idea, there are only a few cases where males advertising for mates have been proven to incur increased risk of predation.

Like most bats, the Fringe-lipped bat (*Trachops cirrhosus*) is nocturnal. A hallmark of the Panamanian jungle at night is the almost constant cacophony of calling male frogs which devote much time and energy to attracting mates. Male Tungara frogs, for example, sometimes call more than 7,000 times in a single night! But the calls do not only attract female frogs. Bats are well known for their ability to hear the very high frequency sounds they use for echolocation, but the Fringe-lipped bat also exploits the relatively low-frequency sounds made by male frogs. The bats simply home in on these calls for a quick meal. At one pond in Panama, several of these bats caught between them an average of 6.6 frogs per hour from a chorus of only 250 frogs.

Male frogs can increase their ability to attract females by making themselves more conspicuous. Depending on the species, they can do this by making more intense calls, calling more frequently, and by producing calls that contain more notes. If bat predation is an important counter-selective force on the evolution of frog vocalizations, then by behaving in ways which attract more females, male frogs also would increase their risk of predation. And that is exactly what happens. In one experiment bats were placed in a flight cage and frog calls were broadcast from two speakers. In all cases bats were attracted to the calls known to be more alluring to females. Bats and female frogs alike selected the more intense calls over the less intense ones, the calls with a faster repetition rate over the ones repeated at a slower rate, and the calls that had more notes over calls with fewer notes. But how do those attractive male frogs avoid being eaten? In further experiments it was shown that bats rarely catch silent frogs and on all but the darkest nights frogs recognize approaching bats by sight and stop calling immediately. Also frogs either ignore smaller insect-eating bats or start calling again quicker. Therefore, the frogs' vocalizations probably have evolved as a compromise between two opposing selective forces. Female choice selects for calls that make the males more conspicuous, while predation selects for calls that make the males less conspicuous.

Not all frogs are subject to predation by the Fringe-lipped bat. A number of species, such as toads, secrete chemicals that are highly toxic to most predators, including the Fringe-lipped bat. All species of frogs, including the poisonous ones, have their own distinctive, species-specific call. These calls enable female frogs to select mates of the correct species. But, once again, the bat is able to exploit information in the call originally intended for females. The Fringe-lipped bat is able to distinguish the calls of different species and use this information to avoid poisonous frogs. Furthermore, not all non-poisonous frogs are appropriate prey. Fringe-lipped bats are of medium size, usually weighing up to 1oz (30g). Some jungle frogs are larger, and one, the South American bullfrog, is known to turn the tables and eat bats. Fringe-lipped bats recognize the calls of such large frogs, as they do those of poisonous species, and avoid them.

Studies of bat–frog interactions demonstrate the important role that predation can have in the evolution of an animal's communication system. As more studies of this nature are conducted, it should become clear that only through an understanding of complex relationships among species can we hope to fully grasp the dynamics of the process of evolution.   MJR/MDT

▶ **Successful hunt**—a Fringe-lipped bat catching a mud puddle frog in a Panamanian pond.

A Myth Exploded

Hunting behavior of vampire bats

No other species has contributed so much to the misunderstanding, even fear, of bats than the Common vampire bat (*Desmodus rotundus*). These bats feed almost exclusively on the blood of domestic stock, for example horses, cattle, burros, goats, pigs etc, with an occasional blood meal from a wild host; rarely do they attack humans.

On a foraging flight, a Common vampire will alight either on the ground near, or directly on, a potential host. It painlessly inflicts a small—0.12in (3mm) diameter, 0.04–0.08in (1–2mm) deep—wound on the hide of the host with its razor-sharp incisors. Its saliva contains anti-coagulants which keep blood flowing freely from the wounds. Common vampires do not "suck" blood; rather, they make use of capillary action and dart their tongues quickly in and out of the wounds. In one feeding (lasting $8\frac{1}{2}$–18 minutes in the case of cattle), a vampire may ingest up to 40 percent of its own body weight; although this is quite a load for the bat, it is rather an insignificant blood loss for the host animal. (In captivity, a single bat will consume 0.5–0.7oz/15–20g each night.) Nevertheless, several bats may feed from the same wound, causing more severe blood loss and possibly weakening of the victim. Some bats also transmit diseases such as rabies to the hosts—a serious threat to livestock in Central and South America.

The Common vampire is active only during the darkest hours of the night, and avoids moonlit periods. This might be a tactic to avoid predation by other nocturnal predators, such as owls, but is more probably related to the activity pattern of its most abundant host—domestic cattle. In the tropics, cattle are active, and therefore sensitive to bat attacks, during moonlit periods of the night; during the dark hours, they bed down in tight clusters.

Exactly how vampires locate their potential hosts remains a mystery. Relative to other bat species they have good eyesight and a well-developed sense of smell. Given the relative volumes of the different brain structures, and the ease with which vampires can be trained in conditioning experiments, learning may play an important role in their daily lives. Vampires often change daytime roosts (hollow trees or caves) to those nearest their preferred cattle herds.

Vampires, like many other bat species, often use riverbeds as "flyways" (flight corridors) to move from one area to another within their home ranges. At one study site, the incidence of animals bearing fresh bites in a population of about 1,200 domestic cattle, decreased from 2–8 animals each

▲ **Hopping to its prey.** Common vampires often land near to their prey then hop and leap forward on the ground. Sight and smell are probably its major senses used to locate prey.

◄ **Razor sharp incisor teeth** and a grotesque head leave little doubt as to why vampires have a bad name.

▼ **Lapping blood** from the head of a pig, a vampire bat takes a meal. Domesticated animals are the major prey of vampire bats.

night at the riverbed to nil at about 1.2mi (2km) on either side of such a river.

Vampires are very efficient at finding prey and most accomplish this within three hours of leaving their daytime roosts. However, males and females show some behavioral differences: although both sexes are equally active throughout the night, females, especially those pregnant or lactating, feed earlier in the evening and appear to give feeding a higher priority than males.

Vampires appear to be selective in their choice of hosts. Within mixed herds of tropical Zebu (Brahman) and Brown Swiss cattle breeds in Costa Rica, vampires preferred members of the Brown Swiss over Zebu animals, calves over their cows and cows in heat (estrus) over non-estrous cows and over bulls! The explanation for these preferences probably lies in the animals' accessibility to the vampires. When a mixed herd of Brown Swiss and Zebu beds down for the night in a tight cluster, the Brown Swiss are most often to be found on the edge of the herd and are thus more easily approached by the vampires. One should not forget that these bats are feeding on animals 10,000 times their own weight—to attempt to secure a blood meal from a host amidst a densely packed herd of such animals is certainly dangerous for the bat. Calves remain bedded down a greater proportion of the night than their cows, and members of herds with both cows and calves bed down with greater spaces between individuals than do members of pure cow herds. Both these factors increase the calves' exposure to vampire attack. Cows in heat are also found

on the perimeter of densely-packed herds. It has also been noted that Brown Swiss are more docile and do not react as vigorously to vampire bites as Zebu.

The onset of the rainy season also heralds changes in vampire/cattle relationships. Normally, vampires inflict their feeding wounds on the neck-shoulder region. However, during the rainy season (wettest month September) there is a notable increase in the number of bites found on the cow's flanks, above the hooves and in the anal region. Furthermore, more animals are bitten during the wet season than in the dry season (lowest rainfall in February), and the degree of preference for Brown Swiss, although still significant, slackens. These changes can also be related to accessibility, since during the rainy season, members of a herd bed down farther apart than during the dry months. This effectively increases the number of animals in a herd exposed to vampire attack, increases the area of a host's body exposed to such attacks, and lessens the importance of Brown Swiss perimeter animals as vampire targets.

It appears that the Common vampire bat is an extremely adaptable species that has almost completely switched over to hosts associated with civilization (domestic forms) over the past 400 years. Due to the elimination of its former natural (wild) hosts and the tremendous increase in domestic herds in many areas throughout its distribution range, the Common vampire has been forced by man to adopt new hunting strategies in order to survive, which it has done with success.   DCT

Unlikely Partners

Mexican long-nosed bats feed on the nectar of desert plants

Bees, butterflies and hummingbirds are familiar nectar feeders and pollinators of plants; the flowers they serve possess elaborate devices to advertise and deliver nectar and pollen. In a similar manner certain bats and plants have evolved together to become unlikely partners in pursuit of food and sex.

New World nectar-feeding bats belong to the subfamily Glossophaginae (family Phyllostomatidae), which comprises 13 genera. The group is basically tropical, but the Mexican long-nosed bat (*Leptonycteris nivalis*) is a nomadic species which follows sequentially blooming plants northward into the desert of Sonora state and summers in Arizona. Here the bats feed from flowers of the giant saguaro cactus and agave.

These small—0.7–0.85oz (20–24g)—bats need a tremendous energy input—their in-flight heart rates may exceed 700 beats per minute. Unlike other bats they lack the ability to conserve energy through a daily lowering of metabolism (torpor). Nor do they store fat or hibernate. Without food, they would starve to death in two days.

As they forage for their summer food plants, Mexican long-nosed bats form flocks which feed at successive plants. Generally flocks contain at least 25 bats comprising adult females and their young (both male and female) of the year. The groups appear to have no social structure while foraging and tests show that there is no difference in food intake dependent on sex, age or weight. There is a lack of antagonistic interactions which is surprising in view of the constant bickering observed in other bat colonies, although the intense mutual grooming which takes place during intermittent roosts every 15–20 minutes may serve a conciliatory function.

While foraging the bats circle above a plant and take turns swooping down over the flower to feed. After feeding for several minutes at one plant, a bat from the flock may move to an adjacent plant and all the other bats follow immediately with no further passes around the original plant. No individual bat "leads" consistently, but the first bat to leave the plant is always the one that most recently visited the flowers.

The groups are truly cooperative, rather than merely congregating at abundant food, and their degree of cohesiveness is impressive. In field experiments, when many of the plants were covered so food was drastically reduced, flocking was tightly maintained, and there was no change in the lack of aggression nor emergence of dominance. When single bats were released from a cage to feed on wild flowers, they were seemingly reluctant to leave the flock. They returned and fluttered in front of their captive flockmates and made repeated sallies to and from the cage as if soliciting company.

The greatest advantage of flocking for these nectar bats is increased foraging efficiency. Because the bats live on such a tight energy budget this benefit of cooperation is critical. The Sonoran desert food plants are only available patchily in both space and time, and the flocking bats make initial energy savings since many eyes search the environment more efficiently than a single pair. The discovery made by one bat soon becomes communal knowledge. This is likewise true for locating especially rich spots within a patch of plants.

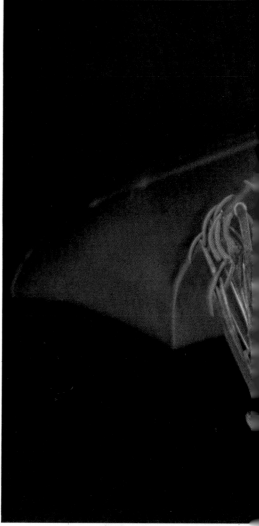

One of the primary decisions for a bat is how long to stay with one patch of flowers before moving on to the next. As the flocks work *Agave* inflorescences, they randomly deplete the nectar in the flowers; as foraging continues, the chances are increased that a bat will visit empty, unrewarding flowers. At a certain point, it will cost the bat more energy to circle around the inflorescence to find a full flower than it would cost to switch to the next plant.

Since no one bat "leads" the flock in switching from one plant to another, each bat must be an equally good decision-maker. The question arises of whether, for the calories the bats invest in feeding behaviors, they are netting the highest possible caloric

◄ Nectar mop. The tongue of a *Leptonycteris* bat can be extended almost the length of its body and is tipped with fleshy bristles.

▼ Quick feeders—*Leptonycteris* feeding from a century plant. Since bats cannot hover, they spend only a fraction of a second feeding during each pass.

reward from the flower population—that is, are they switching patches at the right time? A computer simulation, considering bat flight metabolism, flight speed and natural plant spacing and nectar data could only improve on the bats' efficiency by one part in 10,000! It has been calculated that the Mexican long-nosed bat uses 0.002 kilocalories (kcal) in its four-second flight around a plant and obtains 0.9kcal from feeding—a profit factor of 45.

In making such good decisions the bats assess such variables as levels of nectar (perhaps using their tongue as a dipstick), nectar concentration, number of empty flowers experienced, etc. They also form expectations. If they happen to feed from a particularly rich patch early in the evening and then switch to an average patch, they will tend to abandon the average one in a very short time. Evidently in comparison with recent experience, they "see" the patch as a poor one.

Young bats are apparently not good decision-makers, so performance appears to be improved through learning. Young bats foraging alone, which some do after the main group has returned to winter in Mexico, tend to spend shorter periods of time feeding at each patch of food, often leaving behind nectar. Thus these "impetuous youths" waste more of their energy traveling between plants than is necessary.

Unfortunately, nectar-feeding bat populations in Texas and Arizona have been decimated over the last 30 years. At best, a few thousand Mexican long-nosed bats now make the summer movement to the United States. A few decades ago, a single cave in Arizona was the maternity site for 20,000 individuals. Fears and superstitions have hindered attempts to conserve bats. General habitat destruction may be partially responsible. Another factor in northern Mexico may be "moonshine" pulque and tequila operations. Agaves have long been a local source of food and drink. In central Mexico, the plants are managed and replanted by the large tequila factories, but in Northern Mexico, "cottage" operations thrive. To make pulque and tequila the plants are harvested (and effectively destroyed) before they flower, leaving huge areas without flowering plants.

In United States agave populations which nectar bats no longer visit, plant reproduction is down to 1/3,000th of that in areas that are still visited by bats. Herbarium studies of fruiting capsules from agaves show a decline in the number of viable seeds over the last 30 years, paralleling the decline in bat pollinators. When agave populations diminish, the decline of the remaining bat populations is hastened. In Arizona, the organ pipe cactus and saguaro are also declining. Since these large, nectar-rich plants provide shelter and food for numerous other animals, the whole community is threatened. Individual animal species do not exist in a vacuum, and destruction even of one bat species can have far-reaching implications for the balance of nature, in consequence threatening the survival of further plants and animals. DJH

Buzzing Bats

The lek mating system of Hammer-headed bats

Hammer-headed bats are one of the few mammalian species which practice lek mating. A lek is an aggregation of displaying males to which females come solely for the purpose of mating. Females usually visit a lek, examine a number of males and then select one with whom to mate. Females are remarkably unanimous in this choice so that only a few males do all the mating. Females undertake all the parental care in lek species. Other forms with lek behavior include the Uganda kob among mammals and some birds, frogs, fish and insects.

Hammer-headed bats (*Hypsignathus monstrosus*) occur in tropical forests from Senegal, through the Congo basin to western Uganda; they form leks and mate during each of two—June–August and January–early March—annual dry seasons. A Hammer-headed bat lek nearly always borders a waterway, and varies from 0.4–0.9mi (0.7–1.5km) in length. Males are spaced about 33–49ft (10–15m) apart along the site and the array is usually about two males (range 1–4) deep. In Gabon, there are calling males on the sites for about $3\frac{1}{2}$ months each dry season. Early and late in the season, only a few males call. The number increases rapidly to a peak in July and February, and then declines more slowly towards the end of the dry season. Each night at sunset during the mating period, males leave their day roosts and fly directly to traditional lek sites. At the lek they hang in the foliage of the canopy edge and emit a loud metallic call while flapping their wings at twice the call rate. Early in the mating season, there is usually some fighting for calling territories. By the time females begin visiting the lek—and they start to do so before they are ready to mate—most territorial squabbles have been settled and there is little subsequent interference between males.

Typical leks contain 30–150 displaying males, each calling at one to four times a second and flapping its wings furiously. Females fly along the male assembly and periodically hover before a particular male. This causes the male to perform a staccato variation of its call and to tuck its wings close against its body. Females will make repeated visits on the same night to a decreasing number of males, each time eliciting a "staccato buzz." Finally, selection is complete, the female lands by the male of her choice, and mating is accomplished in 20–30 seconds. Females usually terminate mating with several squeals, and then fly off.

The importance of display in enabling a male to breed has obviously favored a heavy investment in the equipment it uses to advertise itself. Males are twice as large as females—15oz compared to 8.8oz (425/250g)—have an enormous bony larynx which fills their chest cavity, and have a bizarre head with enlarged cheek pouches, inflated nasal cavities, and a funnel-like mouth. The larynx and associated head structures are all specializations for producing the loud call.

Females can first mate at an age of six months and reach adult size at about nine months of age. They can thus produce their first offspring (only one young is born at a time) as yearlings. Females come into heat immediately after birth (post-partum estrus) and thus can produce two successive young each year. In fact, many of the females mating during any dry season are carrying newborn young conceived at the last mating or lek period. As with many lek species, males mature later.

Despite early reports to the contrary, these bats are entirely fruit-eaters. The fruit of several species of *Anthocleista* and figs form the major part of their diets in Gabon. Females and juvenile males appear to feed more on the easily located and closer (0.6–2.5mi/1–4km from the roost) but less profitable *Anthocleista* on which fruits ripen

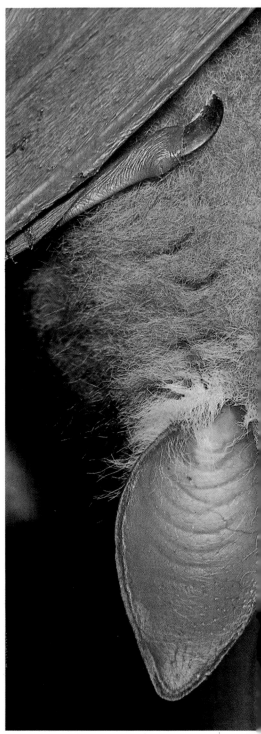

slowly and a few at a time. By contrast adult males fly 6.2mi (10km) or more to find the less predictable but more profitable patches of ripe figs where large numbers of fruit are available on a single trip, but only for a short while. This extra effort by males presumably pays off by providing more energy for vigorous display. It has the cost that, if unsuccessful, males may starve. The effects of variable food levels and the high energetic outlays during display may explain the higher parasitic loads (primarily hemosporidians in the blood cells) in adult males and the higher

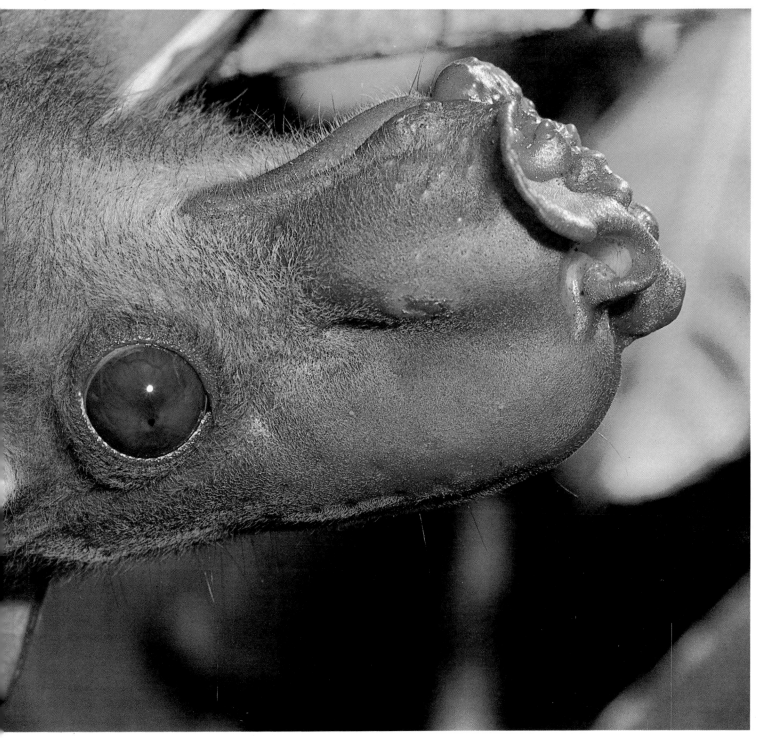

◄ ▲ **Genteel females, grotesque males**—
sexual differences in Hammer-headed bats. LEFT
female; ABOVE male. Young males quickly
become heavier than females of identical age,
but continue to have female-like heads until
yearlings. During the ensuing six months, males
become mature, complete development of the
enormous larynx, and develop the bizarre head
shape of an adult. They are then ready to join
leks for mating and, on average, live long
enough to attend 3–4 consecutive lek seasons.

annual mortality rates of adult males. It is
also reflected by the abandonment of display
by all males, even though females may be
visiting for mating, following days of colder
than average weather.

Lek mating is often considered a "default"
mating system, adopted when males cannot
provide parental care, defend resources
which females require, or defend groups of
females. It is easy to understand that the
expensive and chancy business of self-
advertisement in competition with other
males might be undesirable for males—

unless it is absolutely necessary. Hammer-
headed bats do appear to fit these gen-
eralizations: there is little males could do to
assist itinerant females with young, females
rarely form groups and those formed are at
best transient aggregations, and neither
roosts nor food sources are defensible, the
latter because fig trees are widely dispersed
and come randomly and unpredictably into
fruit. The costs of display are certainly
significant, yet males are committed both
physically and behaviorally to this system.

JWB

MONOTREMES

ORDER: MONOTREMATA
Two families; 3 genera; 3 species.

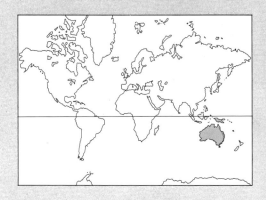

Echidnas **Platypus**

v Vulnerable.

Family Tachyglossidae

Short-beaked echidna

Tachyglossus aculeatus
Short-beaked or Common echidna (or spiny anteater).
Distribution: Australia, Tasmania, New Guinea.
Habitat: almost all types, semi-arid to alpine.
Size: head-body length 12–18in (30–45cm);
weight 5.5–17.6lb (2.5–8kg). Males 25 percent
larger than females.
Coat: black to light brown, with spines on back
and sides; long narrow snout without hair.
Gestation: about 14 days.
Longevity: not known in wild (extremely long-
lived in captivity—up to 49 years).

WHILE the description of monotremes as "the egg-laying mammals" clearly distinguishes them from any other living animals, it exaggerates the significance of egg-laying in the group. The overall pattern of reproduction is clearly mammalian, with only a brief, vestigial period of development of the young within the egg. The eggs are soft-shelled and hatch after 10 days, whereupon the young remain (in a pouch in the echidnas) dependent on the mother's milk for 3–4 months in the platypus and about six months in echidnas. Nonetheless, the term "egg-laying mammal" has long been synonymous with "reptile-like" or "primitive mammal," regardless of the fact that monotremes possess all the major mammalian features: a well-developed fur coat, mammary glands, a single bone in the lower jaw and three bones (incus, stapes and malleus) in the middle ear. Monotremes are also endothermic; their body temperature, although variable in echidnas, remains above environmental temperatures during winter.

Monotremes have separate uteri entering a common urino-genital passage joined to a cloaca, into which the gut and excretory systems also enter. The one common opening to the outside of the body gave the name to the group to which the animals are now known to belong—the order Monotremata ("one-holed creatures").

Although clearly mammals, monotremes are highly specialized ones, particularly in regard to feeding. The platypus is a semi-aquatic carnivorous mammal that feeds on invertebrates living on the bottom of fresh-water streams. Echidnas are terrestrial carnivorous mammals, specializing in ants and termites (Short-beaked or Common echidna) or noncolonial insects and earthworms (Long-beaked echidna). Such diets require grinding rather than cutting or tearing, and monotremes lack teeth as adults. In the platypus, teeth actually start to develop and may even serve as grinding surfaces in the very young, but the teeth never fully develop and regress to be replaced by horny grinding plates at the back of the jaws. Reduction of teeth is common among ant-eating mammals, and echidnas never develop teeth, nor are their grinding surfaces part of the jaw. A pad of horny spines on the back of the tongue grinds against similar spines on the palate, so breaking up the food.

In the platypus the elongation of the front of the skull and the lower jaw to form a bill-like structure is also a foraging specialization. The bill is covered with shiny black skin which contains many sensory nerve endings. Echidnas have a snout which is based on exactly the same modifications of

Long-beaked echidna ⓥ

Zaglossus bruijni
Long-beaked or Long-nosed echidna (or spiny anteater).
Distribution and habitat: mountains of New Guinea.
Size: head-body length 18–35in (45–90cm); weight 11–22lb (5–10kg).
Coat: brown or black; spines present but usually hidden by fur except on sides; Spines shorter and fewer than Short-beaked echidna; very long snout, curved downwards.
Gestation: unknown.
Longevity: not known in wild (to 30 years in captivity).

Family Ornithorhynchidae

Platypus

Ornithorhynchus anatinus
Platypus or duckbill.
Distribution: E Australia from Cooktown in Queensland to Tasmania. Introduced in Kangaroo Island, S Australia.
Habitat: most streams, rivers and some lakes which have permanent water and banks suitable for burrows.
Size: lengths and weights vary from area to area, and weights change with season. Male: head-body length 17.7–23.6in (45–60cm); bill length average 2.3in (5.8cm); tail length 4.1–6in (10.5–15.2cm); weight 2.2–5.3lb (1–2.4kg). Female: head-body length 15.4–21.7in (39–55cm); bill length average 2in (5.2cm); tail length 3.3–5.1in (8.5–13cm); weight 1.5–3.5lb (0.7–1.6kg).
Coat: dark brown back, silver to light brown underside with rusty-brown midline, especially in young animals which have lightest fur. Short, dense fur (about 0.4in/1cm depth). Light patch below eye/ear groove.
Gestation: not known (probably 2–3 weeks).
Incubation: not known (probably about 10 days).
Longevity: 10 or more years (17-plus in captivity).

▶ **The Long-beaked echidna** of New Guinea highlands feeds on earthworms and solitary insects.

▼ **From snowy regions to deserts,** the smaller Short-beaked echidna makes its home where there is a plentiful supply of termites and ants on which it feeds.

skull and jaws but is relatively smaller and is cylindrical in shape. The mouth of an echidna is at the tip of this snout and can only be opened enough to allow passage of the cylindrical tongue.

Monotremes are one of the two groups of venomous mammals (the other is certain shrews). In echidnas, the structures which produce and deliver the venom are not functional, though present. It is only the male platypus that actually produces and is capable of delivering the venom. The venom-producing gland is located behind the knee and is connected by a duct to a horny spur on the back of the ankle. This spur can be erected from a fold of covering skin and is hollow to deliver the venom, which causes agonizing pain in man, and can kill a dog. Venom is delivered by a forceful jab of the hindlimbs. Because the venom gland enlarges at the beginning of the breeding season, it has long been assumed to be connected with mating behavior. The marked increase in aggressive use of the spurs observed between males in the breeding season may serve to decide spatial relationships in the limited river habitat. However, that does not explain why

in echidnas the system is present but non-functional. The spur in male echidnas makes it possible to distinguish them from females, which is otherwise difficult in monotremes since the testes never descend from the abdomen. However the echidnas' venom duct and gland are degenerate, and the male cannot erect the spur. If it is pushed from under its protective sheath of skin, few echidnas can even retract the spur. It may be that the venom system in monotremes originated as a defense against some predator long since extinct. Today adult monotremes have few, if any, predators. Dingoes occasionally prey on echidnas, but dingoes are themselves a relatively recent arrival in Australia.

The platypus is confined to eastern Australia and Tasmania, while the Long-beaked echidna is confined to New Guinea, and the Short-beaked echidna is found in almost all habitats in all of these regions. But these distributions are relatively recent, as there are Pleistocene fossils of, for example, Long-beaked echidnas at numerous sites in Australia and Tasmania. Fossil monotremes from the Pleistocene epoch (after about 2 million years ago) are much the same as the living types. There is a platypus fossil from the mid-Miocene (about 10 million years ago), but it, too, is much like the living platypus, although the adult may have had functional teeth. The logical assumption is that monotremes are an old, specialized derivative of a very early mammal stock that has survived only by being isolated in the Australian region. But there is little direct evidence to show what that ancestral stock was. Australia and South America are assumed to have some special relationship because of their marsupial faunas, but no monotreme fossils have been found in South America, or indeed elsewhere. It has recently been suggested that modern monotremes are descendants of a long-extinct (and much wider spread, although unknown from Australia) group of early mammals known as multituberculates, but there is little supporting evidence. So the zoogeography and evolution of monotremes remain an enigma.   MLA

Echidnas are readily recognized by their covering of long spines (shorter in the Long-beaked species). Fur is present between the spines. In the Long-beaked echidna and the Tasmanian form of the Short-beaked echidna the fur may be longer than the spines. The spiny coat provides an excellent defense. When suddenly disturbed on hard ground, an echidna curls up into a spiky ball; if disturbed on soft soil it may rapidly dig straight down, like a sinking ship, until all that can be seen are the spines of the well-protected back. By using its powerful limbs and erecting its spines, an echidna can wedge itself securely in a rock crevice or hollow log.

Echidna spines are individual hairs and are anchored in a thick layer of muscle (panniculus carnosus) in the skin. The spines obscure the short, blunt tail and the rather large ear openings, which are vertical slits just behind the eyes. Spines are lacking on the underside and limbs. The snout is naked and the small mouth and relatively large nostrils are located at the tip. Echidnas walk with a distinctive rolling gait, although the body is held well above the ground.

Males can be distinguished from females by the presence of a horny spur on the ankle of the hind limb. Males are larger than females within a given population. Yearling Short-beaked echidnas usually weigh less than 2.2lb (1kg), but beyond that there is no way of determining age.

Echidnas have small, bulging eyes. Although they appear to be competent at making visual discriminations in laboratory

studies, in most natural habitats vision is probably not important in detecting food or danger. Their hearing is very good, and echidnas hear a person approaching and take cover long before they can be seen. In locating prey, usually by rooting through the forest litter or undergrowth, the sense of smell is used. When food items are located they are rapidly taken in by the long, thin, highly flexible tongue, which Short-beaked echidnas can extend up to 7in (18cm) from the tip of the snout. The tongue is lubricated by a sticky secretion produced by the very large salivary glands. The ants and termites which form the bulk of the Short-beaked echidna's diet are available throughout the year. One variation of foraging strategy occurs during the early months of spring (August–September), when Short-beaked echidnas attack the mounds of the meat ant *Iridomyrmex detectus* to feed on the fat-laden females: this is done regardless of spirited defense by the stinging workers, although the mounds are prudently avoided the rest of the year when males and females have left.

Short-beaked echidnas are essentially solitary animals, inhabiting a home range the size of which varies according to the environment. In wet forest with abundant food the home range area is about 124 acres (50ha). The home range appears to change little, and within it there is no fixed shelter site. Echidnas take shelter in hollow logs, under piles of rubble and brush and under various thick clumps of vegetation when inactive. Occasionally they dig shallow burrows as long as 4ft (1.2m), which may be reused. A female incubating an egg or suckling young has a fixed burrow. The home ranges of several individuals overlap.

▲ **Digging into an ant's nest** TOP, a Short-beaked echidna searches for food.

▲ **Near-buried sleeper** ABOVE, this Short-beaked echidna retires from the heat of the Australian summer. Disturbed on soft soil, the echidna will dig down, disappearing like a "sinking ship."

▶ **Unmistakable beak-tip nostrils** ABOVE, small protruding eyes and digging foreclaws of a Short-beaked echidna. The echidna draws termites and ants into its mouth on its long saliva-coated tongue.

▶ **Snorkel swimmer** BELOW, a Short-beaked echidna demonstrates the species' ability to cross most types of terrain.

During the mating season (June–August on mainland Australia) the female leaves a scent track by everting the cloaca, the wall of which contains numerous glands. This presumably attracts males in overlapping ranges. The only time echidnas are observed in groups is during the mating season, and on the only occasion when the sex of individuals in such a group was determined, the group consisted of one female being followed by a line of five males. In captivity echidnas kept in spacious accommodation do not form any sort of groups and are mutually tolerant. If kept in confined overcrowded quarters echidnas may form a size-related dominance order, but this does not seem to be a natural behavior.

The chief periods of activity are related to environmental temperature. Short-beaked echidnas are usually active at dusk and dawn, but during the hot summer echidnas are nocturnal and during cold periods they may be active during the middle of the day.

They avoid rain and will remain inactive for days if rain continues. Echidnas do not hibernate. It should be noted, in view of reports that echidnas hibernate, that the mating season is mid-winter in the southern hemisphere.

The female pouch is barely detectable for most of the year. Before the breeding season, folds of skin and muscle on each side of the abdomen enlarge to form an incomplete pouch with milk patches at the front end. There are no teats. The single egg is laid into the pouch by extension of the cloaca while the female lies on her back. After about 10 days the young hatches, using an egg tooth and a horny caruncle at the tip of the snout. The single young remains in the pouch until the spines begin to erupt. For a further six months or so the young continues to suckle. The young become fully independent and move out to occupy their own home ranges about one year after being born.

The Short-beaked echidna is widespread

and common (although little seen) on mainland Australia and Tasmania. However its status in New Guinea is uncertain.

The Long-beaked echidna and several other similar genera were once distributed throughout Australia but disappeared by the late Pleistocene (10,000 years ago). Today there is only one species, restricted to the New Guinea highlands. It is likely that the disappearance of Long-beaked echidnas from Australia, while Short-beaked echidnas have remained, is related to climatic changes in Australia and to differences in diet. Long-beaked echidnas feed largely, if not solely, on earthworms. Their tongue is equipped with horny spines located in a groove that runs from the tip about one-third of the way back. Worms are hooked by these spines when the long tongue is extended. It is necessary to take the worm into the long snout by either the head or tail, and if necessary the forepaws are used to hold the worm while the beak is positioned. Other details of the biology of Long-beaked echidnas are unknown although most of the information given above for Short-beaked echidnas applies to both species.

Like the Short-beaked echidna, which also occurs in New Guinea, the status of this animal is uncertain and zoologists who have visited New Guinea in recent times are concerned that Long-beaked echidnas are widely hunted for food.   MLA

Ever since the first **platypus** (a dried skin) arrived in Britain from the Australian colonies around 1798, this animal has been surrounded by controversy. Initially it was thought that the specimen was a fake, that a taxidermist had stitched together the beak of a duck and body parts of a mammal! Even when it was found to be real, the species was not accepted as a mammal. It did have fur but was found to have a reproductive tract similar to birds and reptiles. Because of this arrangement of the reproductive system it was suggested that the species laid eggs, instead of bearing its young live as did all mammals known at that time. But this suggestion (now known to have been correct) was discredited when it was found that the animal had the essential characteristic from which the class Mammalia takes its name—mammary glands.

Controversy did not end there however, and because the platypus has some skeletal features similar to reptiles (especially the pectoral or shoulder girdle) and because it does actually lay eggs, the species has been described as a "primitive mammal" or even a "furred reptile." As late as 1973 it was thought that the animal could not regulate its body temperature in the precise manner of most mammals, and that it became hypothermic when swimming in water and frequently had to retire to its burrow to warm up. This seemed strange for an animal which must obtain all of its food in water at all seasons of the year, and recent studies have shown that the species is truly mammalian in this respect also.

The platypus is smaller than most people think. The females are significantly smaller than males and the young are about 85 percent of adult size when they first become independent. The animal is streamlined, with a covering of dense waterproof fur over all of its body except the feet and the bill. The bill looks a bit like that of a duck with the nostrils on top just back from the tip, but it is soft and pliable. It is well supplied with nerves and is used by the animal in locating food and in finding its way around underwater, as the eyes and ears are both closed when diving. Behind the bill are two internal cheek pouches opening from the mouth. These contain horny ridges which functionally replace the teeth lost by the young soon after they emerge from the burrows. The pouches are used to store food while it is being chewed and sorted.

The limbs are very short and held close to the body. The hindfeet are only partially webbed, being used in water only as rudders while the forefeet have large webs and are the main organs of propulsion. The webs of the front feet are turned back when the animal is walking or burrowing to expose large broad nails. The rear ankles of the males bear a horny spur which is hollow and connected by a duct to a venom gland in the thigh (see p91). The tail is broad and

▲ **Scouring the water-bottom** for insect larvae, the platypus uses its touch-sensitive, pliable bill as its "ears and eyes" (the real ones are closed underwater).

◄ **"Beak of a duck, body of a mammal."** The glistening, streamlined surface presented by the long guard hairs of the platypus's coat conceals the thick, dry underfur that insulates the body from water temperatures which may in winter drop below zero in certain localities. The platypus can also increase the metabolic rate of its body chemistry so as to maintain normal body temperatures around 89.6°F (32°C).

experience water temperatures close to, and air temperatures well below, freezing in winter. When the platypus is exposed to such cold conditions it can increase its metabolic rate to produce sufficient extra heat to maintain its body temperature around the normal level of 89.6°F (32°C), lower than in many mammals, but certainly much warmer than that of reptiles in cold conditions. Good fur and tissue insulation help the animal to conserve body heat, and their burrows also provide a microclimate that moderates the extremes of outside temperature in both winter and summer.

Although mating is reputed to occur earlier in northern Australia than in the south, it occurs sometime in the spring (August–October). Mating apparently takes place in water after initial approaches by the female, followed by chasing and grasping of her tail by the male. Two (occasionally one or three) eggs are laid. When hatched the young are fed on milk, which they suck from the fur of the mother around the openings of the mammary glands (there is no pouch) for 3–4 months while they are confined to the special breeding burrow. This burrow is longer and more complex than the burrows normally inhabited, as it may be up to 100ft (30m) long and be branched with one or more nesting chambers. The young emerge from these burrows in late summer (late January–early March in New South Wales). They continue to take milk from their mothers for some time.

Although normally two eggs are laid, it is not known how many young are successfully weaned each year. Not all females breed each year, and new recruits to the population probably do not breed until they are at least two years of age. In spite of this low reproductive rate, the platypus has returned from near extinction in certain areas since its protection and the cessation of hunting at the turn of the century. This indicates that the reproductive strategy of having only a few young, but looking after them well, is effective in this long-lived species.

The platypus owes its success to its occupation of an ecological niche which has been a perennial one, even in the driest continent of the world. By the same token, because the platypus is such a highly specialized mammal it is extremely susceptible to the effects of changes in its habitat. Changes wrought by man in Australia have so far only affected individual populations of platypuses, but care and consideration for the environment must be maintained if this unique species is to remain. TRG

flat and is employed as a fat-storage area.

The food of the platypus is almost entirely made up of bottom-dwelling invertebrates, particularly the young stages (larvae) of insects. Two introduced species of trout feed on the same sort of food and are possible competitors of the platypus. However, both the fish and the platypus are common in many rivers, so that it can be assumed that they do not compete seriously. Recent studies in one river system have shown that the trout eat more of the swimming species of invertebrates, while the platypus feed almost exclusively on those inhabiting the bottom of the river. Waterfowl may also overlap in their diets with platypuses, but most consume plant material which does not appear to be eaten by the platypus.

Certain areas occupied by platypuses

MARSUPIALS

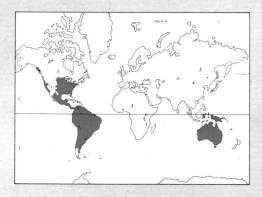

THE first marsupials brought from South America to Europe in the 16th century were considered zoological curiosities. It was not until the exploration and settlement of Australia from 1770 onwards that a sufficient variety of species was collected for European zoologists to realize that, rather than a few aberrant rodents, they were dealing with a natural group of mammals which shared a most unusual mode of reproduction.

Fossil evidence suggests that the ancestors of modern marsupials and placental mammals became distinct about 100 million years ago. The first undoubted marsupial fossils are known from the late Cretaceous of North America, about 75 million years ago, mainly from the family Didelphidae. Although there was at first some development in North America, marsupials later declined there as placental mammals increased in diversity, and they became extinct in North America about 15–20 million years ago. A few didelphid marsupials had spread to Europe by about 50 million years ago, but they were not conspicuously successful, and disappeared about 20–25 million years ago.

South America, on the other hand, had a considerable diversity of marsupial fossil forms only slightly later than the earliest known fossil marsupials in North America. This diversity persisted for the more than 60 million years that South America was isolated from North America. Seven families of living and fossil marsupials are known from South America, where they filled the omnivore and carnivore niches. About 2–5 million years ago, a land connection to North America was again established, and more placental mammals reached South America, including carnivores such as the jaguar. In the face of such competition, the large carnivorous marsupials disappeared, but the small omnivores have persisted successfully to the present day. Some marsupials moved north to recolonize North America, most notably the Virginia or Common opossum.

The earliest marsupials found in Australia so far are from some 23 million years ago, at which time most modern families and forms were clearly established. There is no clear fossil evidence to establish whether marsupials originated in North America, South America or Australia. Extremely primitive marsupials are known from the Cretaceous in both South and North America, making them a more likely point of origin than Australia, with no fossil record at this time. The lack of fossil marsupials in Europe, Africa and Asia makes the most likely route of the spread from South America to Australia via Antarctica. At this time the three southern continents were still united in the land mass known as Gondwanaland.

▼ **Fossil marsupials** include many instances of gigantism and flesh-eaters. In South America, the hyena-like *Borhyaena* (1) preyed on marsupial and placental mammals alike during the Miocene (26–7 million years ago); the jaguar-sized Pliocene genus *Thylacosmilus* (2) was similar to the saber-toothed cats living at the same time in other continents; when North and South America rejoined 2–5 million years ago, placental carnivores moved south, and forced large marsupials into extinction. In Australia, and related to today's kangaroos, was the enormous Pleistocene short-headed browser *Procoptodon goliah* (3) standing 9.8ft (3m) high. The 7ft (2m) long *Diprotodon* (4) may have survived until 20,000 years ago and the "marsupial lion" *Thylacoleo carnifex* (5) only died out some 30,000 years ago.

Bandicoots
Family Peramelidae
Seventeen species in 7 genera.

Rabbit-eared bandicoots or bilbies
Family Thylacomyidae
Two species in 1 genus.

Diprotodonts
Suborder Diprotodonta

Cuscuses and brushtails
Family Phalangeridae
Fourteen species in 3 genera.

Pygmy possums
Family Burramyidae
Seven species in 4 genera.

Ringtail possums
Family Pseudocheiridae
Sixteen species in 2 genera.

Gliders
Family Petauridae
Seven species in 3 genera.

Kangaroos and wallabies
Family Macropodidae
Fifty species in 11 genera.

Rat kangaroos
Family Potoroidae
Ten species in 5 genera.

Koala
Family Phascolarctidae
One species, *Phascolarctos cinereus*.

Wombats
Family Vombatidae
Three species in 2 genera.

Honey possum
Family Tarsipedidae
One species, *Tarsipes rostratus*.

Gradually, Gondwanaland broke up as each continental piece was moved over the surface of the earth by convection currents deep within the earth. This breakup began 135 million years ago with the separation of India, followed by Africa, Madagascar and New Zealand. Australia and Antarctica remained connected until about 45 million years ago and South America and Antarctica separated about 30 million years ago. Forty-five million years ago the climate of the southern land mass was much more congenial than it is now—Antarctica supported forests of Southern beech. The first (and so far the only) fossil land mammal to be found in Antarctica was a marsupial of the extinct didelphoid family Polydolopidae, in rocks about 40 million years old, which indicates that marsupials did exist in Antarctica at about the time when Australia became isolated.

The Australian crustal plate (including the southern part of New Guinea) gradually drifted northward for some 30 million years before reaching its present latitude, during which time its plants and animals were isolated from other continents, until Southeast Asia was approached about 10–15 million years ago. It is this long isolation which allowed the extensive development of marsupials in Australia in the absence of any competition from placental mammals.

Early Australian fossil marsupials of 20–15 million years ago include a preponderance of arboreal and browsing terrestrial forms. From the mid-Miocene (15 million years ago) extensive forests became confined to coastal areas and savanna woodlands took over large areas of the interior. The changes in climate and vegetation were matched by an increase in terrestrial grazing marsupials. Kangaroos formed an increasingly significant part of the fauna, and today are the most numerous marsupials over much of inland Australia. As recently as 30,000 years ago, there existed many now extinct giant herbivores, such as the 9.8ft (3m) tall browsing kangaroo *Procoptodon* and *Diprotodon*, the largest marsupial that ever lived, the size and shape of a living rhinoceros, a member of the now extinct family Diprotodontidae.

As the marsupials evolved in Australia filling the same ecological niches as placental mammals filled elsewhere so, in many cases, they adopted similar morphological solutions to ecological problems. One example of this convergent evolution, the carnivorous Tasmanian wolf or thylacine, is very similar in overall form to wolves and dogs of other continents. The so-called

Marsupial mole is very similar in form to placental moles, likewise burrowing insectivores. The marsupial Sugar glider and the two flying squirrels of North America have developed a similar gliding membrane (patagium).

Today's marsupials are found only in the New World and in the Australian region. In the USA and Canada there are only 2 species in one family, from Panama north, 9 didelphid species. South America has 81 species in three families, mostly small insectivores or omnivores, some of which are arboreal. Australia has about 120 species in 15 families and New Guinea about 53 species in six families. These range from tiny, 0.18oz (5g) or even less, shrew-like insectivorous dasyures to large grass-eating kangaroos (males may reach 200lb/90kg) with, in between, a great variety of medium-sized carnivores, arboreal leaf-eaters and terrestrial omnivores in a range of habitats from desert to rain forest.

Although there are many other anatomical differences, it is their reproduction that sets marsupials apart from other mammals. In its form and early development in the uterus, the marsupial egg is like that of reptiles and birds and quite unlike the egg of placental mammals (eutherians). Whereas eutherian young undergo most of their development and considerable growth inside the female, marsupial young are born very early in development. For example, a female Eastern gray kangaroo of about 66lb (30kg) gives birth after 36 days' gestation to an offspring which weighs under 0.03oz (about 0.8g). This young is then carried in a pouch on the abdomen of its mother where it suckles her milk, develops and grows until after about 300 days it weighs about 11lb (5kg) and is no longer carried in the pouch. After it leaves the pouch the young follows its mother closely and continues to suckle until about 18 months old.

Immediately after birth, the newborn young makes an amazing journing from the opening of the birth canal to the area of the nipples. Forelimbs and head develop far in advance of the rest of the body, and the young is able to move with swimming movements of its forelimbs. Although it is quite blind, the young locates (how is not yet known) a nipple and sucks it into its circular mouth. The end of the nipple enlarges to fit depressions and ridges in the mouth, and the young remains firmly attached to the nipple for 1–2 months until, with further development of its jaws, it is able to open its mouth and let go.

In many marsupials the young is protected by a fold of skin which covers the nipple area, forming the pouch (see diagram).

In marsupials the major emphasis in the nourishment of the young is on lactation, since most development and all growth occurs outside the uterus. For the short time that the embryo is in the uterus, it is nourished by transfer of nutrients from inside the uterus across the wall of the

BODY PLAN OF MARSUPIALS

▼ **Marsupial skulls** generally have a large face area and a small brain-case. There is often a sagittal crest for the attachment of the temporal muscles that close the jaws, and the eye socket and opening for the temporal muscles run together, as in most primitive mammals. There are usually holes in the palate, between the upper molars. The rear part of the lower jaw is usually turned inward, unlike placental mammals.

Many marsupials have more teeth than placental mammals. American opossums for instance have 50. There are usually three premolars and four molars on each side in both upper and lower jaws.

Marsupials with four or more lower incisors are termed polyprotodont. The Eastern quoll (*Dasyurus viverrinus*), has six. Its chiefly insectivorous and partly carnivorous diet is reflected in the relatively small cheek teeth each with two or more sharp cusps and the large canines with a cutting edge. Its dental formula is I4/3, C1/1, P2/2, M4/4 = 42. The largely insectivorous bandicoot (*Perameles*) has small teeth of even size with sharp cusps for crushing the insects which it seeks out with its long pointed snout (I4–5/3, C1/1, P3/3, M4/4 = 46–48).

Diprotodont marsupials have only two lower incisors, usually large and forward-pointing. The broad, flattened skull of the leaf-eating Brush-tailed possum contains reduced incisors, canines and premolars, with simple low-crowned molars (I3/2, C1/0, P2/1, M4/4 = 34). The large wombat has rodent-like teeth and only 24 of them (I1/1, C0/0, P1/1, M4/4), all rootless and ever-growing to compensate for wear in chewing tough fibrous grasses.

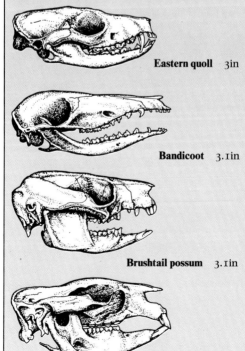

Eastern quoll 3in

Bandicoot 3.1in

Brushtail possum 3.1in

Common wombat 7in

Evolution of marsupial families. The fossil record of marsupials is very thin (in Australia for example no fossil is more than 23 million years old) and the early dates shown here are accordingly approximate. For the same reason much of the left-hand side of this "tree" is speculative. The evolution of the marsupial moles, cats, tiger, mice etc is a prime example of the convergent evolution of similar forms to fit similar ecological "niches" to those exploited on other continents by carnivores, rodents and herbivores.

Honey possum (Tarsipedidae)
Kangaroos (Macropodidae, Potoroidae)
Cuscuses, brushtails (Phalangeridae)
Ringtails, gliders (Petauridae, Cheirogaleidae)
Pygmy possums (Burramyidae)
Wombats (Vombatidae)
Koala (Phascolarctidae)
Marsupial carnivores (Dasyuridae)
Numbat (Myrmecobiidae)
Thylacine (Thylacinidae)
Bandicoots (Peramelidae)
Bilbies (Thylacomyidae)
Marsupial mole (Notoryctidae)
American opossums (Didelphidae)
Monito del monte (Microbiotheriidae)
Shrew opossums (Caenolestidae)

PLEISTOCENE
PLIOCENE
MIOCENE
OLIGOCENE
EOCENE
PALEOCENE
CRETACEOUS

2
7
26
38
54
65
100 Million years ago

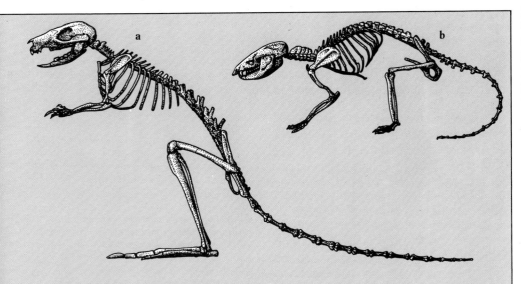

▲ **Skeletons** of (**a**) Tasmanian bettong and (**b**) Virginia opossum. The Virginia opossum is medium-sized, with unspecialized features shared with its marsupial ancestors. These include the presence of all digits in an unreduced state, all with claws. The skull and teeth are those of a "generalist," the long tail is prehensile, acting as "a fifth hand," and there are epipubic or "marsupial bones" that project forward from the pelvis and help support the pouch. The hindlimbs in this quadruped are only slightly longer than the forelimbs. The larger kangaroo has small forelimbs, and larger hindlimbs for leaping. The hindfoot is narrowed and lengthened (hence macro-podid, "large-footed"), and the digits are unequal. Stance is more, or completely, upright, and the tail is long, not prehensile but used as an extra prop of foot.

▼ **Feet of marsupials:** (**a**) opposable first digit in foot of the tree-dwelling Virginia opossum; (**b**) long narrow foot, lacking a first digit, of the kultarr, a species of inland Australia with a bounding gait; both these species have the second and third digits separate (didactylous); in many marsupials (eg kangaroos and bandicoot) these digits are fused (syndactylous), forming a grooming "comb": (**c**) opposable first digit and sharp claws for landing on trees in Feathertail glider; (**d**) first digit much reduced in long foot of terrestrial Short-nosed bandicoot—fourth digit forms axis of foot; (**e**) first digit entirely absent in foot of kangaroo.

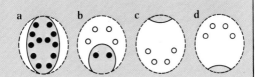

▲ **Pouches** (marsupia) occur in females of most marsupials. Some small terrestrial species have no pouch. Sometimes a rudimentary pouch (**a**) is formed by a fold of skin on either side of the nipple area that helps protect the attached young (eg mouse opossums, antechinuses, quolls). In (**b**) the arrangement is more of a pouch (eg Virginia and Southern opossums, Tasmanian devil, dunnarts). Many of the deepest pouches, completely enclosing the teats, belong to the more active climbers, leapers or diggers. Some, opening forward (**c**), are typical of species with smaller litters of 1–4 (eg possums, kangaroos). Others (**d**) open backward and are typical of digging and burrowing species (eg bandicoots, wombats).

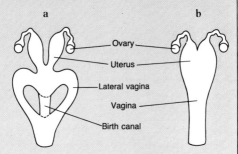

▲ **Anatomy of reproduction**, and its physiology, set marsupials (**a**) apart. In the female, eggs are shed into a separate (lateral) uterus, to be fertilized. The two lateral vaginae are often matched in the male by a two-lobed penis. Implantation of the egg may be delayed, and the true placenta of other mammals is absent. The young are typically born through a third, central, canal; this is formed before each birth in most marsupials, such as American opossums: in the Honey possum and kangaroos the birth canal is permanent after the first birth. The shape of uterus in placental mammals is shown in (**b**).

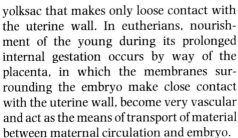

yolksac that makes only loose contact with the uterine wall. In eutherians, nourishment of the young during its prolonged internal gestation occurs by way of the placenta, in which the membranes surrounding the embryo make close contact with the uterine wall, become very vascular and act as the means of transport of material between maternal circulation and embryo.

A further peculiarity of reproduction, similar to the delayed implantation found in some other mammals, occurs in most kangaroos and a few species in other marsupial families. Pregnancy in these marsupials occupies more or less the full length of the estrous cycle but does not affect the cycle, so that at about the time a female gives birth, she also becomes receptive and mates. Embryos produced at this mating develop only as far as a hollow ball of cells (the blastocyst) and then become quiescent, entering a state of suspended animation or "embryonic diapause." The hormonal signal (prolactin) which blocks further development of the blastocyst is produced in response to the sucking stimulus from the young in the pouch. When sucking decreases as the young begins to eat other food and to leave the pouch, or if the young is lost from the pouch, the quiescent blastocyst resumes development, the embryo is born, and the cycle begins again. In some species which do not breed all year round, such as the Tammar wallaby, the period of quiescence of the blastocyst is extended by seasonal variables such as changes in day length. The origin of embryonic diapause may have been to prevent a second young being born while the pouch was already occupied, but it has other advantages, allowing rapid replacement of young which are lost, even in the absence of a male.

In marsupials, the only teeth replaced during the animal's lifetime are the posterior premolars. Relatively unspecialized marsupials such as American opossums, Australian dasyures and bandicoots have many more incisor teeth than placental mammals (10 or eight in the upper jaw and eight in the lower jaw, compared with a maximum of six upper and six lower incisors in the lower jaw). Those marsupials with at least four incisors in the lower jaw are termed polyprotodont, in contrast to the diprotodonts, which have only two incisors, generally large and directed forwards, in the lower jaw. Although the original function of these two teeth may have been for holding and stabbing insect prey, in herbivores they make, with the upper incisors, a wonderfully precise instrument for the selection of individual leaves or, indeed, blades of grass.

The Australian diprotodonts have the second and third toes of the hindfoot joined (syndactylous). So too do the polyprotodont bandicoots, suggesting that they share a syndactylous ancestor.

The most important senses of marsupials are hearing and smell. Most species are nocturnal, so vision is not particularly important. Arboreal species in particular use sound for communication at a distance, and all marsupials seem to live in a world dominated by smells. As well as urine and feces, each species has several odor-producing skin glands which are used to mark important sites, other animals, or themselves. It is known that the Sugar glider can recognize strangers to its group on the basis of scent alone, and it is likely that most marsupials recognize by scent other individuals, places and sexual condition.

The historical accident of their late discovery has led to marsupials being originally classified as a single order of the class Mammalia. Some modern authorities recognize that the antiquity and diversity of the group warrant division into a number of orders within a superorder Marsupialia. However, authorities do not agree on what the orders should be, because the affinities of the marsupial families are still constantly debated and uncertain, owing to the paucity of early fossil history. Here we divide the marsupials into 18 living families grouped into two suborders: the Polyprotodonta and Diprodota (see p96). The numbers of genera and species are only approximate, because new collections and modern work on old specimens are producing many changes in classification.

South American marsupials are mostly small terrestrial or arboreal insectivores or omnivores, but in Australia marsupials have adopted many of the life-styles found in placental mammals in other parts of the world: terrestrial grazing and browsing herbivores (kangaroos and rat kangaroos), arboreal folivores (koala and possums), arboreal omnivores (Sugar glider and pygmy possums), in addition to small terrestrial insectivores/omnivores (dasyurids and bandicoots), and nectarivores (Honey possum).

The "primitive" tag that was applied to marsupials for a long time was taken as sufficient explanation of why marsupial societies do not have the subtleties and complexities of primate and carnivore societies. Now it is clear that there is a range of social systems in marsupials which is the product of an independent evolution in response to ecological circumstances. However, the starting point of marsupial evolution in this respect was different, because the pattern of reproduction, with the young carried in a pouch or on the abdomen of the mother, was in itself an important factor in social evolution.

The common stereotype of marsupial parental care is a female kangaroo with one large young in her pouch, but there are other very different patterns. For example, in most species of the families Didelphidae (American opossums) and Dasyuridae (Australian carnivores), large litters of eight or more are born and, in contrast to the large deep bag of the kangaroos, the pouch is no more than a raised fold of skin around the nipples and does not enclose the litter. Immediately after birth, young didelphids or dasyurids stay firmly attached to the nipples, and are carried wherever their mother goes. As soon as the young are able to release the teat, the mother leaves the litter in a nest when she goes out to feed. At this stage the young have very little hair, their eyes are not open, and they are unable to stand, but the whole litter may weigh more than their mother, and is just too much for her to carry while she forages.

In the bandicoots and some of the smaller diprotodonts (eg gliders, Mountain pygmy possum, Honey possum), 2–4 young are born and the nipples are completely enclosed by the pouch. The smaller litter is carried until later in development, although it, too, is left in a nest when the young become too heavy for the mother to carry, but before they are able to follow her. Only those species which give birth to a single young carry it in the deep pouch until it is able to keep up with its mother on the ground or ride on her back.

In all mammals, because of the milk produced by the mother, male assistance in feeding the young is less important than in, for example, birds, where both parents may feed the young. In many marsupials, the role of the male is even further reduced because the pouch takes over the functions of carrying and protecting the young and keeping it warm. A female's need for assistance in rearing young does not appear to be an important factor promoting the formation of long-lasting male-female pairs or larger social groups.

The majority of marsupial species mate promiscuously, show few examples of long-term bonds and do not live in groups. That some species do form monogamous pairs or harems suggests that their general absence is due to the lack of external pressures

▶ **Life in the pouch**—the single young of an Australian Common brushtail possum attached to a teat in its mother's deep pouch. At birth the young weigh less than a hundredth of an ounce. Unlike other marsupials such as the Virginia opossum, whose much more numerous young are "parked" by the mother while she forages, this one will develop in the pouch for 5–6 months.

▼ **A "North Australian tiger"** depicted in an Aboriginal rock painting in Kakado National Park, Northern Territory. Better known as the Tasmanian wolf or tiger, or thylacine, the species became extinct on the mainland before Europeans arrived, probably as the dingo spread from the northwest. It survived in Tasmania, where there were no dingos, only to be hunted to extinction by Europeans.

For Aboriginal man, the animals of his world were an important part of his view of life, which saw him in a three-sided relationship with mythical beings and nature. Everything in his life was thought to be fitted into a pattern established when the world was made in the dreamtime, enshrined in the lore passed on by the storytellers. Specific reasons for the form and behaviour of every living creature were contained in the dreamtime stories. Every Aboriginal was linked to the mythical beings of the dreamtime by some creature of the present. Membership of a particular totem dictated the whole pattern of life, who should marry whom and which animals could be hunted.

predation and his domestic pets. Hunting (by small family parties with very limited equipment) by itself probably had little effect on marsupial populations. Less certain is the effect of the practice of burning large tracts of land both to drive out game which could be killed and to produce new growth that would attract kangaroos at a later time.

The second period of major change began with the arrival of Europeans with their sheep, cattle, rabbits, foxes, cats, dogs, donkeys and camels, and large-scale modification of habitat for pastoral and agricultural enterprises. Approximately nine species have become extinct and another 15–20 have suffered a gross reduction in range, persisting only in small isolated populations. The species which have suffered most from the changes wrought by European man are small kangaroos, bandicoots and large carnivores such as the thylacine and native cats. Habitat degradation by sheep, cattle and rabbits seems to have had most effect on the species of more arid regions, such as the Greater bilby or Rabbit-eared bandicoot, numbat and various rat kangaroos (eg Brush-tailed and Lesueur's rat kangaroos).

The environmental changes brought about by European man have not all been unfavorable to marsupials. A few of the large grazing herbivores, the kangaroos (eg Red, Eastern and Western gray kangaroos, and wallaroos), have increased in numbers and range with the spread of grasslands and watering points for stock, and in some areas are numerous enough to provide significant competition for sheep or cattle, mainly when food and water are scarce during droughts. These kangaroos, which at times are seen as pests, present the problem of keeping numbers below a level at which competition becomes significant. Harvesting is controlled by the fauna authorities throughout Australia with a quota of kangaroos to be shot each year determined on the basis of population surveys.

Most species of marsupial have little or no importance as pests and their continued existence depends largely on the maintenance of sufficient habitat to support secure populations and also on the control of feral foxes and cats, which have spread over the whole Australian continent and are significant predators of the small marsupials.

Of the marsupials outside Australia, the Virginia opossum in North America appears to coexist happily with man. Despite the widespread destruction of habitat in South America, no species of marsupial is classified as endangered.   EMR

favoring them, and not because marsupials are incapable of their development.

The marsupials lived in Australia without man for more than 45 million years. Since then they have lived first with Aboriginal man and subsequently with European man for less than 100,000 years (see LEFT).

The time since the arrival of man has shown some marked changes in the marsupial fauna of Australia. The first major change was in the late Pleistocene, with the extinction of whole families of some large terrestrial marsupials, most notably *Diprotodon* and the large browsing kangaroos. It is probable that the climatic fluctuations, increasing aridity and reduction of favorable habitat at this time placed many forms under increasing stress, and early man placed the final nails in the coffin with fires,

AMERICAN OPOSSUMS

Family: Didelphidae
Seventy-five species in 11 genera.
Distribution: throughout most of S and
C America, north through eastern N America to
Ontario, Canada. Virginia opossum introduced
into the Pacific coast.

Habitat: wide-ranging, including temperate
deciduous forests, tropical forests, grasslands,
and regions, mountains, and human settlements. Terrestrial, arboreal and semi-aquatic.

Size: ranges from the small Formosan mouse
opossum with head-body length 2.7in (6.8cm),
tail length 2.2in (5.5cm), and Kuns' short-
tailed opossum with head-body length 2.8in
(7.1cm), tail length 1.7in (4.2cm), to the
Virginia opossum with head-body length
13–19.7in (33–55cm), tail length 9.8–21.3in
(25–54cm) and weight 4.4–12.1lb (2–5.5kg).

Gestation: 12–14 days.
Longevity: 1–3 years (to about 8 in captivity).

Coat: either short, dense and fine, or woolly, or
a combination of short underfur with longer
guard hairs. Dark to light grays and browns,
golden; some species with facial masks or
stripes.

Subfamily Didelphinae

Seventy species in 8 genera, distribution as family.
Virginia or **Common opossum** (*Didelphis
viriginiana*), **Southern opossum** (*D. marsupialis*),
and **White-eared opossum** (*D. albiventris*);
mouse opossums, 47 species of *Marmosa*,
including the **Common mouse opossum**
(*M. murina*), **Ashy** (*M. cinerea*), **Elegant**
(*M. elegans*), **Formosan** (*M. formosa*) and **Pale-
bellied** (*M. robinsoni*) **mouse opossums**; the
yapok or **Water opossum** (*Chironectes
minimus*); **Lutrine** or **Little water** or **Thick-
tailed opossum** (*Lutreolina crassicaudata*);
short-tailed opossums, 14 species of
Monodelphis, including the **Gray short-tailed
opossum** (*M. domestica*) and **Kuns' short-tailed
opossum** (*M. kunsi*); **Patagonian opossum**
(*Lestodelphys halli*); **Brown four-eyed opossum**
(*Metachirus nudicaudatus*); **Gray four-eyed
opossum** (*Philander opossum*) and **Mcilhenny's
four-eyed opossum** (*P. mcilhennyi*).

Subfamily Caluromyinae

Five species in 3 genera, from S Mexico through
C America and most of northern S America.
Woolly opossums (*Caluromys philander*,
C. derbianus, *C. lanatus*); **Black-shouldered
opossum** (*Caluromysiops irrupta*); **Bushy-tailed
opossum** (*Glironia venusta*).

WHEN marsupials were first introduced
to Europeans in 1500, it was a female
Southern opossum from Brazil that the
explorer Pinzón presented to the royal court
of Spain's Ferdinand and Isabella. The mon-
archs examined this female with young in
her pouch and dubbed her an "incredible
mother." Despite this royal introduction,
the popular image of the opossum has never
been as lofty; they are often viewed as rather
slow-witted animals with a dreadful smell.
In fact, although not as diverse as the well-
known Australian marsupials, the American opossums are a successful group with a
variety of different species, ranging from the
highly specialized tree-dwelling woolly
opossums to generalists such as the Southern and Virginia opossums.

American opossums range in size from
that of a mouse to that of a cat. The nose is
long and pointed with long tactile hairs
(vibrissae). Eyesight is generally well-
developed and, in many species, the eyes are
round and somewhat protruding. When an
opossum is aroused it will often threaten the
intruder, with mouth open and lips curled
back revealing its 50 sharp teeth. Hearing is
acute and the naked ears are often in
constant motion as an animal tracks different sounds. Most opossums are proficient
climbers, with hands and feet well adapted
for grasping. Each foot has five digits and the
big toe on the hind foot is opposable. The
round tail is generally furred at the base
with the remainder either naked or sparsely
haired. Most opossums have prehensile tails
which are used as grasping organs as
animals climb or feed in trees. Unlike the
Southern opossum which was introduced to

Spanish royalty, not all female opossums
have a well-developed pouch. In some
species there are simply two lateral folds of
skin on the abdomen, whereas in others the
pouch is absent altogether. In males the
penis is forked and the pendant scrotum
often distinctly colored.

The Virginia or Common opossum of
North and Central America, the Southern
opossum of Central and South America, and
the White-eared opossum of higher elevations in South America are generalized
species, occurring in a variety of habitats
from grasslands to forests. They have cat-
sized bodies, but are heavier with shorter
legs. Although primarily terrestrial, these
opossums are capable climbers. In tropical
grasslands, the Southern opossum becomes
highly arboreal during the rainy season
when the ground is flooded. Opportunistic
feeders, these opossums vary their diets
depending upon what is seasonally or locally abundant. Their diet includes fruit,
insects, small vertebrates, carrion and gar-
bage. In tropical forests of southeastern Peru
the Southern opossum climbs to heights of
80ft (25m) to feed on flowers and nectar
during the dry season.

The four-eyed opossums from the forests
of Central and northern South America are
also rather generalized species. They are
smaller than the Virginia opossum with
more slender bodies. They have distinct
white spots above each eye, from which
their common name is derived. These
opossums are adept climbers, but the degree
to which they climb seems to vary between
habitats. The four-eyed opossums are also
opportunistic feeders; earthworms, fruit,

▲ **Possum up a tree.** The Virginia opossum is at home on the ground but may inhabit woodlands and is well able to climb trees. Its diet ranges from insects and fruit to carrion. Opposable first digits on hind feet are found in all American opossums.

◄ **A Woolly opossum** (*Caluromys lanatus*) peers through the leaves in the Amazon rain forest. The large forward-facing eyes are those of a specialized tree-dweller. Woolly opossums eat fruit and nectar.

insects and small vertebrates are all eaten.

The yapok, or Water opossum, is the only marsupial highly adapted to the aquatic habit. The hindfeet of this striking opossum are webbed, making the big toe less opposable than in other didelphids. When swimming, the hindfeet alternate strokes while the forefeet are extended in front, allowing them to either feel for prey or carry food items. Yapoks are primarily carnivorous, feeding on crustaceans, fish, frogs and insects. Although yapoks can climb, they do so rarely and the long, round tail is not very prehensile. Both male and female yapoks possess a pouch, which opens to the rear. During a dive, the female's pouch becomes a watertight chamber; fatty secretions and long hairs lining the lips of the pouch form a seal and strong sphincter muscles close the pouch. In males, the scrotum can be pulled into the pouch when the animal is swimming or moving swiftly.

The Lutrine or Little water opossum is also a good swimmer, although it lacks the specializations of the yapok. Unlike the yapok, which is found primarily in forests, Lutrine opossums often inhabit open grasslands. Known as the "comadreja" (weasel) in South America, this opossum has a long, low body with short, stout legs. The tail is very thick at the base and densely furred. Lutrine opossums are able predators, being excellent swimmers and climbers and also agile on the ground. They feed on a variety of prey including small mammals, birds, reptiles, frogs and insects.

The mouse, or murine, opossums are a diverse group, with individual species varying greatly in size, climbing ability and habitat. All are rather opportunistic feeders. The largest species, the Ashy mouse opossum, is one of the most arboreal, whereas others are more terrestrial (eg *Marmosa fuscata*). The tail in most species is long and slender and very prehensile, but in some species (eg the Elegant mouse opossum) can become swollen at the base for fat storage. The large thin ears can become crinkled when the animal is aroused. The females lack a pouch and the number and arrangement of mammae vary between species. Mouse opossums inhabit most habitats from Mexico through South America; they are absent only from the high Andean páramo and puna zones, the Chilean desert and Patagonia. In Patagonia, mouse opossums are replaced by another small species, the Patagonian opossum, which has the most southerly distribution of any didelphid. This opossum broadly resembles the mouse opossums. The muzzle is shorter, which allows for greater biting power. For this, and because insects and fruit are rare in their habitat, Patagonian opossums are believed to be more carnivorous than mouse opossums. The feet, which are stronger and possess longer claws than in mouse opossums, suggest burrowing (fossorial) habits. As in some of the mouse opossums, the tail of the Patagonian opossum can become swollen with fat.

The short-tailed opossums are small didelphids inhabiting forest and grasslands from eastern Panama through most of northern South America east of the Andes. The tail of these shrew-like opossums is short and naked and their eyes are proportionately smaller than in most didelphids and not as protruding. As these anatomical features suggest, short-tailed opossums are primarily terrestrial, but they can climb. Like mouse opossums, females lack a pouch and the number of mammae varies between species. Short-tailed opossums are omnivorous,

The Monito del Monte—a Hibernator

In the forests of south-central Chile is found a small marsupial known as the "monito del monte" or "colocolo." Once thought to belong to the same family as the widespread American opossums (Didelphidae), the monito del monte is now believed to be the only living member of an otherwise fossil family, the Microbiotheriidae. About 20 million years ago at least six other species of this family inhabited southern South America. Now the single remaining species, *Dromiciops australis*, has a limited distribution extending south from the city of Concepción to the island of Chiloe and east from the coast of Chile to the high Andes.

Monitos (little monkeys) have small bodies with short muzzles, small round ears, and thick tails. Their head-body length is 3.2–5.1in (8–13cm), tail length 3.5–5.1in (9–13cm) and they weigh just 0.6–1.1oz (16–31g). Their fur is short, dense and silky. They have a light gray face with black eye-rings. Their upper body is gray-brown with cinnamon on the crown and neck and several light gray patches on the shoulders and hips. This alternation of colors results in a slightly marbled appearance which may help camouflage the animal. The underparts are pale buffy. The tail is covered with dense body fur at the base and brown hair for the remainder.

These arboreal marsupials are found in cool, humid forests, especially in bamboo thickets. Environmental conditions are often harsh in this region, and monitos del monte exhibit various adaptations to the cold. The dense body fur and small, well-furred ears help prevent heat loss. During winter months when temperatures drop and food (primarily insects and other small invertebrates) is scarce, monitos del monte hibernate. Prior to hibernation, the base of the tail becomes swollen with fat deposits. The nests of these marsupials also protect them from the cold. They construct spherical nests out of water-repellent bamboo leaves and line them with moss or grass. The nests are placed in well-protected areas such as tree holes, fallen logs, or under tree roots.

Female monitos del monte have small but well-developed pouches with four teats. Breeding takes place in the spring and the number of young produced ranges from two to four. Initially the young monitos remain in the pouch, then the female leaves them in the nest. After emerging from the nest the young will ride on the female's back and, later, mother and young forage together. Both males and females become sexually mature during their second year.

There are various local superstitions about these harmless animals. One is that the bite of a monito del monte is venomous and produces convulsions in humans. Another is that it is bad luck to see a monito del monte; some people have even been reported to burn their house to the ground after seeing a monito del monte in their home.

▷ **A portrait of alertness** OVERLEAF This Southern opossum has the sensitive whiskers on a long snout, naked ears that move as they track sounds, and hands adapted for grasping that are typical of American opossums.

▼ **Representative species of American opossums** (family Didelphidae), plus single species from the families Caenolestidae and Microbiotheriidae. (**1**) Red-sided short-tailed opossum (*Monodelphis brevicaudata*) eating centipede. (**2**) Brown four-eyed opossum (*Metachirus nudicaudatus*) grooming. (**3**) White-eared opossum (*Didelphis albiventris*) showing strength of prehensile tail. (**4**) Ashy mouse opossum (*Marmosa cinerea*) climbing tree. (**5**) Yapok (*Chironectes minimus*) with fish. (**6**) Lutrine or Little water opossum (*Lutreolina crassicaudata*) in aggressive stance. (**7**) Woolly opossum (*Caluromys lanatus*). (**8**) Patagonian opossum (*Lestodelphys halli*) hunting spider. (**9**) Shrew opossum (*Lestoros inca*—family Caenolestidae). (**10**) Gray four-eyed opossum (*Philander opossum*) foraging for fruit. (**11**) Monito del monte or colocolo (*Dromiciops australis*—family Microbiotheriidae) in nest. (**12**) Black-shouldered opossum (*Caluromysiops irrupta*) eating nut. (**13**) Bushy-tailed opossum (*Glironia venusta*).

feeding on insects, earthworms, carrion, fruit etc. Often they will inhabit human dwellings, where they are a welcome predator on insects and small rodents.

The three species of woolly opossum, the Black-shouldered and Bushy-tailed opossum are placed in a separate subfamily (Caluromyinae) from other didelphids on the basis of differences in blood proteins, anatomy of the females' urogenital system, and males' spermatozoa. The woolly opossums and the Black-shouldered opossum are among the most specialized of the didelphids. Highly arboreal, they have large protruding eyes which are directed somewhat forward, making their faces reminiscent of that of a primate. Inhabitants of humid tropical forests, these opossums climb through the upper canopy of trees in search of fruit. During the dry season, they also feed on the nectar of flowering trees and serve as pollinators for the trees they visit. While feeding they can hang by their long prehensile tails to reach fruit or flowers.

Although the Bushy-tailed opossum resembles mouse opossums in general appearance and proportions, dental characteristics, such as the size and shape of the molars, indicate that it is actually more closely related to the woolly and Black-shouldered opossums. This species is known from only a few museum specimens, all of which were taken from humid tropical forests.

One popular misconception was that opossums copulated through the nose and that young were later blown through the nose into the pouch! The male's bifurcated penis, the tendency for females to lick the pouch area before birth, and the small size (0.5in/0.005oz) of the young at birth all probably contributed to this notion. Reproduction in didelphids is typical of marsupials: gestation is short and does not interrupt the estrous cycle. Young are poorly developed at birth, and most of the development of the young takes place during lactation.

Most opossums appear to have seasonal reproduction. Breeding is timed so that first young leave the pouch when resources are most abundant. For example, the Virginia opossum in North America breeds during the winter and the young leave the pouch in the spring. Opossums in the seasonal tropics breed during the dry season and the first young leave the pouch with the commencement of the rainy season. Up to three litters can be produced in one season, but the last litter is often produced at the beginning of the period of food scarcity and often these young die in the pouch. Opossums in aseasonal tropical forests may reproduce throughout the year. Year-round breeding may also occur in the White-eared opossum in the arid region of northeast Brazil.

There are no elaborate courtship displays nor long-term pair-bonds. The male typically initiates contact, approaching the female while making a clicking vocalization. A non-receptive female will avoid contact or be aggressive, but a female in estrus will allow the male to mount. In some species courtship behavior involves active pursuit of the female. Copulation can be very prolonged, up to six hours in Pale-bellied mouse opossums.

Many of the newborn young die, as many never attach onto a teat. A female will often produce more young than she has mammae. For example, most female Virginia opossums have 13 mammae, some of which may not even be functional, but they may produce as many as 56 young. The number of young in an opossum litter which do attach ranges from one to 15, but varies both within and between species. Older females tend to have fewer young and litters born late in the season are often smaller. Litter sizes in the Virginia and Southern opossums seem to increase with increasing latitude. The number of mammae provides an indication of maximum possible litter size. In general, some species (Virginia or Common opossum, short-tailed opossums, Pale-bellied mouse opossum) have comparatively large litters (about seven young), whereas others (Gray four-eyed opossum, Woolly opossum) have 3–5 young. Females of some species (eg Virginia opossum) cannot usually raise a single offspring because there is insufficient stimulus to maintain lactation.

The rearing cycle in species which have been studied ranges from about 70 to 125 days. For example, the Gray four-eyed opossum and Woolly opossum are similar in size (usually about 14oz/400g), but the time from birth to weaning is 68–75 days in the former and 110–125 days in the latter. Initially young remain attached to the teats. Later, the young begin to crawl about the female and/or are left in a nest while the female forages. Toward the end of lactation, young begin to follow the female. Female Pale-bellied mouse opossums will retrieve detached young within a few days of birth; in contrast, female Virginia opossums do not respond to distress calls of detached young until after the young have left the pouch (at about 70 days). During the nesting phase young opossums become more responsive to clicking vocalizations of the female.

Although individual vocalizations and odors allow for some mother-infant recognition, maternal care in opossums does not appear to be restricted solely to a female's own offspring. Female Pale-bellied mouse opossums will retrieve young other than their own, and Virginia opossums and woolly opossums have been observed carrying other females' young in their pouches. Toward the end of lactation, females cease any maternal care and dispersal is rapid. Sexual maturity is attained within six to 10 months. Age at sexual maturity is not related directly to body size. Considering the Gray four-eyed opossum and the woolly opossums again, the former can breed at six months, the latter not until 10 months.

In general, opossums are not long-lived. Few Virginia opossums live beyond two years in the wild and the smaller mouse opossums may not survive much beyond one reproductive season. Woolly opossums and the Black-shouldered opossum may live longer. Although animals kept in captivity may survive longer, females are generally not able to reproduce after two years. Thus, among many of these didelphids there is a trend towards the production of a few large litters during a limited reproductive life. Indeed, a female Pale-bellied mouse opossum may typically reproduce only once in a lifetime.

The American opossums appear to be locally nomadic animals, without defended territories. Radio-tracking studies reveal that individual animals occupy home ranges, but do not exclude others of the same species (conspecifics). How long a home range is occupied varies both between and within species. In the forests of French Guiana, for example, some woolly opossums have been observed to remain up to a year in the same home range whereas others shifted home range repeatedly. Gray four-eyed opossums were more likely to shift home range. In contrast to some other mammals, didelphids do not appear to explore their entire home range on a regular basis. Movements primarily involve feeding and travel to and from a nest site and are highly variable depending upon food resources and/or reproductive condition. Thus home range estimates for Virginia opossums in the central United States vary from 31 to 96 acres (12.5–38.8ha). An individual woolly opossum's home range may vary from 0.75 to 2.5 acres (0.3–1ha) from one day to the next. In general, the more carnivorous species have greater movements than similar-sized species which feed more on fruit. During the breeding season male didel-

Shrew Opossums of the High Andes

Seven small, shrew-like marsupial species are found in the Andean region of western South America from southern Venezuela to southern Chile. Known sometimes as shrew (or rat) opossums, they are unique among American marsupials in having a reduced number of incisors, the lower middle two of which are large and project forward.

The South American group represents a distinct line of evolution which diverged from ancestral stock before the Australian forms did, and its members are placed in a separate family, the Caenolestidae. Fossil evidence indicates that about 20 million years ago seven genera of caenolestids occurred in South America. Today the family is represented by only three genera and seven species. There are five species of *Caenolestes*. They are: the Gray-bellied caenolestid (*C. caniventer*), Blackish caenolestid (*C. convelatus*), Ecuadorian caenolestid (*C. fuliginosus*), Colombian caenolestid (*C. obscurus*) and Tate's caenolestid (*C. tatei*). Placed in separate genera are the Peruvian caenolestid (*Lestoros inca*) and the Chilean caenolestid (*Rhyncholestes raphanurus*). Known head-body lengths of these small marsupials are in the range of 3.5–5.5in (9–14cm), tail lengths mostly 3.9–5.5in (10–14cm), and weights 0.5–1.4oz (14–41g).

The elongated snouts are equipped with numerous tactile whiskers. The eyes are small and vision is poor. The well-developed ears project above the fur. The rat-like tails are about the same length as the body (rather less in the Chilean caenolestid) and are covered with stiff, short hairs. The fur on the body is soft and thick and is uniformly dark brown in most species. Females lack a pouch and most species have four teats (five in the Chilean caenolestid). Caenolestids are active during

the early evening and/or night, when they forage for insects, earthworms and other small invertebrates, and small vertebrates. They are able predators, using their large incisors to kill prey. Caenolestids travel about on well-marked ground trails or runways. More than one individual will use a particular trail or runway. When moving slowly, they have a typically symmetrical gait, but when moving faster the Colombian and Peruvian caenolestids, and possibly other species, will bound, allowing the animal to clear obstacles. During locomotion, the tail is used as a counter-balance. Although primarily terrestrial, caenolestids can climb.

The Blackish, Colombian, and Ecuadorian caenolestids are distributed in the high-elevation wet, cold cloud forests, intermontane forests, and páramos in the Andes of western Venezuela, Colombia and Ecuador. In these habitats they are most common on moss-covered slopes and ledges that are protected from the cold winds and rain. The Gray-bellied and Tate's caenolestids of southern Ecuador occur at lower elevations. The Peruvian caenolestid is found at high elevations in the Peruvian Andes, but in drier habitats than that of the other species. Peruvian caenolestids have been trapped in areas with low trees, bushes and grasses. The Chilean caenolestid inhabits the cool humid forests of southern Chile. Prior to the winter months the tail of this species becomes swollen with fat deposits.

Very little is known about the biology of these Marsupials. Shrew opossums inhabit inaccessible and (for humans) rather inhospitable areas, which makes them difficult to study. They have always been considered rare, but recent collecting trips suggest that at least some species may be more common.

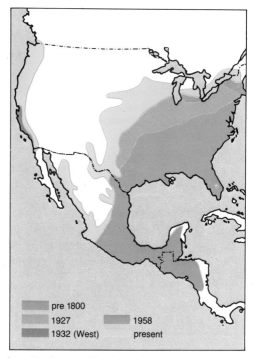

▲ **Recolonizing North America** where didelphids were once widespread, the Virginia opossum has extended its range well over 800,000 sq mi (2 million sq km) during the past 50 years.

pre 1800
1927   1958
1932 (West)   present

◄ **One of 47 mouse opossum species,** BELOW, this Alston's mouse opossum (*Marmosa alstoni*) of Monteverde, Costa Rica, will eat a variety of foods. Here the victim is a grasshopper.

▼ **Harassed mother**—Virginia opossum mother and young. Only six offspring are visible here, but the average litter is 10 or more. Newborn may number many more but the female has only 13 teats (some of these may not produce milk), so many newborn American opossums die as they cannot attach to a teat.

phids become more active, whereas reproductive females generally become more sedentary.

Most opossums use several to many nest sites within their range. Nests are often used alternately with conspecifics in the area. Virginia and Southern opossums use a variety of nest sites, both terrestrial and arboreal, but hollow trees are a common location. Four-eyed opossums also nest in trees (in holes and open limbs) and on the ground (rock crevices, tree roots and under fallen palm fronds). Mouse opossums nest either on the ground (under logs and tree roots) or in trees (holes, abandoned birds' nests), depending upon arboreal tendencies and local conditions. Occasionally mouse opossums make nests in banana stalks and more than once animals have been shipped to grocery stores in the United States and Europe! In the open grasslands, the Lutrine opossum constructs globular nests of leaves or uses abandoned armadillo burrows. In more forested areas, these opossums may use tree holes. Unlike other didelphids, yapoks construct more permanent nests. Underground nesting chambers are located near the waterline and are reached through holes dug into stream banks.

Opossums are solitary animals. Although many opossums may congregate at common food sources during periods of food scarcity, there is no interaction unless animals get too close. Typically, when two animals do meet, they threaten each other with open-mouth threats and hissing and then continue on their way. If aggression does persist (usually between males) the hissing changes into a growl and then to a screech. Communication by smell is very important. Many species have well-developed scent glands on the chest. In addition, male Virginia opossums, Gray four-eyed opossums, and Gray short-tailed opossums have been observed marking objects with saliva. Marking behavior is carried out primarily by males and is thought to advertise their presence in an area.

In tropical forests up to seven species of didelphids may be found at the same locality. Competition between these species is avoided through differences in body size and tendency to climb. For example, woolly opossums and the Ashy mouse opossum may be found in the tree canopy, the Common mouse opossum in lower branches, Southern and Gray four-eyed opossums on the ground and in the lower branches, and short-tailed opossums on the ground. Some species appear to vary their tendency to climb depending upon the presence of similar-sized opossums: For example, in a Brazilian forest where both Gray and Brown four-eyed opossums were found together, the former was more arboreal than the latter. However, in a forest in French Guiana where only the Gray four-eyed opossum was present, it was primarily terrestrial, and elsewhere the Brown four-eyed opossum is primarily arboreal.

North American fossil deposits from 70–80 million years ago are rich in didelphid remains. From North America didelphids probably entered South America and Europe (see p96). By 10–20 million years ago didelphids were extinct in Europe and North America. When about 2–5 million years ago South America again became joined to Central America, northern placental mammals entered South America and many South American marsupials became extinct, but didelphids persisted and even moved northward into Central and North America. During historical times, the early European settlers of North America found no marsupials north of what is now Virginia and Ohio. Since then the Virginia opossum has extended its range to New Zealand and southern Canada. After introductions on the West Coast in 1890, this opossum has expanded from southern California to southern Canada, a change most likely related to man's impact on the environment. Despite being hunted for food and pelts, the Virginia opossum thrives on both farms and in towns and even cities. Elsewhere in the Americas, man's impact on the environment is detrimental to didelphids. Destruction of humid tropical forests results in loss of habitat for the more specialized species. MAO'C

MARSUPIAL CARNIVORES

A VARIETY of marsupials feed upon the flesh of animals, including American opossums, bandicoots, the thylacine (see p113), the numbat (see p116) and the dasyurids. In Australia and New Guinea most of the marsupial carnivores are dasyurids and of the marsupial families inhabiting those lands they are among the most successful. Dasyurids are found in all major terrestrial habitats. A higher proportion of dasyurid species occurs in the deserts of Australia than of any other family of marsupials. They are also found in tropical rain forest, temperate eucalypt forest and woodland, flood plain, alpine and coastal heaths and even in the vegetation of coastal dunes. Yet, despite their success, they are "conservative" in appearance and body form. A large part of their success may, instead, be due to the surprising array of life-cycles they display.

Dasyurids are mostly small and mouse-like. Over 50 percent of the species weigh less than 3.5oz (100g) as adults and they include some of the smallest mammals. The ningauis of central and northwestern Australia may weigh as little as 0.07oz (2g) as adults. Many of these small dasyurids resemble shrews in appearance and habits. They have long conical snouts which presumably enable them to remove their insect prey from crevices.

In the 2.1–10.6oz (60–300g) size range are the kowari and the mulgara of central Australia and, also inland, the two species of *Phascogale* which resemble the tree shrews of Asia (order Scandentia). They too have a pointed snout, but also have conspicuous, large eyes, large ears, and bushy tails which may have a signaling function.

The largest dasyurids, the quolls (Eastern quoll male 2–4.4lb/0.9–2kg) and the much larger Tasmanian devil, bear some resemblance to placental carnivores of similar size, both in appearance and in their coat pattern of dark brown or black with conspicuous white markings.

Dasyurids are easily distinguished from the other major groups of Australian marsupials by a simple combination of characters: they possess three pairs of incisors in the lower jaw, and have front feet with five toes, hind feet with never less than four toes, and all toes are separately developed. These are considered to be primitive marsupial features from which the more specialized dentition and feet of bandicoots, possums and kangaroos have been derived. Because of this, dasyurids are often considered closest to the stock from which other Australian marsupial groups have arisen. Until recently, the largest of the marsupial carnivores, the thylacine, was also classified as a dasyurid, but although closely related to this group, it is now placed in a separate family, the Thylacinidae.

Most dasyurids are insectivorous, but include items such as earthworms, spiders,

▼ **Representative species of marsupial carnivores** (dasyurids). (1) Kultarr (*Antechinomys laniger*). (2) Pilbara ningaui (*Ningaui timealeyi*) eating beetle. (3) Three-striped marsupial mouse (*Myoictis melas*). (4) New Guinea marsupial cat (*Satanellus albopunctatus*). (5) Fat-tailed or Red-eared antechinus (*Pseudantechinus macdonnellensis*). (6) Marsupial mouse (*Phascolosorex dorsalis*. (7) Red-tailed phascogale (*Phascogale calura*). (8) Little red antechinus (*Dasykatula rosamondae*), (9) Long-tailed marsupial mouse (*Murexia longicaudata*). (10) Fat-tailed dunnart (*Sminthopis crassicaudata*). (11) Common planigale (*Planigale maculata*) eating caterpillar.

DICK TWINNEY 84

small lizards, flowers and fruit in their diets. Even the larger quolls feed extensively upon beetle larvae. One survey showed that insect remains occurred in 97 percent of the feces of the Eastern quoll, while vertebrate remains occurred in only 17 percent. The largest dasyurid, the Tasmanian devil, is remarkably inefficient in capturing and killing active vertebrates and is thought to subsist on vertebrate carrion, principally from wombats, on Bennet's wallaby and sheep. When feeding upon large carcasses they detach and bolt large portions, crushing bones with their powerful jaws. One description tells how they use their forepaws to cram lengths of intestine into their mouths like eating spaghetti. Only the largest bones remain after they have fed upon a carcass.

The mulgara kills both invertebrate and vertebrate prey with a series of bites, each accompanied by a vigorous shake of the prey. The prey is dropped between bites. With large insects and small lizards the first bites are randomly directed, but the final bite is always directed at the head. There are no preliminary bites with snakes and mice. Mulgara eat mice head first and do not skin the prey. Although there have been few studies of prey capture and feeding by dasyurids, the overall impression is that they capture prey by stealth and not by chase.

Little is known about the social organization of dasyurids but they appear for the most part to be solitary. The Fat-tailed dunnart is found in drier habitats over much of the southern two-thirds of Australia. It nests in groups, but the relationships between individuals in these groups is not known. Out of the breeding season, groups are most commonly of two or three individuals. Nesting in groups is most common in April and May, just before the start of the breeding season, and is lowest in August and November–February, when females are frequently with litters. During the breeding season females, except when in heat (estrus), usually exclude males from the nest.

Recent observations of the Brown antechinus of eastern Australia have shown that males disperse from the maternal nest at weaning and nest with other unrelated females, some of which remain at the maternal nest. As the breeding season approaches, males and females visit a number of nests and increase the number of individuals with which they associate. Males copulate with a number of females.

Many species use mate-attracting calls. Males tend to call at night throughout the

breeding season, but females may confine calling to periods of receptivity. It has been suggested that these calls have arisen as a consequence of the solitary nature of dasyurids and of their occurrence in many open habitats where communication by other means would endanger their lives.

Most small placental mammals ovulate more than once during a breeding season and usually produce more than one litter. A number of dasyurids also show this pattern. For example, the Fat-tailed dunnart breeds between July, in the middle of the Australian winter, and January or February, in summer. Females usually produce two litters during this period, one before and one after October. Gestation lasts about 12–13 days,

▲ **Tools of a carnivore**—powerful jaws and sharp teeth of the Tasmanian devil. This largest of Australian marsupial carnivores will take living prey, including lambs and poultry, but it prefers carrion, and can chew and swallow all parts of a sheep carcass, including the bones.

▶ **Four-month old Eastern quolls** OPPOSITE ABOVE in their grass-lined den. Usually six young of this species attach to teats in the pouch. In mid-August, about 10 weeks after birth, the mother deposits them in the nest.

▶ **"Tiger cat" of Tasmania** BELOW. The Spotted-tailed quoll is nearly as large as the Tasmanian devil and a much more active hunter. It kills its prey—gliders, small wallabies, reptiles—with a bite to the back of the head.

which is short even for a marsupial. The young are at first suckled continuously within the pouch and later within a grass-lined nest located within a hollow log or under a large stone. Lactation occupies 60–70 days. Young Fat-tailed dunnarts mature rapidly for a marsupial and are capable of breeding at six months. Even so, they do not breed in the breeding season of their birth, but in the following season. Few if any individuals live beyond 18 months of age and so do not breed in a second season.

In tropical Australia and New Guinea there are some small dasyurids which breed year-round but little else is known of their life-cycles. It is thought that many dasyurids like the Fat-tailed dunnart coincide breeding with spring and summer because this is the time of greatest insect, and therefore food, abundance. If this is so, then it is likely that year-round reproduction is possible in some tropical species because of the year-round abundance of insects.

The quolls and Tasmanian devil may also be able to ovulate more than once a year but only produce a single litter. This is because it takes these large dasyurids longer to raise a litter. Mating occurs in March in the Tasmanian devil and most births occur in April. The young are suckled for 8–9 months and are weaned in November or December. The young may take two years to reach sexual maturity, rather than the one year typical of most dasyurids, but they may live to at least six years of age.

The Thylacine or Tasmanian Wolf

The thylacine, Tasmanian wolf or Tasmanian tiger was the largest of the recent marsupial carnivores. Fossil thylacines are widely scattered in Australia and New Guinea, but the living animal was confined in historical times to Tasmania, where it now appears to be extinct.

Superficially the thylacine resembled a dog. It stood about 24in (60cm) at the shoulders, head-body length averaged 31.5in (80cm), and weight 33–77lb (15–35kg). The head was dog-like, the neck was short and the body sloped away from the shoulders. The legs were short, as in large dasyurids. The features which clearly distinguish it from dogs are the long (20in/50cm) stiff tail which is thick at the base, and the coat pattern of black or brown stripes across the back on a sandy yellow ground. The thylacine (*Thylacinus cynocephalus*) is placed in its own family, the Thylacinidae.

Most of the information we have on the behavior of the thylacine is either anecdotal or has been obtained from old film. It ran with diagonally opposing limbs moving alternately. It could sit upright on the hindlimbs and tail rather like a kangaroo, and leap 6–10ft with great agility. Thylacines appear to have hunted alone or in pairs, and before Europeans settled in Tasmania probably fed upon wallabies, possums, bandicoots, rodents and birds. It is suggested that they caught prey by stealth rather than by chase.

At the time of European settlement the thylacine appears to have been widespread in Tasmania and was particularly common where settled areas adjoined dense forest. It was thought to rest during the day in dense forest on hilly terrain and emerge to feed at night in grassland and woodland. Its extinction on mainland Australia some time in the last 3,000 years may have been a consequence of competition with the dingo.

From the early days of European settlement of Tasmania the thylacine developed a reputation for killing sheep. As early as 1830 bounties were offered for killing thylacines and their destruction led to fears for the species as early as 1850. Even so, the Tasmanian Government introduced its own bounty scheme in 1888 and in the next 21 years, before the last bounty was paid, 2,268 animals were officially accounted for. The number of bounties paid had declined sharply by the end of this period and it is thought that an epidemic disease as well as hunting led to the thylacine's final disappearance.

The last thylacine to be captured was obtained in western Tasmania in 1933 and died in the Hobart zoo in 1936. Since then there have been a number of very thorough searches of Tasmania and despite alleged sightings of this animal, even to this day, the most recent survey concluded that there has been no positive evidence of the survival of thylacines since 1936. AKL

Roughly one-third of the dasyurid species are unusual among small mammals in that females only ovulate once a year and so are only able to produce a single litter annually. Some of these species, such as the Sandstone antechinus in the north of the Northern Territory, live up to 30–36 months and breed in two breeding seasons. Once again, mating usually occurs in winter and the young are weaned in late spring to early summer when insects are most abundant.

The most unusual life-cycle is found among seven species of *Antechinus* and two of *Phascogale*. These species also ovulate once a year and produce a single litter, but males only live for 11.5 months and mate in one two-week mating period. In the Brown antechinus, females may live to three years of age but they rarely if ever produce more than two litters.

Births in the Brown antechinus usually occur in September or October, that is, in very early spring, and usually within a one- to two-day period within a given population. The young are then attached firmly to teats in a saucer-like pouch for about a month. They grow substantially during this period and hang beneath the body as the female moves about foraging. Subsequently the young are placed in a nest in a tree hollow and suckled for a further 2–3 months. These young are weaned by December or January and mature and mate in the following winter. Mating is intense. Males tend to disperse widely during the mating period, and may mount and copulate with females for prolonged periods. Males caged with a female have been observed to remain mounted for up to 12 hours and may repeat this for up to 13 nights.

At the end of the mating period in July or August, all males die, and the females are free to raise young in their absence. Like the onset of mating, births and weaning, this male die-off (see below) occurs at precisely the same time each year within a population and usually occupies 5–10 days.

The size of the litters varies considerably among dasyurids and is usually greatest in the small species. *Planigale* and *Antechinus* may have litters of 12 young whereas the much larger Tasmanian devil has litters of 2–4 young. However, not all the small dasyurids have large litters; the two New Guinea species of *Antechinus*, which breed year-round, have litters of three or four young.

Because the young attach firmly to a teat for a period after birth, the number of young raised is limited by the number of teats available. Dasyurids produce more young

The Marsupial Mole

The Marsupial mole is the only Australian mammal that has become specialized for a burrowing (fossorial) life. Others, including small native rodents, have failed to adapt to the use of this niche, apart from a few species nesting in burrows.

Because of its extensive and distinct modifications the Marsupial mole (*Notoryctes typhlops*) is placed in a separate family, the Notoryctidae. Its limbs are short stubs. The hands are modified as excavating instruments, with rudimentary digits and greatly enlarged flat claws on the third and fourth digits. Excavated soil is pushed back behind the animal with the hindlimbs, which also give forward thrust to the body and, like the hands, are flattened with reduced digits and three small flat claws on the second, third and fourth digits. The naked skin (rhinarium) on the tip of the snout has been extended into a horny shield over the front of the head, apparently for thrusting through the soil. The coat is pale yellow and silky. The nostrils are small slits, there are no functional eyes or external ears, and the ear openings are concealed by fur. The neck vertebrae are fused together, presumably to provide rigidity for thrusting motions. Females have a rear-opening pouch with two teats. The tail, reduced to a stub, is said to be used sometimes as a prop when burrowing. Head-body length is approximately 5.1–5.7in (13–14.5cm), tail length 1in (2–2.5cm) and weight 1.4oz (40g). Dentition is I4/3, C1/1, P2/3, M4/4 = 44.

Little is known of these moles in the wild. They occur in the central deserts, using sandy soils in river-flat country and sandy spinifex grasslands. They are thought to prefer to feed on insects, particularly burrowing larvae of beetles of the family Scarabaeidae and moths of the family Cossidae. In captivity Marsupial moles will seek out insect larvae buried in the soil and consume them underground. They also feed on the surface. They are not known to make permanent burrows, the soil collapsing behind them as they move forward, and in this respect they are most unusual among fossorial mammals, which usually construct permanent burrows. Animals in captivity have been observed to sleep in a small cavity which collapses after they leave.

Compared to other burrowing animals (eg true moles and golden moles), the Marsupial mole shows differences of detail in the adaptive route it has followed. The head shield is much more extensive than in many others, the eyes are more rudimentary than in most, and the rigid head/neck region with fused vertebrae appears to be specific to the Marsupial moles. GG

than they have teats and, in most species, all or all-but-one of the teats are occupied by a young. The small species tend to have more teats than the larger species.

How do these life-cycles relate to the habitats used by dasyurids? Most of the species from the desert habitats, such as the Fat-tailed dunnart and the kowari, have 6–8-month breeding seasons in which the females produce two litters, each containing 5–8 young. These habitats are harsh and it is difficult to predict when conditions will favor successful reproduction. By reproducing twice during a breeding season these species increase the chance of successfully rearing at least one litter. They are presumably restricted to breeding in spring and summer by the seasonal distribution of food. Insects would be reduced in abundance during dry and cold periods of fall and winter.

The larger dasyurids are restricted to a single litter annually, probably because it

◄ ▲ ► **Competition in small dasyures.** The Brown antechinus RIGHT is abundant in forests and heathlands of southeastern Australia, where it does however face competition for food. The larger and more terrestrial Dusky antechinus ABOVE will force its Brown relative into more open country, or up into the trees. Consequently Brown antechinus populations may be 70 percent lower where the two overlap. The Brown antechinus competes more successfully with other marsupials such as the smaller Common dunnart (*Sminthopsis murina*) LEFT or the White-footed dunnart, and expels them from favorable habitat.

Brown antechinus females carry more female than male young in the pouch (58 percent of the total). Since females only breed once they can produce more daughters without having to "worry" about future competition from them.

In the Dusky antechinus these percentages are reversed, and more males are carried, probably because most females breed twice in their life-time and the mother can thus reduce competition from stay-at-home daughters. (Males on the other hand disperse from their natal homes before they breed.)

takes longer for large mammals to raise young and this is especially true of marsupials. Here the ability to ovulate more than once during a breeding season provides an opportunity to replace a litter if one is lost. These large dasyurids are found in arid as well as wet forest habitats and their success in a variety of habitats, some of which are harsh, may be related to their size. Generally large mammals live longer than small mammals and are able to spread their breeding over a number of years.

The small dasyurids which can only produce one litter a year fall into two groups. Those species where both males and females reproduce in two years tend to occur where there is some risk of losing a litter, as in habitats marginal to deserts. Others, such as the White-footed dunnart of southern Victoria and Tasmania, use vegetation which is regenerating after a fire and suitable for only a few years. They tend to produce large litters of 10 young, and may have opted to produce one large litter a year rather than two smaller litters.

The second group of such species are those typified by a male die-off after the first breeding season. They are restricted to the forests and heathlands of Australia, where their chances of successfully raising a litter are good. In these habitats the abundance of insects is highly seasonal, reaching peaks in

The Numbat
—Termite-eater

The numbat is highly specialized to feed upon termites and, perhaps because of the diet, it is the only fully day-active Australian marsupial. Because of its distinctive coat markings and delicate appearance, it is also one of the most attractive marsupials.

The numbat (*Myrmecobius fasciatus*) is the sole member of the family Myrmecobiidae. Head-body length averages 9.7in (24.5cm), tail length 7in (17.7cm) and males weigh 1.1lb (0.5kg), females 0.9lb (0.4kg). The black-and-white bars across the rump fade into reddish-brown on the upper back and shoulder. A prominent white-bordered dark bar passes from the base of each ear through the eye to the snout. The long tail is bushy.

The numbat spends most of its active hours searching for food. It walks, stopping and starting, sniffing at the ground and turning over small pieces of wood in its search for shallow underground termite galleries. On locating a gallery, the numbat squats on its hind feet and digs rapidly with its strong clawed forefeet. Termites are extracted with the extremely long, narrow tongue which darts in and out of the gallery. Some ants are eaten but (despite alternative names of Banded or Marsupial anteater) it seems that the numbat usually takes these in accidentally, while picking up the termites. It does not chew its food, and also swallows grit and soil acquired while feeding.

Numbats are solitary for most of the year, each individual occupying a territory of up to 370 acres (150ha). During the cooler months a male and female may share the same territory, but they are still rarely seen together. Hollow logs are used for shelter and refuge throughout the year, although numbats also dig burrows and often spend the nights in them during the cooler months. The burrows and some logs contain nests of leaves, grass and sometimes bark. In summer numbats sunbathe on logs.

Four young are born between January and May, and attach themselves to the nipples of

the female, which lacks a pouch. In July or August the mother deposits them in a burrow, suckling them at night. By October, the young numbats are half grown and are feeding on termites themselves while remaining in their parents' area. They disperse in early summer (December).

Numbats once occurred across the southern and central parts of Australia, from the west coast to the semi-arid areas of western New South Wales. They are now found only in a few areas of eucalypt forest and woodland in the southwest of Western Australia. Destruction of their habitat for agriculture and predation by foxes have probably been the major contributors to this decline. While most of their habitat is now secure from further clearing, remaining numbat populations are so small that the species is considered rare and endangered. Efforts are being made to set up a breeding colony from which natural populations may be reestablished.   AKL

▶ **Mulgara** eating a locust. This widespread species of inland Australia digs burrows in the sand. A black crest on the short, fat tail identifies the mulgara.

▼ **The kowari** is another small burrowing carnivore of the inland deserts, but restricted to southwestern Queensland. The black brush tips a longer tail than the mulgara's.

spring and early summer and lows in the dry fall and cold winters. Because of the long period required by these small marsupials to raise litters it is probably not feasible for them to raise two litters in a year without a high chance of losing at least one of the litters. Instead they have concentrated their breeding into producing a single annual litter. Males faced with the probability of dying before a second breeding season go all out to father as many young as possible during their first short breeding season and die abruptly as a result of this effort.

Considerable attention has been focused on the die-off of males which occurs at the conclusion of the breeding season of these dasyurids. Once again, we have most information for the Brown antechinus, in which the death of males seems to result from a variety of diseases, including stomach and intestinal ulcers. These ulcers, often called "stress ulcers," and other evidence suggest that the males are severely stressed during the mating period. At first it was thought that their stress resulted from their behavior during that period, when they may spend much of their time mating, chasing females and fighting with other males. But recently it has become obvious that the stress response in males is to their advantage as breeding animals, allowing them to give up feeding and concentrate upon finding and mating with females. Stressed animals convert body protein into energy which may replace the energy usually obtained from food. But while being stressed may be beneficial in allowing the males to mate with more females and father more offspring, it also makes the males more susceptible to disease.

The ranges of most dasyurids have almost certainly shrunk since the advent of European settlement in Australia. In most instances this has probably resulted from the destruction of habitat by clearing for agriculture or from frequent burning which is used to create pasture for sheep and cattle. Restrictions in the ranges of the larger species such as the quolls have been most obvious and some of these, such as the Eastern quoll, are endangered over parts of their range. Whether or not this reduction in numbers is due to competition from feral cats is unknown.

Five dasyurids are considered threatened with extinction. They are the dibbler, which is restricted to Cheyne Beach, Jerdacuttup, Western Australia, the Red-tailed phascogale of southwestern Australia, and three *Sminthopsis* species. The dibbler may already be extinct. AKL

BANDICOOTS AND BILBIES

Families: Peramelidae and Thylacomyidae
Nineteen species in 8 genera.
Distribution: Australia and New Guinea.

Habitat: all major habitats in Australia and New Guinea from desert to rain forest and semi-urban areas.

Size: ranges from head-body length 6–7in (15–17.5cm), tail length 4.3in (11cm) in the Mouse bandicoot to head-body length 15–22in (39–56cm), tail length 4.7–13.4in (12–34cm) and weight up to 10.4lb (4.7kg) in the Giant bandicoot. Males of larger species 60–80 percent heavier than females.

Gestation: 12.5 days in Long-nosed and Brindled bandicoots; others probably similar.

Longevity: not known, but 3 or more years in Brindled bandicoot.

Bandicoots (family Peramelidae)
Australian long-nosed bandicoots, 4 species of *Perameles*: the **Long-nosed bandicoot** (*P. nasuta*), **Eastern barred bandicoot** (*P. gunnii*); **Desert** or **Orange bandicoot** [EX] (*P. eremiana*) and **Western barred bandicoot** or **marl** [R] (*P. bougainville*); **New Guinea long-nosed bandicoots**, 4 species of *Peroryctes* including the **Giant bandicoot** (*P. broadbenti*) and **Striped bandicoot** (*P. longicauda*); **Mouse bandicoot** (*Microperoryctes murina*); **spiny bandicoots**, 3 species of *Echymipera* including the **Rufescent** or **Rufous spiny bandicoot** (*E. rufescens*) and **Spiny bandicoot** (*E. kalubu*); the **Ceram Island bandicoot** (*Rhynchomeles prattorum*); **short-nosed bandicoots**, 3 species of *Isoodon*: the **Brindled** or **Northern brown bandicoot** (*I. macrourus*), **Golden bandicoot** (*I. auratus*) and **Southern brown** or **short-nosed bandicoot** or **quenda** (*I. obesulus*); and the **Pig-footed bandicoot** [EX] (*Chaeropus ecaudatus*).

Rabbit-eared bandicoots or **bilbies** (family Thylacomyidae)
Two species of *Macrotis*, the **Greater bilby**, **Greater rabbit-eared bandicoot**, or **dalgyte** [R] (*M. lagotis*) and **Lesser bilby** [EX] (*M. leucura*).

[EX] Extinct. [R] Rare.

BANDICOOTS have the highest reproductive rate of all marsupials. In this respect they are the marsupials showing greatest similarity with placental groups such as rodents whose life-cycle centers on producing many young with little maternal care. Otherwise these small insectivores and omnivores fit into an ecological niche somewhat similar to that of many members of the order Insectivora (shrews and hedgehogs).

Most bandicoots are rabbit-sized or smaller, have short limbs, a long pointed muzzle, and a thickset body with a short neck. The ears are normally short, the forefeet have three prominent toes with strong flattish claws, and the pouch opens backward. The furthest from this pattern is the recently extinct Pig-footed bandicoot which developed longer limbs and small footpads as adaptations to a more cursorial (running) life on open plains. Ear length is only prominent in the Pig-footed bandicoot and Rabbit-eared bandicoots. Teeth are small, relatively even-sized and with pointed cusps, as in typical insectivore teeth. These animals are basically designed for digging out invertebrate food in the ground, poking into crevices and rooting around with their powerful foreclaws.

Bandicoots are distinguished from all other marsupials by the combined presence of fused (syndactylous) toes on the hindfeet, forming a comb for grooming, and polyprotodont dentition (see p98).

The rear-opening pouch normally has eight teats. It extends forward along the abdomen as the young enlarge, eventually occupying most of the mother's underside and contracting again after departure of the young.

The sense of smell is well developed but eyesight seems variable, as eye diameter varies noticeably between species. Loud calls are either absent or uncommon. Only the Long-nosed bandicoot is known to have a loud vocalization; it produces a sharp squeaky alarm call when disturbed at night. A very low sibilant "huffing" with bared teeth is uttered as a threat by the Brindled bandicoot and probably others.

The dental formula is I5/3, C1/1, P3/3, M4/4 = 48, except in spiny bandicoots, which have four pairs of upper incisors (I4/3). Sexual dimorphism occurs in the larger species, males being about 60–80 percent heavier and 15 percent longer, with larger canines.

In recent (Pleistocene) times bandicoots have to a large extent evolved separately in mainland Australia and New Guinea, as a result of the intermittent separation of the two land masses and the marked habitat differences between the tropical rain-forested island and the drier continent. All genera of the New Guinea region are exclusive to these northern islands, or nearly so. Only one species, the Rufescent bandicoot, extends into northern Australia. The remaining genera are essentially Australian although one species, the Brindled bandicoot, intrudes into the grassy woodlands in lowland southern New Guinea, as the Rufescent bandicoot does in the opposite direction where it uses the small rainforest patches of Cape York Peninsula. These two intrusions indicate that an important—perhaps even the dominant—influence on the different bandicoot fauna of the two land masses is habitat, and not just the water barrier. Where suitable habitat exists, animals have managed to colonize the other land mass in spite of its geographic isolation.

Within New Guinea, different species occur at different altitudes. The Spiny bandicoots range from sea level to about 5,250ft (1,600m). On the other hand the Mouse bandicoot and two of the four New Guinea long-nosed bandicoots are restricted to altitudes above 4,000ft (1,200m).

Within Australia, there are pronounced

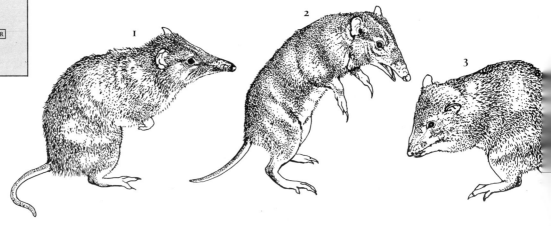

▼ ▲ **The short-nosed Brindled bandicoot**
ABOVE inhabits low ground cover in coastal
areas of eastern and northeastern Australia
and south New Guinea. BELOW One of the large
bandicoots, it is active at night and frequently
sniffs the air (1) to detect any danger. The usual
gait is on all fours, but the larger hindlimbs are
used in an aggressive hop (2) characteristic of
males. The Brindled bandicoot digs out fungi,
tubers, insects, worms and other invertebrate
prey with its strong foreclaws (3). After the
shortest gestation of perhaps any mammal, the
newborn young crawl into their mother's rear-
opening pouch (4), where they are carried for
seven weeks, by which time the mother's pouch
is bulging (5).

climatic influences on distribution of species, which tend to fall into two groups. A number of species are restricted to the dry semi-arid and arid areas; all of these have suffered big population declines in recent times. They include the Desert bandicoot, Western barred bandicoot, the Golden bandicoot, Pig-footed bandicoot and the rabbit-eared bandicoots. The remaining Australian bandicoots occur in coastal or sub-coastal zones. This pattern is an effect, whether direct or indirect, of rainfall. The Brindled bandicoot, a coastal species of eastern and northern Australia, is widely distributed as far inland as about the 29.5in (75cm) isohyet (rainfall line). Beyond this it tends to be largely confined to watercourses (riverine) and extends much farther inland in

this manner, almost to the 23.6in (60cm) isohyet. Other distribution patterns reflect apparent latitudinal influences on distribution in both the above groups.

The classification of bandicoots is not fully resolved, although all genera and the two families are clearly defined. Groups in need of revision include the Southern short-nosed bandicoot and Western barred bandicoot and possibly several others. Characteristic adaptive changes from the primitive condition include lengthening of the rostrum of the skull permitting animals to probe further into holes and crevices; longer ears; larger auditory bullae and longer limbs in species from more open habitats, particularly arid areas; shortening of the tail; and enlarged molars (development of a fourth cusp).

The short-nosed bandicoots are stocky, short-eared, plain-colored animals. They favor areas of close ground cover, tall grass or low shrubbery, although actual habitat may vary from this. They occur throughout Australia. Important differences between species or populations are: an increase in the size of auditory bullae in more arid areas which may assist earlier detection of predators; overall size differences including dwarfed forms, particularly on islands, and in more open areas, perhaps an adaptation to scarcer food; variation in the angle of the ascending rear portion of the lower jaw; and the presence of an extra cusp on the last upper molar. There is little overlap between different species' distributions.

The long-nosed bandicoots are more lightly built, with a relatively longer skull, longer ears, barred body markings, and a preference for areas of open ground cover such as bare forest floors or short grassland, although again habitat use is extremely flexible. They have exploited most of the continent with some noticeable gaps—there has been a failure to fully utilize tropical humid areas other than rain forest. Important variables between species are: increased ear length and bullae size in more arid areas; different degrees of barring, which is absent in the forest species, the Long-nosed bandicoot, and conspicuous in grassland species either as disruptive camouflage in grass cover or as species recognition marks in more open areas.

The Pig-footed bandicoot is highly specialized, with adaptations for a running (cursorial), plains-dwelling life. In the forefeet only the second and third digits remain functional, forming a paired foot pad like an even-toed ungulate (artiodactyl) foot. In the hindfeet, the fourth digit forms a single functional pad. The syndactylous "comb" also remains. The limbs are correspondingly lengthened for better running. This bandicoot also has longer ears.

The several New Guinea genera are poorly known. They tend to be little modified, short-eared forest bandicoots. However, lengthening of the rostrum is marked in some, particularly spiny bandicoots and the Ceram Island bandicoot. Spiny bandicoots also have shorter tails.

Rabbit-eared bandicoots have lengthened ears, rostra and limbs, highly developed auditory bullae with twin chambers, and a long crested tail. They are the only burrowing bandicoots and are an offshoot from the main bandicoot stock that has become highly specialized for arid areas. The main differences between species and populations are: size; tail coloration; coat coloration; and bulla size (larger in Lesser bilby).

Although bandicoots are specialized for feeding on soil invertebrates, the few dietary studies have shown that feeding is opportunistic and omnivorous. Their diets include insects, other invertebrates, fruits, seeds of non-woody plants, subterranean fungi and occasional plant fiber. Diet can also include a high proportion of surface food and it is likely that bandicoots switch to other food

when insects are unavailable. Food in the ground is dug out with the strong foreclaws, usually leaving characteristically conical holes. The elongation of the muzzle is presumably associated with probing down into holes and other crevices and under logs etc for food. The Brindled bandicoot has a characteristic foraging pattern, moving slowly over its whole 2.5–12 acre (1–5ha) range, and spending little time in any one spot. This is an adaptation for finding food that occurs as small isolated and scattered items rather than concentrated in a few areas.

The biology of bandicoots has been poorly studied, although there are indications that the life-cycle of the Brindled bandicoot is typical of the group. Its gestation of 12.5 days is less than half that of most other marsupials and perhaps the shortest of any mammal. Development of the embryo is aided by a form of chorioallantoic placentation that is unique to bandicoots among marsupials. It resembles the placenta of

▶ **The Long-nosed bandicoot** of eastern Australia, in addition to living up to its common name, has longer ears than the short-nosed bandicoots. It is well known for the conical holes it leaves in the ground after nighttime foraging for insects.

▶ **Distinctive white markings** BELOW RIGHT on the rump give the Eastern barred bandicoot its name. Grasslands are its preferred habitat, in Tasmania and south Victoria.

▼ **Big ears**—the Greater bilby or Rabbit-eared bandicoot is a desert species now much reduced in distribution. Apart from the long ears, the long furry tail and burrowing habits set this rare animal apart from other surviving bandicoots.

eutherian mammals. Other marsupials form only a yolk-sac placenta, whereas bandicoots and eutherians have independently evolved both types of placentation. Young at birth are about 0.4in (1cm) long, and about 0.007oz (0.2g) in weight, with well-developed forelimbs. The allantoic stalk anchors the young to the mother whilst the newborn crawls to the pouch, where it attaches to a nipple. Litter size ranges from 1 to 7 (commonly 2–4). Young leave the pouch at about 49–50 days and are weaned about 10 days later. In good conditions, sexual maturity may occur at about 90 days of age, although it is normally attained much later. Females are polyestrous and breed throughout the year in suitable climates, elsewhere breeding seasonally. Mating can occur when the previous litter is near the end of its pouch life. Since the gestation is 12.5 days, the new litter is born at about the time of weaning the earlier litter.

The reproductive cycle is one of the most distinctive characteristics of bandicoots, setting them well apart from all other marsupials. They have become uniquely specialized for a high reproductive rate and reduced parental care. In the Brindled bandicoot, and possibly in all bandicoots, this is achieved by accelerated gestation, rapid development of young in the pouch, early sexual maturity and a rapid succession of litters in the polyestrous females. In one Brindled bandicoot population with 6–8-month breeding seasons, females produced an average 6.4 young in one season, and 9.6 in the next. Litter size, however, while higher than in many marsupial groups, is not exceptional, being smaller than in others, such as dasyurids.

Bandicoot society is poorly studied in most species, but again is likely to follow a common pattern throughout the group. The Brindled bandicoot is solitary, animals come together only to mate, and there appears to be no lasting attachment between mother and young, contact being lost at weaning or

soon after. Males are larger than females and socially dominant, dominance correlating approximately with body size. Dominance between closely matched males may be established by chases or, rarely, by fights, in which the males approach each other standing on their hind legs. Either the two combatants lock jaws and wrestle onto the ground, or one may jump high above the other and rake out with its hindfoot in an endeavor to wound it. Male home ranges are larger, 4.2–12.8 acres (1.7–5.2ha) in one study, compared to 2.2–5.2 acres (0.9–2.1ha) for females. Characteristically there is a "core area," apparently where most time is spent foraging. The ranges of both sexes overlap, although core areas do not. Males do a rapid tour around most of the home range each night, perhaps as a patrolling action to detect other males or receptive (estrous) females. Caged animals show intense interest in nest sites, and dominant males may commonly evict others from nests. Nests may therefore be a significant focus of social interactions in the wild. Nests consist of heaps of raked-up ground-litter with an internal chamber. A scent gland is present behind the ear of many species in both sexes. The Brindled bandicoot uses it to mark the ground or vegetation during aggressive encounters between males. The ground cover of Brindled bandicoots is subject to frequent destruction by fire or drought. Their high reproductive rate and mobility enable them to colonize quickly as suitable habitat becomes available.

Australian bandicoots have suffered one of the greatest declines of all marsupial groups. All species of the semi-arid and arid zones have either become extinct or suffered massive declines, being reduced now to a few remnant populations that are still endangered. An important feature of most extinctions appears to be grazing by cattle, sheep or rabbits and the consequent changes in the nature of ground cover. Some authorities alternatively blame introduced predators, including foxes and cats. Removal of sheep and cattle is an important conservation measure in these areas. Control of rabbits and introduced predators is desirable but extremely difficult. Most bandicoots of higher rainfall areas have been little affected by European settlement, or are thriving, and are not yet in need of specific conservation measures. An exception is the Eastern barred bandicoot, which has been rendered almost extinct in Victoria by cultivation and grazing on the grassy plains to which it is restricted, but remains common in Tasmania.   GG

CUSCUSES AND BRUSHTAIL POSSUMS

Family: Phalangeridae
Fourteen species in 3 genera.
Distribution: Australia, New Guinea (including Irian Jaya) and adjacent islands west to Sulawesi, east to Solomon Islands. Common brushtail possum introduced to New Zealand. Gray cuscus possibly also to some Solomon Islands.

Habitat: rain forest, moss forest, eucalypt forest; temperate, arid and alpine woodland.

Size: ranges from the "Lesser" Sulawesi cuscus *Phalanger ursinus* with head-body length 13.4in (34cm), tail length 11.8in (30cm) and weight unknown, to the Black-spotted cuscus with head-body length to 27.6in (70cm), tail length 19.7in (50cm) and weight about 11lb (5kg).

Coat: short, dense, gray (Scaly-tailed possum); long, woolly, gray-black (brushtail possums); long, dense, white-black or reddish brown, some species with spots or dorsal stripes (cuscuses).

Gestation: 16–17 days (brushtail possums).
Longevity: to 13 years (at least 17 in captivity).

Cuscuses or phalangers, 10 species of *Phalanger*: **Spotted cuscus** ⋆ (*P. maculatus*); **Gray cuscus** ⋆ (*P. orientalis*); **Woodlark Island cuscus** ⓡ (*P. lullulae*); **Sulawesi cuscuses** (*P. ursinus* and *P. celebensis*); **Ground cuscus** (*P. gymnotis*); **Stein's cuscus** ⓡ (*P. interpositus*); **Mountain cuscus** (*P. carmelitae*); **Silky cuscus** (*P. vestitus*), **Black-spotted cuscus** ⓡ (*P. rufoniger*).

Brushtail possums, 3 species of *Trichosurus*: **Common brushtail possum** (*T. vulpecula*); **Mountain brushtail possum** or bobuck (*T. caninus*); **Northern brushtail possum** (*T. arnhemensis*).

Scaly-tailed possum, 1 species of *Wyulda*, *W. squamicaudata*.

⋆ CITES listed.   ⓡ Rare.

▶ **Plain, spotted species?** ABOVE This Spotted cuscus female represents an unspotted color phase.

▶ **The rare Scaly-tailed possum** BELOW was only discovered early this century in the remote Kimberley region of north Western Australia.

▷ **The Spotted cuscus** OVERLEAF is a tree-dwelling species common in New Guinea, rare in Cape York, Queensland, Australia.

Dwelling in the remote outback as well as in the suburbs of most Australian cities, the Common brushtail possum is perhaps the most frequently encountered of all Australian mammals. Yet this species is only one of 14 in the phalanger family, which includes the rare Scaly-tailed possum of the Kimberley region, and the Woodlark Island cuscus of which only eight specimens have been reported.

The phalangers are nocturnal, usually arboreal, and they possess well-developed forward-opening pouches; they are distinguished from other tree-dwelling marsupials by their relatively large size, simple, low-crowned molar teeth, lack of a gliding membrane and variable amount of bare skin on the tail. All species have curved and sharply pointed foreclaws for climbing, and clawless but opposable first hind toes which aid in grasping branches. Most species are leaf-eaters and have a long cecum in the gut, but their relatively unspecialized dentition allows them to eat a wide variety of plant products (leaves, fruits, bark) and occasionally eggs and invertebrates.

Seven subspecies of the Common brushtail possum have been named (the last as recently as 1963), but only three are currently accepted. The most widespread form is found in wooded habitats in all Australian states and varies considerably in size (4.4–7.7lb/2–3.5kg) and color (light gray to black). The other subspecies are slightly heavier (up to 9lb/4.1kg) and form geographically isolated populations in Tasmania and in northeastern Queensland. Population density of the Common brushtail varies with habitat, from 1 animal per acre (0.4 per ha) in open forest and woodland, to 3.5 per acre (1.4/ha) in suburban gardens and 5.2 per acre (2.1/ha) in grazed open forest.

Like their widespread congenor, the Mountain and Northern brushtail possums are sharp-faced, with medium-large upright ears, and a tail that is fully furred above with the tip naked below. But they are geographically much more restricted and are not split into subspecies. The solidly built Mountain brushtail occupies dense wet forests in southeastern Australia and may attain population densities of 1–4.5 per acre (0.4–1.8/ha), whereas the little-known Northern brushtail occurs in woodland from the top end of the Northern Territory to Barrow Island, Western Australia.

The very wide distribution of the Common brushtail possum is probably due to its considerable flexibility of feeding and nesting behavior and high reproductive poten-

tial. Where it occurs with the larger and more terrestrial Mountain possum, it eats mostly mature eucalypt leaves and obtains only 20 percent of its food from shrubs in the forest understory. However, in the absence of the larger species, the Common brushtail may spend most of its time on the ground eating a wide range of plant leaves, even grass and clover. In suburban gardens, it has developed an unwelcome taste for rose buds.

The Common brushtail is no less flexible in its nesting behavior. Although, like the other two species, it prefers to nest above ground in tree cavities (dens), the Common brushtail also uses hollow logs and holes in creek banks, while in suburbia it hides under house roofs. In the dense forests of New Zealand it is even known to roost koala-like, exposed on tree forks.

Common brushtail females begin to breed at one year and produce 1–2 young annually. In most populations 90 percent of females breed in the fall (March–May), but up to 50 percent may also breed in spring (September–November). Only one young is born at a time, and the annual reproductive rate of females averages 1.4. In the Mountain brushtail, by contrast, females begin to breed at 2–3 years, produce at most only one young each year, in the fall, and reproduce at an annual rate as low as 0.73. The growth rates of the two species also differ markedly. Both give birth to pink, naked young weighing only 0.008oz (0.22g), but the young of the Common brushtail are weaned first at the age of six months (eight months for the Mountain brushtail) and disperse first at 7–18 months (18–36 months for the Mountain brushtail).

Common brushtails are solitary, except when they are breeding and rearing young. By the end of their third or fourth year, individuals establish small exclusive areas—den trees—within their home ranges, which they defend against individuals of the same sex and social status. Individuals of the opposite sex or lower social status are tolerated within the exclusive areas but, even though the home ranges of males (7.5–20 acres/3–8ha) sometimes completely overlap the ranges of females (2.5–12.4 acres/1–5ha), individuals almost always nest alone and overt interactions are rare.

Despite the ability of the Common brushtail to use a wide variety of dens, defense of den trees suggests that preferred nest sites are in short supply. Because few young die before weaning (15 percent), relatively large numbers of independent young enter the population each year. These young use small, poor-quality dens, and up to 80 percent of males and 50 percent of females die or disperse within their first year. In contrast, in the Mountain brushtail, many young die before weaning (56 percent), so the numbers entering the population—and hence competition for scarce dens—are relatively small. About 80 percent of Mountain brushtail young survive each year after becoming independent, and males and females, far from being solitary, appear to form long-term pair-bonds.

The dispersion of Common brushtails, and in particular the defense of den trees, appears to be maintained through scent marking and to a lesser extent by means of calls, and direct aggression. At least nine scent-producing glands have been recorded in the Common brushtail—more than in

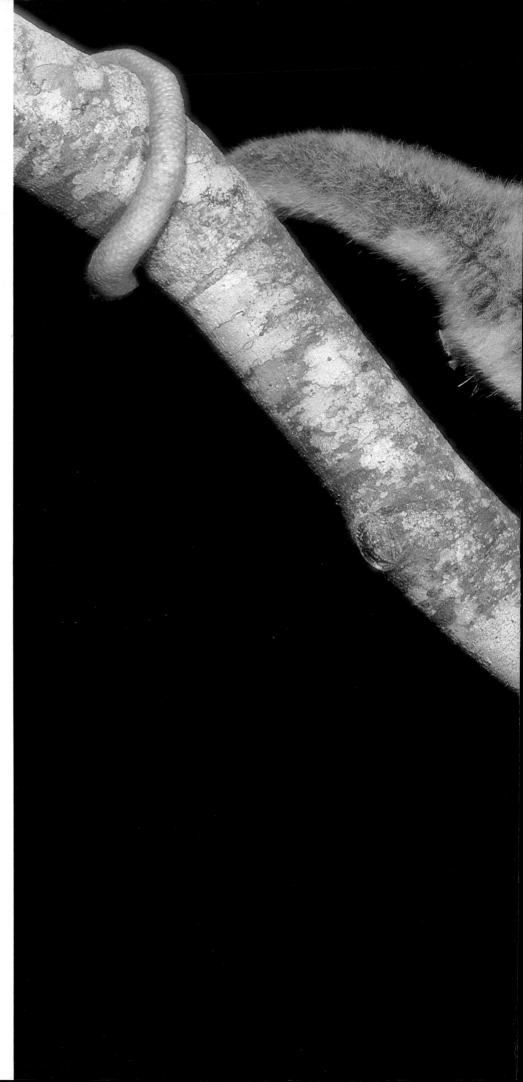

any other species of marsupial. In males, secretions from mouth and chest glands are wiped on the branches and twigs of trees, especially den trees, and these are thought to advertise both the presence and the status of the marker to potential rivals. Females also advertise themselves, but they distribute scent more passively, in urine and feces. Auditory signals probably play a smaller role in maintaining the dispersion of Common brushtails, but a very wide repertoire of screeches, hisses, grunts, growls and chatters is nevertheless known. Many calls are loud—audible to humans at up to 980ft (300m)—and may be given in face-to-face encounters.

The brushtail possums are of considerable commercial importance. The Mountain brushtail causes damage in exotic pine plantations in Victoria and New South Wales, while in Queensland it frequently raids banana and pecan crops. The Common brushtail also damages pines, and in Tasmania it is believed to damage regenerating eucalypt forest. A potentially much more serious problem is that the Common brushtail may become infected with bovine tuberculosis. This discovery, made in New Zealand in 1970, led to fears that brushtails may reinfect cattle. A widespread and costly poisoning program was set up, but infected brushtails remain firmly established at a couple of dozen sites on the North and South islands of New Zealand.

On the other side of the economic coin, the Common brushtail has long been valued for its fur. The rich, dense fur of the Tasmanian form has found special favor and between 1923 and 1959 over 1 million pelts were exported. Exports from New Zealand have also grown rapidly (see box). However, in eastern Australia the last open season on possums was in 1963, and the future for all three species of brushtail seems to be quite secure.

The Scaly-tailed possum was discovered only in 1917. It is known from seven localities in the Kimberley region of Western Australia, and is distinguished by its naked, prehensile, rasp-like tail, very large eyes, small ears, sharp face and short dense gray fur. The Scaly-tailed possum is strictly nocturnal, solitary and feeds on the flowers and leaves of *Eucalyptus* trees; unlike other phalangers it probably nests among rocks. One female has been found with a single, naked young in her pouch in June, but no further details of reproductive behavior are available. The Scaly-tailed possum occupies one of the remotest corners of Australia and, although quite rare, it is considered to be

currently safe from the depredations of man.

In terms of numbers of species, the curious, round-headed cuscuses are the most successful representatives of the family. They are small-eared, and the tail is prehensile, and naked for the outer half or two-thirds of its length. Eight species occur in the rain forests of New Guinea (where they evolved) and two further species occur as far west as Sulawesi and neighboring islands. The Sulawesi cuscuses were probably derived from the ancestors of Spotted and Gray cuscuses, which rafted the 470mi (750km) across the Banda Sea long before the end of the last Ice Age about 11,000 years ago. In a later invasion, the Spotted and Gray cuscuses also crossed Torres Strait to establish populations on Cape York Peninsula, northern Queensland.

On mainland New Guinea, the geographical ranges of some species of cuscus overlap, whereas others fall within more or less exclusive (allopatric) altitudinal zones. These allopatric species are very similar in body size and habits and are apparently unable to coexist. The rarity of Stein's cuscus, for example, which is to be found only at altitudes of 4,000–5,000ft (about 1,200–1,500m), has been attributed to competition from the Gray cuscus, which occurs abundantly below 4,000ft, and the Mountain cuscus, which occurs at altitudes of 5,000–7,500ft (1,500–2,300m). A fourth species, the Silky cuscus, which differs from

A Marsupial Invader: the Common Brushtail in New Zealand

When the first Australian Common brushtail possums were imported to New Zealand around 1840, it was hoped that they would form the basis of a lucrative fur industry. The venture was manifestly successful. Aided by further importations until 1924 and by freeing of captive-bred animals, populations increased prodigiously, so that sales of pelts are now an important source of revenue: in 1976, 1.5 million pelts worth NZ$4.5m were sold. However, the blessings of this marsupial invader are mixed. As well as carrying bovine tuberculosis (see p124), the possum has recently been shown to have subtle but potentially damaging effects on the indigenous vegetation.

New Zealand forest trees evolved in the absence of leaf-eating mammals and, unlike the Australian eucalypts that produce poisonous oils and phenols, the leaves of most species are palatable and lack defenses against predators. When first introduced to particular New Zealand forests, the possums rapidly exploited the new food source and increased in population density up to 120 animals per

acre (50/ha)—some 25 times more than in Australia. By the time numbers had stabilized at 15–25 per acre (6–10/ha), trees such as ratas (*Metrosideros* species) and konini (*Fuchsia excorticata*) had all but disappeared from many areas, and possums were turning their attention to less favored species.

Possums hasten tree death by congregating on individual trees and almost completely defoliating them. These normally solitary creatures evidently abandon their social inhibitions when food and other resources are abundant and, in contrast to their Australian kin, the New Zealand possums occupy small (2.5–5 acres/1–2ha) and extensively overlapping home ranges.

The final verdict on possum damage is unclear. Young individual ratas and other exploited tree species are appearing in many localities, but they now appear to be distasteful to possums. Presumably possums are conferring a selective advantage on "unpalatable" trees, and so continue to subtly but surely alter the structure of the forest.

CRD

▼ ▲ **Most familiar of Australia's possums,** the Common brushtail is one of three species with large ears, pointed muzzle and furry tail that contrast with the mainly New Guinean cuscuses. They inhabit most areas with trees, through which they move by reaching from one branch to another. The Common brushtail exists in several color phases, including the widespread silver-grey ABOVE and the striking copper-red color of the Queensland form BELOW.

▶ **The Gray cuscus of Cape York, Queensland,** on New Guinea and adjacent islands, is a more lightly built member of the same genus as the Spotted cuscus.

the three lower-altitude species principally in its possession of long dense fur, occupies altitudes above 7,500ft. Where two species do overlap, they usually differ in size and habits. Often the larger of the pair is strictly herbivorous and spends most of its life in the forest canopy, whereas the smaller species dwells in the forest understory and feeds to a greater extent on fruits and insects. The Ground cuscus differs markedly from all other cuscuses in being partly carnivorous and semi-terrestrial (on Kobroor Island in the Aru group it reputedly lives in caves); it is accordingly able to coexist with several other cuscuses and its altitudinal range (0–8,900ft/2,700m) is the greatest of any species.

Anecdotal accounts suggest that individuals of all cuscus species usually feed and nest alone. Interactions between individuals are often aggressive; captive Ground cuscuses threaten each other by snarling and hissing, gaping and standing upright, and they attempt to subdue opponents by biting, kicking and cuffing. This species also distributes saliva on the branches and twigs of trees (as well as on itself) and has been observed to dribble urine and drag its cloaca on the ground surface. As in the Common brushtail possum, these activities provide olfactory information for other individuals and presumably mediate social interactions.

Courtship between the male and female cuscus is rather circumspect, and is usually conducted with great deliberation on the limbs of trees. In the Ground cuscus, the male follows the female prior to mating and attempts to sniff her head, flanks and cloaca; it may also utter soft, short clicks. Behavior during copulation has not been described, but the two sexes evidently go separate ways shortly afterwards. In the wild, female Gray and Spotted cuscuses (and probably other species) seldom suckle more than two young, although they possess four teats, and breeding is continuous throughout the year.

Although cuscuses are harmless to man and fortunately of no economic importance, the larger species have long been valued by traditional hunters for their coats and meat. Three species with restricted ranges—the Black-spotted cuscus, Stein's cuscus and the Woodlark Island cuscus—appear to be particularly susceptible to overhunting, and also to the more recent threat of habitat destruction. New Guinea has no national parks, but unless protected areas can be established within the next few years, the continued survival of the susceptible mainland species and the numerous island forms will be gravely threatened.   CRD

RINGTAILS, PYGMY POSSUMS, GLIDERS

Families: Pseudocheiridae, Petauridae, Burramyidae
Thirty species in 9 genera.
Distribution: SE, E, N and SW Australia, Tasmania, New Guinea.

Habitat: forests, woodland, shrublands and heathland.

Size: ranges from head-body length 2.5in (6.4cm), tail length 2.8in (7.1cm) and weight 0.25oz (7g) in the Little pygmy possum to head-body length 13–15in (33–38cm), tail length 7.9–10.6in (20–27cm) and weight 2.9–4.4lb (1.3–2kg) in the Rock ringtail possum.

Coat: grays or browns with paler underside; often darker eye patches or forehead or back stripes; tail long, well-furred (most gliders), prehensile and part naked, or feather-like.

Gestation: 12–50 days (all young are less than 0.035oz/1g at birth).

Longevity: 4–15 years (shorter in pygmy possums with large litters and longer in gliders and ringtails with single young).

Ringtail possums
(family Pseudocheiridae)
Sixteen species in 2 genera: 15 species of *Pseudocheirus* (SE, E, N, SW Australia, Tasmania, New Guinea and W Irian). including **Common ringtail possum** (*P. peregrinus*) and **Rock ringtail possum** (*P. dahli*); **Greater glider** (*Petauroides volans*), E Australia.

Gliders (family Petauridae)
Seven species in 3 genera: 4 species of *Petaurus* (Tasmania, SE, E, N, NW Australia, New Guinea), including **Yellow-bellied** or **Fluffy glider** (*P. australis*) and **Sugar glider** (*P. breviceps*); **Leadbeater's possum** [E] (*Gymnobelideus leadbeateri*), Victoria; **striped possums**, 2 species of *Dactylopsila*, NE coastal Queensland, New Guinea.

Pygmy possums
(family Burramyidae)
Seven species in 4 genera: **pygmy possums** (4 species of *Cercartetus*, including the **Eastern pygmy possum**. *C. nanus*), Tasmania, Kangaroo Island, SE, E, NE, SW Australia, New Guinea; **Feathertail glider** or **Pygmy glider** or **Flying mouse** (*Acrobates pygmaeus*), SE to NE Australia; **Feathertail possum** (*Distoechurus pennatus*), New Guinea; **Mountain pygmy possum** [*] (*Burramys parvus*), SE Australia.

[E] Endangered. [*] CITES listed.

THE ringtail possums, gliders and pygmy possums inhabit the unique forested environments of Australia and New Guinea. When the Australian continent was invaded some 40–60 million years ago by primitive possum-like marsupials, it was blanketed in a wet, misty and humid rain forest. Opening of these forests in the mid to late Tertiary (32–5 million years ago) and their gradual replacement by the marginal eucalypt and acacia forests of today, forced this early fauna to seek refuge in the high-altitude regions of northern Queensland and Papua New Guinea, where the ringtail possums radiated to form a diverse family of leaf- and fruit-eating specialists. At the same time the new nectar-, gum- and insect-rich Australian eucalypt and wattle (*Acacia*) forests provided many abundant niches for the predominantly nectarivorous pygmy possums and the sap- and gumivorous petaurid gliders. This diversification has led to some remarkable convergences of form, function and behavior with the arboreal lemurs, bush babies, monkeys and squirrels of other continents.

The ringtail possums, pygmy possums and gliders are arboreal marsupials with hand-like feet, an enlarged opposable big toe on the hindfoot and a range of adaptations suited to moving about in the forest. The modern possum families of Australasia, although superficially similar to one another, differ in external form, internal anatomy and physiology, and the biochemistry of blood proteins as much from one another as from kangaroos and the koala. Previously included with the brushtail possums and cuscuses (the family Phalangeridae), the gliders, pygmy and ringtail possums are now separated into three additional families. In non-gliding species the tail is prehensile and may be used for grasping branches and transporting nest material; a naked under-surface effectively increases friction. In gliders (but not the Feathertail glider) the tail is heavily furred and straight or tapering; it may be used for controlling the direction of flight. Gliding species are specialized for rapid movement in the open forests and are thought to have evolved independently in three families during the mid-late Tertiary. In the nine glider species that survive today, gliding is achieved by use of a thin, furred membrane (patagium) that stretches from fore- to hindlimbs (wrist to ankle in the Sugar glider, wrist to knee in the Feathertail glider), increasing surface area in flight to form a large rectangle. It is retracted when not in use and may be visible

as a wavy line along the side of the body. The effective gliding surface area has been increased by lengthening of arm and leg bones and some species are able to cover distances of over 330ft (100m) in a single glide, from the top of one tree to the butt or trunk of another. The heavier Greater glider, with a reduced (elbow-to-ankle) gliding membrane, descends steeply with limited control, but the smaller gliders are accomplished acrobats that weave and maneuver gracefully between trees, landing with precision by swooping upwards. What appears to be a gentle landing to the human eye is in fact shown by slow motion photography to be a high speed collision. The animals bounce backward after impact and must fasten their long claws into the tree trunk to avoid tumbling to the ground. The fourth and fifth digits of the hand are elongated and have greatly enlarged claws which assist clinging after the landing impact.

All these possums are nocturnal and have large, protruding eyes. Most are also quiet, secretive and hence rarely seen. The only audible sign of their presence may be the gentle "plop" of gliders landing on tree trunks, the yapping alarm call of the Sugar glider or the screeching or gurgling flight call of the Yellow-bellied glider. Ringtail possums are generally quiet but occasionally emit soft twittering calls. Most possum species make loud screaming and screeching calls when attacked or handled.

Four major dietary groups can be recognized: folivores, sapivores and gumivores, insectivores, and nectarivores. Ringtail possums and the Greater glider together form a highly specialized group (family Pseudocheiridae) of arboreal leaf-eaters (folivores), characterized by enlargement of the cecum to form a region for microbial fermentation of the cellulose in their highly fibrous diet. Fine grinding of food particles in a battery of well-developed molars with crescent-shaped ridges on the crowns (selenodont molars) enhances digestion. Rates of food intake in these groups are slowed by the time required for cellulose fermentation, and nitrogen and energy is often conserved by slow motion, relatively small litter sizes (1–1.5), coprophagy (reingestion of feces) and adoption of medium to large body size (0.4–4.4lb/ 0.2–2kg). The preferred diet of the Greater glider of eastern Australia is eucalypt leaves. The greatest diversity of species in this widespread group is in the high-altitude dripping rain forests and cloud forests of northern Queensland and New Guinea.

The four species of petaurid glider and Leadbeater's possum (all of the family

◄ ▼ Denizens of inland forests of eastern Australia, these female and male Squirrel gliders (*Petaurus norfolcensis*) LEFT show the long, bushy, soft-furred tail that gives them their name. The larger Yellow-bellied glider BELOW lives in more coastal forest areas with higher rainfall. Both species are uncommon and both have a diet chiefly of gum and sap from *Eucalyptus* trees. Long, sharp claws grip the bark when the animal lands on a trunk at the end of a glide.

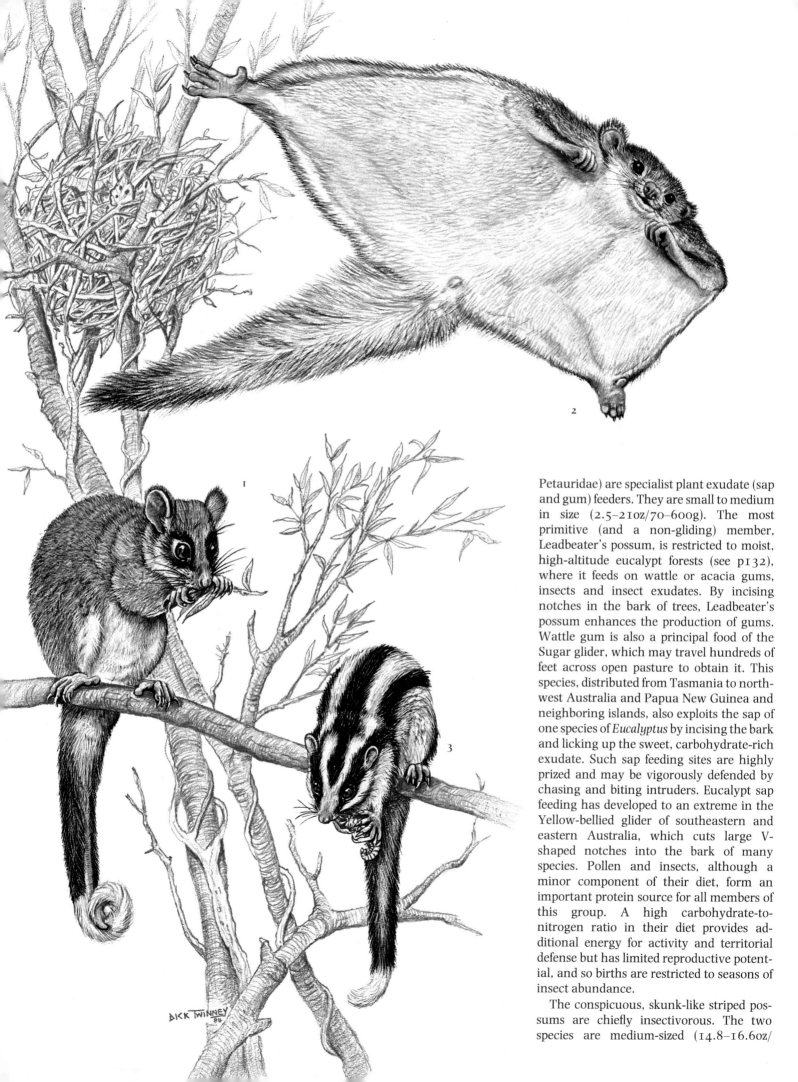

Petauridae) are specialist plant exudate (sap and gum) feeders. They are small to medium in size (2.5–21oz/70–600g). The most primitive (and a non-gliding) member, Leadbeater's possum, is restricted to moist, high-altitude eucalypt forests (see p132), where it feeds on wattle or acacia gums, insects and insect exudates. By incising notches in the bark of trees, Leadbeater's possum enhances the production of gums. Wattle gum is also a principal food of the Sugar glider, which may travel hundreds of feet across open pasture to obtain it. This species, distributed from Tasmania to north-west Australia and Papua New Guinea and neighboring islands, also exploits the sap of one species of *Eucalyptus* by incising the bark and licking up the sweet, carbohydrate-rich exudate. Such sap feeding sites are highly prized and may be vigorously defended by chasing and biting intruders. Eucalypt sap feeding has developed to an extreme in the Yellow-bellied glider of southeastern and eastern Australia, which cuts large V-shaped notches into the bark of many species. Pollen and insects, although a minor component of their diet, form an important protein source for all members of this group. A high carbohydrate-to-nitrogen ratio in their diet provides additional energy for activity and territorial defense but has limited reproductive potential, and so births are restricted to seasons of insect abundance.

The conspicuous, skunk-like striped possums are chiefly insectivorous. The two species are medium-sized (14.8–16.6oz/

420–470g) and are specialized for exploitation of social insects, ants, bees, termites and other wood-boring insects in tropical lowland rain forests of northern Queensland and New Guinea. A suite of adaptations, including an extremely elongated fourth finger (like that of the aye-aye of Madagascar), elongated tongues and enlarged and forward-pointing upper as well as lower incisors, aid in the noisy extraction of insects from deep within wood crevices. Feeding activity may produce a shower of woodchips.

Pygmy possums in the genus *Cercartetus* and the Feathertail or Pygmy glider form a fourth group (family Burramyidae) that has diversified in the nectar-rich sclerophyllous Australian heathlands, shrublands and eucalypt forests. The brush-tipped ton-

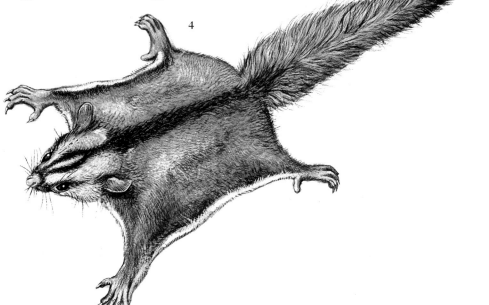

gue of the Feathertail glider is used for sipping nectar from flower capsules, and the small size (under 1.2oz/35g) and extreme mobility of all five species increase nectar-harvesting rates. In poor seasons aggregations of many individuals may be found on isolated flowering trees and shrubs. Most species are also thought to take the abundant pollen available at flowers, and occasionally insects, to provide protein. The small size and abundant dietary nitrogen permit unusually large litter sizes (4–6) and rapid growth and development rates, similar to those of carnivorous marsupials (family Dasyuridae).

The rare and poorly studied Mountain pygmy possum is superficially similar. It spends up to six months of the year active

▲ **Possums and gliders—diet and movement**. (1) Common ringtail possum (*Pseudocheirus peregrinus*) eating leaves, with its spherical nest made of grass and bark in the background. (2) Greater glider (*Petauroides volans*) gliding. (3) Striped possum (*Dactylopsila trivirgata*) eating an insect. (4) Sugar glider (*Petaurus breviceps*) gliding. (5) The omnivorous Feathertail possum (*Distoechurus pennatus*) eating an insect. (6) Yellow-bellied glider (*P. australis*) feeding on sap of *Eucalyptus* by biting into bark. (7) Mountain pygmy possum (*Burramys parvus*), a chiefly nectar- and pollen-eating species.

▶ **Nectar and pollen** are important in the diet of the Eastern pygmy possum, which uses its brush-tipped tongue to collect nectar from the flowers of *Eucalyptus* (as here): fruits and insects may also be taken.

◀ **Feather-like tail** adds maneuverability and distance to the flight of the Feathertail glider of eastern Australia. Another nectar-eating species, it is the only feather-tailed marsupial in Australasia—the non-gliding Feathertail possum inhabits only New Guinea.

beneath a blanket of snow in the high-altitude heaths of the Snowy Mountains. This scansorial (ground- and tree-foraging) species has a unique diet of seeds, fleshy fruit, some plant foliage, insects and other invertebrates. The remarkable sectorial premolar tooth is adapted for husking and cracking seeds. Excess seeds may be cached for use during periods of winter shortage.

The other member of the pygmy possum family, the Feathertail possum of Papua New Guinea, has a tail like that of the Feathertail glider but is larger (1.8–1.9oz/ 50–55g) and has no gliding membrane. Its diet includes insects, fruit and possibly plant exudates.

Patterns of social organization and mating behavior in possums and gliders are remarkably diverse, but to some extent predictable from species' body size, diet and habitat characteristics. The larger folivorous ringtail possums and Greater glider are primarily solitary; they sleep singly or occasionally in pairs, in tree hollows or vegetation clumps, by day and emerge to feed on foliage in home ranges of up to 7.4 acres (3ha) at night. Male home ranges are generally exclusive but may partially overlap those of one or two females. The occupation of exclusive home ranges by males and overlapping home ranges by females is associated with greater mortality of males among juveniles and a consequent female-biased sex ratio.

The tendency towards gregariousness increases with decreasing body size, the Common ringtail of eastern Australia forming nesting groups of up to 3 individuals, the Yellow-bellied glider groups of up to 5, the Sugar glider up to 12, and the Feathertail glider up to 25. Most nesting groups consist of mated pairs with offspring, but the

Rediscovery of Leadbeater's Possum

An hour after nightfall one evening in 1961, at a tourist spot in the wet misty mountains just 68mi from Melbourne, the attention of a fauna survey group from the National Museum of Victoria was caught by a small, bright-eyed and alert, gray possum leaping nimbly through the forest undergrowth. Its size at first suggested a Sugar glider but the absence of a gliding membrane and the narrow bushy tail led to the exciting conclusion that here, alive, and only the sixth specimen known to science, was the long-lost Leadbeater's possum.

This rare little possum, now the State of Victoria's faunal emblem, was first discovered in 1867 in the Bass River Valley. Only five specimens were collected, all prior to 1909, and in 1921 it was concluded that the destruction of the scrub and forest in the area had resulted in complete extermination.

Surveys following the rediscovery led to its detection at some 40 separate sites within a 15.5 × 25mi (25 × 40km) area. Its preferred

habitat was the zone of Victoria's Central Highland forests dominated by the majestic Mountain ash (*Eucalyptus regnans*), the world's tallest hardwood and Australia's most valued timber producing tree. Standing beneath such forest giants provides the most reliable method of catching a glimpse of Leadbeater's possum as the animals emerge at dusk from their family retreat in a hollow branch to feed in the surrounding forest. Now, only 22 years after its discovery, the possum is again threatened with extinction by forest clearance. inappropriate forest management, and natural disappearance of the large dead trees that provide nest sites in regrowth forests (in 1939 a fire destroyed two-thirds of Victoria's Mountain ash forests). The species' survival, along with that of the only other nationally endangered possum, the Mountain pygmy possum (threatened by ski-run and general tourist development at alpine resorts),depends upon effective government action which is yet to be forthcoming.

petaurids may form truly mixed groups with up to four or more unrelated adults of both sexes (Sugar glider), one male and one or several females (Yellow-bellied glider), or with one female and up to three males (Leadbeater's possum). The chief reason for nesting in groups is thought to be improved energy conservation through huddling during winter. Larger nesting groups of one species, the Sugar glider, disband into small groups during summer. The aggregation of females during winter enables dominant males to monopolize access to up to three females in the petaurid gliders, and a harem-defense mating system prevails.

An entirely different mating system occurs in the closely related Leadbeater's possum. Individual females occupy large nests in hollow trees and actively defend a surrounding 2.5–3.7 acres (1–1.5ha) exclusive territory from other females. Mating is strictly monogamous and male partners assist females in defense of territories. Additional adult males may be tolerated in family groups by the breeding pairs but adult females are not, and an associated higher female mortality results in a male-biased sex ratio. This pattern appears to be associated with the construction of well-insulated nests, avoiding the necessity for females to huddle during winter, and with the occupation of dense, highly productive habitats in which food resources are readily defensible and surplus energy is available to meet the cost of territorial defense.

Selective pressures exerted during competition for mating partners (sexual selection) have led to the prolific development of scent-marking glands in the petaurid group, for use in marking other members of the social group. Leadbeater's possum, the most primitive and only monogamous member, shows least development of special scent glands, and scent-marking between partners involves the mutual transfer of saliva to the tail base with its adjacent anal glands. Males of the promiscuous Sugar glider, in contrast, possess forehead, chest and anal glands. Males use their head glands to spread scent on the chest of females, and females in turn spread scent on their heads by rubbing the chest gland of dominant males. Male Yellow-bellied gliders have similar glands but scent transfer is achieved quite differently, by rubbing the head gland against the female's anal gland. Females in turn rub their heads on the dominant male's anal gland. Such behavior probably facilitates group cohesion by communicating an individual's social status, sex, group membership and reproductive position. AS

KANGAROOS AND WALLABIES

Families: Macropodidae and Potoroidae
About 60 species in 16 genera.
Distribution: Australia, New Guinea.
Habitat: wide ranging, from inland plains to tropical rain forests.

Size: ranges from head-body length 11.2in (28.4cm), tail length 5.6in (14.2cm) and weight 1.2lb (0.5kg) in the Musky rat kangaroo to head-body length 65in (165cm), tail length 42in (107cm) and weight 198lb (90kg) in the male Red kangaroo.

Gestation: newborn attach to a maternal teat within a pouch and there further develop for 6–11 months.

Longevity: variable according to species and climatic conditions. Larger species may attain 12–18 years (28 years in captivity).

SOME 224 modern mammals have been described from Australia since the first European settlement in 1788, but the popular image of an Australian mammal both in that country and abroad is still perhaps that of a hopping female kangaroo, with an attractive offspring protruding from its abdominal pouch. Among the approximately 120 species of marsupials in Australia itself, some 45 are recognized as belonging to the families Potoroidae and Macropodidae. There are 10 further kangaroo species in New Guinea and nearby islands, in addition to two also present in Australia.

Most of the kangaroo species had been collected and described by the mid-19th century. Although argument about the taxonomy and nomenclature of some kangaroos is not yet settled, their recorded history is frequently first associated with early explorers. Thus when in 1770 James Cook's vessel struck the Barrier Reef and repairs were undertaken at Endeavour River, near the present site of Cooktown, the party's naturalists, Banks and Solander, together with the artist Parkinson, collected specimens throughout the seven-week delay, including three kangaroos. Descriptions of these specimens aroused great interest in Europe at the time, but nearly 200 years later the descriptions were revealed to be

Families of Kangaroos and Wallabies

Rat kangaroos
(Family Potoroidae)
Genus *Hypsiprymnodon*. One species, the **Musky rat kangaroo** (*H. moschatus*).

Genus *Potorous*. Three species, including the **Long-nosed potoroo** or **rat kangaroo** (*P. tridactylus*) and the **Long-footed potoroo** [I] (*P. longipes*).

Genus *Caloprymnus*. One species, the **Plains** or **Desert rat kangaroo** [I] (*C. campestris*).

Genus *Bettongia* [*] Four species, the **bettongs** or **short-nosed rat kangaroos**: the **Brush-tailed rat kangaroo** or **bettong**, or **woylie** [E] (*B. penicillata*); **Lesueur's** or **Burrowing rat kangaroo**, or **boodie** [R] (*B. lesueur*); **Northern rat kangaroo** or **bettong** (*B. tropica*) and **Gaimard's rat kangaroo** or **Tasmanian bettong** (*B. gaimardi*).

Genus *Aepyprymnus*. One species, the **Rufous rat kangaroo** or **bettong** (*A. rufescens*).

Kangaroos
(Family Macropodidae)
Genus *Dendrolagus*. Seven species, the **tree kangaroos**.

Genus *Lagostrophus*. One species, the **Banded hare wallaby** [R] (*L. fasciatus*).

Genus *Lagorchestes*. Four species, including the **Spectacled hare wallaby** (*L. conspicillatus*); and **Western** or **Rufous hare wallaby** [R] (*L. hirsutus*).

Genus *Onychogalea*. Three species, including the **Bridled nailtail wallaby** [E] (*O. fraenata*) and the **Crescent nailtail wallaby** [EX] (*O. lunata*).

Genus *Petrogale*. Ten species, including the **Yellow-footed** or **Ring-tailed rock wallaby** (*P. xanthopus*).

Genus *Thylogale*. Four species, the **pademelons** or **scrub wallabies**.

Genus *Setonix*. One species, the **quokka** (*S. brachyurus*).

Genus *Wallabia*. One species, the **Swamp** or **Black wallaby** (*W. bicolor*).

Genus *Dorcopsis*. Three species, the **greater forest** or **New Guinea wallabies**.

Genus *Dorcopsulus*. Two species, the **lesser forest** or **mountain wallabies**.

Genus *Macropus*. Fourteen species, including the **Red kangaroo** (*M. rufus*), **Eastern gray kangaroo** or **forester** (*M. giganteus*), **Western gray** or **Mallee** or **Blackfaced kangaroo** (*M. fuliginosus*), the **wallaroo** or **euro**, or **Hill kangaroo** (*M. robustus*), the **Tammar** or **Dama wallaby** (*M. eugenii*), **Whiptail** or **Prettyface wallaby**, or **flier** (*M. parryi*) and **Parma wallaby** (*M. parma*).

[*] CITES listed. [E] Endangered.
[EX] Extinct. [I] Threatened, but status indeterminate.

▲ **Largest and most typical of marsupials**— the Red kangaroo. A family group, with the head, tail and one foot of a joey protruding after it has jumped into its mother's pouch. The single young does not finally leave the pouch until about eight months old. In most kangaroos the male's coat is russet to brick red; female "blue fliers" have blue-grey fur.

◄ **Sheltering from the sun**, a Spectacled hare wallaby hides beneath hummocks of grass on Barrow Island, off Western Australia. In this harsh location, the hare wallaby feeds on tips of spinifex grass leaves and does not drink even when water is present.

composites of all three animals, and it became necessary to identify what were the species collected in order to ensure the application to the correct species of the first used scientific name. The problem was finally settled in 1966 by determination No. 760 of the International Commission on Zoological Nomenclature, which assigned the name *Macropus giganteus* to the Eastern gray kangaroo, the first specimen of a kangaroo collected on the Australian mainland by Europeans for scientific study.

The rat kangaroos are often regarded as ancestral to other kangaroos. They are placed in a separate family, the Potoroidae, on the basis of their dentition (see below), which is adapted to a more generalized diet. Other ancestral features include the pre-

sence of the first toe in the Musky rat kangaroo, and possum-like morphology of the brain. Among the Macropodidae, the use of the names kangaroo and wallaby to indicate large and small species is now largely a matter of tradition. The original discrimination between the two on the basis of length of hindfoot and basal length of the skull has long proved unsatisfactory and the term kangaroo is used here to cover both.

Kangaroos and rat kangaroos have adapted to a great range of habitats, including open plains, woodlands and forests, rocky outcrops, slopes and cliffs, with a few species becoming arboreal. Such adaptations have led to a wide variation in size and form. Common features which distinguish the group from other marsupials include the characteristic body shape and structure of their jaw and teeth. With the exception of the Musky rat kangaroo, which has a simple stomach, all have a large sacculated stomach akin to that found in ruminants. The distinctive shape includes short forelimbs as opposed to elongated hindlimbs adapted to hopping, and a large and often heavy tail used as a balance in this form of locomotion or as an additional prop to support the animal's weight during slow forward movement, particularly when grazing. On horizontal surfaces tree kangaroos can move in a similar hopping manner to the ground-dwelling forms, from which they differ in that their forelimbs are stouter and more muscular, while their hindlimbs are relatively shorter, bearing squat broad feet. Tree kangaroos climb by gripping branches with their stout foreclaws and walking backwards or forwards with alternate movements of their hindfeet. This independent movement of the hindlimbs is a feature not present in other kangaroos, except for swimming when hindlimbs move independently. The forelimbs of all kangaroos have five clawed digits while the long foot bears two major toes, of similar shape and bearing prominent claws, the larger corresponding to the fourth and the smaller to the fifth digit. A first digit equivalent to a "big toe" is absent in all species except the Musky rat kangaroo, while the second and third digits are very small and, except for the claws, are bound in a common sheath. Despite their small size these bound toes provide an extremely flexible grooming organ.

Both males and females have a prominent cloacal protuberance that encloses the rec-tal opening and the uro-genital passage in the female or the retracted penis in the male. In front of the cloacal protuberance a pendulous scrotum is obvious in mature males, while females possess a pouch bearing on the abdominal wall four independent mammary glands each with a teat, to one of which the newborn young attaches after climbing up the outer body wall and over the lip of the pouch.

Apart from two forward-projecting (procumbent) incisors which move laterally against six upper incisors, and a wide gap (diastema) between the incisors and cheek teeth in both upper and lower jaw, the two families possess characteristic grinding (molariform) teeth. In young animals the first two teeth in the cheek row are a shearing (sectorial) premolar and the only "milk" tooth, a molar-like premolar. Both these are eventually shed and replaced by a single sectorial premolar. Four robust molariform teeth follow and erupt in sequence over a relatively long period of the animal's life span, and with advancing age gradually move toward the front of the jaw with an associated loss in turn of those teeth further forward. In rat kangaroos the first upper incisor is much longer than the other two, whereas in kangaroos and wallabies the three teeth tend to be much the same size. The molars of the rat kangaroos bear four cusps and decrease in size towards the rear, but those of kangaroos and wallabies bear two transverse ridges with a prominent longitudinal connecting link between them. The size of successive molars may increase slightly or remain much the same.

Marked sexual dimorphism in size and, in

▶ **The Rufous bettong** or Rufous rat kangaroo spends the day in a nest in the grass, as do other rat kangaroos and potoroos. At night it feeds on grasses, herbs, roots and tubers on the floor of the open forests where it prefers to live.

▼ **Representative species of larger kangaroos and wallabies**, shown in a hopping sequence. (**1**) Bridled nailtail wallaby (*Onychogalea fraenata*). (**2**) Wallaroo (*Macropus robustus*). (**3**) Quokka (*Setonix brachyurus*). (**4**) Red-legged pademelon (*Thylogale stigmatica*). (**5**) Yellow-footed rock wallaby (*Petrogale xanthopus*). (**6**) Gray forest wallaby (*Dorcopsis veterum*).

some cases, coat color, is readily observed among kangaroos. Male and female young develop at much the same rate within the parental pouch but on emergence the rate of male growth increases so that fully developed adult males are larger than females and in some species, such as the Red and both gray kangaroos, may exceed twice the size of females of comparable age. Examples of differences in color are well known; thus the soft dense and woolly coat of Red kangaroos, for example, may be pale to dark russet-red in the male and in the female a distinct blue-gray, while the coarse and shaggy-haired male wallaroos are black and their females silver-gray. However, differences in coat color between the sexes of gray kangaroos are not marked. The eastern species is predominantly gray-colored and the western brown. Both possess soft fur which may vary from short and sparse in the tropics to dense and woolly in colder regions.

Members of this group are primarily associated with habitats containing herbs, grasses and shrubs. In Australia these are found in relatively open communities that merge into forests on the one hand and through woodlands into grasslands on the other. The woodland fauna includes the large kangaroos, large and small wallabies and several of the rat kangaroos. Many of these species are widespread but some have even more specialized requirements. The somewhat sedentary wallaroos or hill kangaroos are usually to be found associated with stony rises, rock hills and escarpments; the colonial rock wallabies, with rock piles, steep rocky hills and cliffs; thus these species'

potential distribution tends to be discontinuous though widespread throughout the woodland zone.

Unfortunately, since the late 18th century human settlement has brought considerable and often dramatic changes to the original habitat, with consequent drastic effects on the distribution and numbers of kangaroos, so that some species are now restricted to a portion of their former ranges, often including offshore islands. Removal or thinning of shrubs and degradation of grasslands by domestic stock and by the introduced rabbit have rendered such areas unsuitable for many of the smaller grass-dwelling and grass-nesting species, as well as exposing them to predation. The total removal of cover for the establishment of improved pastures, crops or monocultures of exotic conifers has had equally disastrous effects on many marsupials. However, in some cases it would appear that the reduction of the original tall coarse dry grasses to a closely cropped sward by introduced stock has allowed the larger kangaroos to thrive, and in other cases some species of forest-dwelling wallabies appear to have prospered when improved pastures have been developed adjacent to timber from which they emerge to graze.

Until quite recently little was known of selection and utilization of native plants by domestic stock, let alone by kangaroos. The possible effects of competition by feral animals including rabbits, goats and an assemblage of other grazing animals was usually overlooked.

Food preferences have been studied in only a few native and domestic species, habitats and widely separate locations. Regrettably the findings of these studies have been extrapolated frequently and uncritically to many other parts of the continent. In general kangaroos prefer to feed from dusk to dawn in habitats with open undergrowth which permits freedom of movement by the animal and promotion of the grasses. These conditions tend to occur on the fringes of forests, in open woodlands or near natural or improved pastures. Investigations to date indicate that domestic and native grazing animals are selective in their choice of food. Kangaroos eat no more than sheep of equivalent size but they do select plants of a lower nitrogen content. At any one time of the year food preferences of sheep differ from those of kangaroos, while different species and sexes of kangaroos within a common habitat may select different varieties or quantities of particular plants.

In one study of the diets of sheep, Red kangaroos and Eastern gray kangaroos within the mulga-box and spinifex plant associations of southwestern Queensland, it

was found that although each group of animals concentrated on particular species of plants, the Eastern gray kangaroos concentrated mainly on grasses (64 percent grass, 36 percent dicotyledons), while the diet of Red kangaroos and sheep had more in common (46 percent grass, 54 percent dicotyledons) through their preference for forbs and browse. With changed seasonal conditions accompanied by a drop in temperature, dicotyledons became less ·abundant and all these species turned their attention to grasses as the food sources became depleted.

In a further example, involving a different group of species, Yellow-footed rock wallabies near Broken Hill, New South Wales (where they are of restricted distribution and relatively rare), were compared with the wallaroo and two feral competitors, the goat and rabbit. During good seasons considerable overlap was reported in the species eaten by all the herbivores present and this overlap increased with deterioration of the

▷ **Gregarious grazers** OVERLEAF, Eastern gray kangaroos move out from the cover of trees to feed on the grasses that are their preferred food. Larger size and safety in numbers may permit such daytime feeding, while most kangaroos feed exclusively in the safety of dusk or darkness.

▼ **Representative small- and medium-sized** kangaroos and wallabies. (**1**) Papuan or Lesser forest wallaby (*Dorcopsulus macleayi*). (**2**) Musky rat kangaroo (*Hypsiprymnodon moschatus*). (**3**) Lumholtz's tree kangaroo (*Dendrolagus lumholtzi*). (**4**) Desert rat kangaroo (*Caloprymnus campestris*). (**5**) Boodie (*Bettongia lesueur*). (**6**) Rufous hare wallaby (*Lagorchestes hirsutus*). (**7**) Long-nosed potoroo (*Potorous tridactylus*). (**8**) Banded hare wallaby (*Lagostrophus fasciatus*). (**9**) Rufous bettong (*Aepyprymnus rufescens*).

vegetation. In good seasons the largest
component of the wallaby's diet was forbs
(42–52 percent), chiefly small herbaceous
ephemeral species. During drought, browse
became the most important dietary component (44 percent), with a marked overlap
of dietary components (75 percent) for all
categories of plants in wallabies and goats.
Competition from the wallaroos appeared
least, with limited overlap of dietary components and little variation from the high
proportion of grasses ingested throughout
the study. The results indicate that small
surviving "island" colonies of rock wallabies are subject to considerable competition, particularly with goats capable of
removing browse to levels beyond the reach
of wallabies, and to a lesser extent with
rabbits.

Patterns of reproduction vary greatly.
Some species such as the Red kangaroo are
opportunistic breeders, mating and producing young when seasonal conditions favor
successful rearing of the offspring; others
such as the gray kangaroos are capable of
breeding throughout the year but tend to be
primarily seasonal breeders with most
young born during the summer months, the
young then leaving the pouch at a most
favorable time, the spring of the following
year. Still other species have a very restricted breeding season, for example the Tammar wallaby, in which the greatest number
of young are born in late January. Onset of
sexual maturity may be less than a year in
the female Tammar, but exceed 15 months
and even attain 2–3 years depending on
seasonal conditions in the larger species of
kangaroos. Courtship may be restricted to a
few hours or may extend over 2–3 days,
with the male closely associated with a
female coming into heat (estrus). Males
generally follow such females, frequently
sniffing the opening of the pouch and urogenital area, while pawing at the female's
tail. During this interaction male wallabies
exhibit a characteristic sideways sinuous
swishing of their tails, an activity less noticeable in the larger kangaroos. Attention by
other males at this time results in chasing or
fighting between the competitors. Mating
may be brief or, as in the case of gray
kangaroos on occasions, exceed one hour.

The gestation period is about one month
(28 days in Tammars; in Eastern gray
kangaroos it is one of the longest at 36
days). Young at birth are small and undeveloped and weigh from 0.01oz (0.3g) in smaller wallabies to under 0.035oz (1g) in the
larger kangaroos. One young is the usual
number born to each female, but twins are

known. The Musky rat kangaroo is an exception in that two young are usually born. Other than in the Swamp wallaby, where the estrous cycle (32 days) is shorter than the gestation period (35 days), the estrous cycle is longer than gestation. In a number of species matings occur when the female is receptive after giving birth (post-partum estrus), in which case a quiescent blastocyst may result, later to develop on vacation of the pouch by the young produced at the preceding mating. Immediate post-partum mating is unknown in the gray kangaroos, where loss of young is followed by return to estrus about one week later. Newborn young attach to one of four teats in the pouch where the young remain for several months until they eventually leave the pouch for short periods and then, depending on species, subsequently vacate the pouch completely some 5–11 months after birth. Young of most species then continue to suckle from the same teat they occupied during pouch life for a further 2–6 months. Young tend to associate with their mothers until they attain sexual maturity.

Like the herbivorous hoofed mammals, kangaroos have social systems which range from solitary to group living according to factors such as habitat, diet, body size and mobility. The principal evolutionary trends within the family have been away from the early forms, believed to have been small omnivorous forest dwellers, probably nocturnal and solitary by nature, towards larger size and grazing habits, with some development of daytime activity and group living. The rat kangaroos are generally solitary. In the Long-nosed potoroo male home ranges (about 47 acres/19ha) overlap those of several females (about 12.5 acres/5ha), but there is some indication that the home ranges of males do not overlap. The Brush-tailed bettong has feeding areas which overlap, but an area of 2.5–5 acres (1–2ha) surrounding several daytime nests

in current use appears to be almost exclusive to individuals, any overlap being between males and adjacent females. Total home ranges of males (67 acres/27ha) are larger than those of females (49 acres/20ha).

The biology of many of the smaller wallabies is little known. Some are solitary, eg in the 9–13lb (4–6kg) Red-necked pademelon the home ranges of about 35 acres (14ha) overlap extensively, but there are no persistent associations. One of the smallest wallabies, the 4.4–11lb (2–5kg) quokka, has individual home ranges of 4–24 acres (1.6–9.7ha) which overlap in areas of suitable habitat. There is some interchange between areas, but the population is in effect divided into subunits. Individuals within an area are not gregarious but remain tolerant of each other except to monopolize particular shelter sites in hot weather.

There is an obvious trend towards increasing sociability in the kangaroos, in which increased size, greater mobility, less completely nocturnal activity and a diet based on the grasses of more open habitat

▲ **The Burrowing bettong or boodie** is the only kangaroo that regularly inhabits burrows. Once common on mainland Australia, it is now extinct there and confined to islands off the coast of Western Australia. It eats tubers, roots, seeds, fruit, fungi and termites.

▼ **Red kangaroo fight.** Before a fight two males may engage in a "stiff-legged" walk (1) in the face of the opponent, and in scratching and grooming (2, 3), standing upright on extended rear legs. The fight is initiated by locking forearms (4) and attempting to push the opponent backward to the ground (5). Fights may occur when one male's monopoly of access to an individual or group of females is challenged. There appears to be no defense of territory for its own sake.

1   2   3   4   5

▲ **Climbing kangaroo.** Lumholtz's tree kangaroo (*Dendrolagus lumholtzi*).

▼ **Reproduction in kangaroos** varies according to whether the fertilized egg develops continuously from fertilization to birth or whether it enters a period of dormancy (diapause) before finally developing. Also kangaroos may give birth at any time of the year (aseasonal) or at fixed times (seasonal). Three types are indicated here. (**a**) The Western gray kangaroo is a seasonal breeder with a continuous gestation of 30 days: the young stay in the pouch for 320 days. When one joey has just been born (white bar) another is still at foot. (**b**) The Tammar wallaby is a seasonal breeder and exhibits diapause. When one joey has just been born the mother has another fertilized egg in her uterus, which will not be born until the following season. (**c**) The Red Kangaroo is an aseasonal breeder with diapause. Thus when one joey has just been born, there is another at foot, suckling, while the mother has a fertilized egg in her uterus which will be born soon after the joey leaves the pouch.

are correlated with an increased tendency for the individual to be one of a group. A similar pattern is known in several species, eg Eastern gray kangaroo, Western gray kangaroo, Whiptail wallaby, Red kangaroo and Antilopine wallaroo, which are usually seen in small groups of 2–10, solitary animals being rare. These may be subunits of a group which shares a common home range, or of a large unstable aggregation the members of which may be locally nomadic (as in the Red kangaroo). In the Whiptail wallaby, whose males attain 55lb (25kg) and females 33lb (15kg), up to 50 individuals share a group home range of about 250 acres (100ha) but are generally found in small, continually changing subgroups of 7–10 animals. Individual home ranges for males are about 185 acres (75ha) and for females about 138 acres (56ha).

In all of these species, the main association between individuals is between mother and offspring, which may stay together after the young is weaned. In most kangaroos mating is promiscuous, with males competing for access to females. The largest, most dominant males are able to monopolize a female in heat, and in a group one male may father most of the offspring. It is presumably selection for increased body size in competing males which has led to the marked sexual dimorphism in the larger kangaroos.

At the time of European settlement nomadic Aboriginal man utilized kangaroos as a source of meat and hides but hunting at this level probably had little effect on kangaroo populations. Early European settlers also valued kangaroos as a source of meat and hides but increasing settlement gradually brought changes in the environment. Habitat destruction, coupled with the introduction of predators such as the European Red fox, domestic dog and cat, and of competitors such as domestic stock and the rabbit, all contributed to the depletion in numbers and in some cases the extinction of a few species of kangaroos. However, for some other species and in particular the larger kangaroos there is circumstantial evidence of an increase in numbers following limitation of predation by dingoes, coupled with changes in pasture conditions and composition, and the increasing provision of watering points with the extension of agricultural and pastoral zones. As some species of kangaroos increased in numbers and competed with stock, settlers gradually came to regard them as pests. Initially numbers were reduced on a local scale by organized drives, shooting and occasionally by poisoning, but in recent years the culling of these species of kangaroos has been under State or Territorial control.

Most species are relatively secure. The greatest threats are associated with destruction of habitat or, in the case of smaller species, predation by foxes. Ten species are regarded as endangered. The Parma wallaby is now reduced to restricted, but well-established, populations in wet sclerophyll forest, rain forest and dry sclerophyll forest in northeastern New South Wales. Of the two nailtail wallabies, and four rat kangaroos of the genus *Bettongia*, some are restricted to inland or relict mainland populations and others have not been sighted for many years. The Banded and Western hare wallabies, both once plentiful in the interior, are now restricted to islands in Shark Bay.

Western gray kangaroo. Seasonal breeder with no diapause — **a**

30 days — 320 days — 30 days — joey at foot and joey in pouch

Tammar wallaby. Seasonal breeder with diapause — 250 days — **b**

27 days — joey in pouch, fertilized egg in uterus

Red kangaroo. Aseasonal breeder with diapause — 235 days — **c**

33 days — joey in pouch, joey at foot, fertilized egg in uterus

0 days — 365 days

☐ True gestation   ☐ Infant in pouch   ☐ Mating
☐ Diapause   ☐ Infant at foot (suckling)   ☐ Birth   ☐ Leaves pouch

KOALA

Phascolarctos cinereus
Sole member of the family Phascolarctidae.
Distribution: mainland E Australia.

Habitat: eucalypt forest below 2,000ft (600m); highly specific in feeding preference for a few eucalypt species.

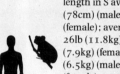

Size: animals from S of range significantly larger. Head-body length in S averages 30.7in (78cm) (male), 28.3in (72cm) (female); average weight in S 26lb (11.8kg) (male), 17.4lb (7.9kg) (female); in N 14.3lb (6.5kg) (male), 11.2lb (5.1kg) (female).

Coat: gray to tawny; white on chin, chest and inner side of forelimbs; ears fringed with long white hairs; rump dappled with white patches; coat shorter and lighter in N of range.

Gestation: 34–36 days.
Longevity: up to 13 years (18 in captivity).

Subspecies: 3; *P. c. victor* (Victoria), *P. c. cinereus* (New South Wales), *P. c. adustus* (Queensland). May be arbitrarily divided, as there is a gradual south-to-north decrease in body size, hair length and darkness of coat.

▶ **Mother and young** OPPOSITE – a young koala of 7–10 months rides on its mother's back. At birth the single young weighs one-fiftieth of an ounce. At five months, before leaving its mother's pouch, the young koala feeds on part-digested leaves provided by the mother. Tree-fork sites such as the one pictured are daytime sleeping sites.

▶ **Protected koala**—this animal lives in the Currumbin Sanctuary, Queensland. At such sites populations can increase to dangerous levels that put food trees at risk.

▷ **Koala feeding** OVERLEAF on *Eucalyptus* leaves, chief food of this specialized leaf-eater.

THE koala was not always the popular and loved animal that it is today. The early white settlers in Australia killed millions for their pelts. This hunting, together with land clearance and an increased frequency and scale of forest fires between 1850 and 1900, so decimated koala populations that by the early 1930s they were thought to be inexorably headed for extinction. Bans on hunting in the various states between 1898 and 1927 and intensive management, particularly from 1944 in the southern populations, has reversed this decline and koalas are now relatively common in their favored habitat, with densities approaching 1.2 animals per acre (3/ha) in some colonies.

Koalas are principally nocturnal and extremely specialized for a life spent almost exclusively in trees. Their stout body is covered with dense fur, the tail is reduced to a stump, the paws are large and the digits strongly clawed. The first and second digits of the forepaw are opposable to the other three and this enables the animal to grip the smaller branches as it climbs. Koalas ascend large trees by clasping the bole with the sharp claws of the forepaws and bringing the hindfeet up together in a bounding movement. They are less agile on the ground but travel using a similar bounding action or a slower quadrupedal walk.

Males are up to 50 percent heavier than females, have a broader face, comparatively smaller ears, and a large chest gland. Females lack this gland. They have a pouch which opens to the rear.

Female koalas are sexually mature at two years of age. Males are fertile at two years old but usually do not mate until they are four, because they require longer to become large enough to compete for females.

The summer breeding season (October–February) is characterized by a great deal of aggression between males and their bellowing is heard throughout the night. These calls, which consist of a series of harsh inhalations each followed by a resonant, growling expiration, advertise an individual's presence and warn other males away. The call of one male usually elicits a response from all the adult males in the area. In contrast, the only vocalization commonly heard from females and subadult males is a harsh wailing distress call, given usually when harassed by adult males.

Koalas are polygynous (males mate with several females) and relatively sedentary. Adults occupy fixed home ranges, the males usually 3.7–7.4 acres (1.5–3ha), females 0.1–2.5 acres (0.5–1ha). The home range of a breeding male overlaps those of females as well as of subadult and nonbreeding males. In the breeding season the adult males are very active at night and constantly move through their range, both ejecting male rivals and mating with any receptive (estrous) females. Copulation is brief, usually lasting less than two minutes, and occurs in the tree. The male covers the female and grasps on to the back of her neck with his teeth while mating.

The females give birth to a single young each year with the majority of births occurring in mid-summer (December–January). The newborn weigh less than 0.02oz (0.5g) and attach to one of the two nipples in the pouch. Weaning commences after five months and is initiated by the young feeding on partially digested leaf material produced from the female's anus. This pap is thought to come from the cecum of the mother and to inoculate the gut of the young with the microbes it needs to digest eucalypt leaf. Growth is rapid once the young begins feeding on leaves. The young departs the pouch for good after seven months and travels around clinging to the mother's back before becoming independent by eleven months of age. It may continue to live close to the mother for a few more months.

Outside the breeding season there is little obvious social behavior. While neighboring animals are doubtless aware of each other's presence, there are few interactions and no

apparent social groupings. While koalas will feed on a large number of eucalypt and non-eucalypt species, the leaves of only a few eucalypt species make up the bulk of their diet. In the south, *Eucalyptus viminalis* and *E. ovata* are the preferred species, while the northern populations feed predominantly on *E. punctata*, *E. camaldulensis* and *E. tereticornis*. An adult koala eats about 1.1lb (500g) daily and its diet of low-protein, highly fibrous eucalypt leaf contains high concentrations of phenolics and volatile oils. The koala has adapted in numerous ways to cope with this diet. The cheek teeth are reduced to a single premolar and four broad, high-cusped molars on each jaw which finely grind the leaves for easier digestion. Some toxic plant compounds appear to be detoxified in the liver through the action of glucuronic acid, and are excreted. Microbial fermentation occurs in the cecum, which is up to four times the body length of the koala and the largest of any mammal in proportion to size. Because of the low quality of the diet, koalas conserve energy by their behavior. They are slow-moving and sleep up to 18 hours out of 24. This has given rise to the popular myth that koalas are drugged by the eucalypt compounds they ingest. Koalas feed from dusk onwards and the animal moves from its favored resting fork to the tree crown to feed. Except in the hottest weather, they obtain all of their water requirements from the leaves.

Koala populations can build up to extremely high densities wherever their favored food species occur. This is illustrated by the fate of a koala population introduced onto a small island off the coast of southeastern Australia. Between 1923 and 1933 a total of 165 koalas were transferred to this island from another colony which was overpopulated. In 1944, when it was apparent that these koalas had multiplied to such numbers that they were killing their food trees and many had already died of starvation, 1,349 koalas were removed. Populations on offshore islands are now managed much more intensively but, because of large-scale clearing of native forest, many of the areas of habitat suitable for koalas now occur in small isolated patches which have similar management problems to island habitats. The future management of these populations is complicated by the shortage of suitable forest areas where surplus animals can be released. Alternative procedures, such as the release of animals into forests with a lower density of preferred *Eucalyptus* species, are now being investigated.   RM

WOMBATS

Family: Vombatidae
Three species in 2 genera.
Distribution: Australia.

Common wombat

Vombatus ursinus
Common, Naked-nosed, Coarse-haired or Forest wombat.
Distribution: SE Australia including Flinders
Island and Tasmania.
Habitat: temperate forests, heaths, mountains.

Size: head-body length 35.4–45in
(90–115cm); tail length about 1in (2.5cm);
height about 14.2in (36cm); weight 48.5–86lb
(22–39kg).
Coat: coarse, black or brown to gray; bare
muzzle, short rounded ears.
Gestation: unknown.
Longevity: over 5 years (up to 26 years in
captivity).
Subspecies: 3.

Southern hairy-nosed wombat

Lasiorhinus latifrons
Southern hairy-nosed or soft-furred wombat or
Plains wombat.
Distribution: central southern Australia.
Habitat: savanna woodlands, grasslands, shrub
steppes.

Size: head-body length 34.3–39in (87–99cm);
weight 42–70lb (19–32kg); tail and height
similar to Common wombat.
Coat: fine, gray to brown, with lighter patches;
hairy muzzle, longer pointed ears.
Gestation: 20–22 days.
Longevity: unknown (to 18 years in captivity).

Northern hairy-nosed wombat [E]

Lasiorhinus krefftii
Northern or Queensland hairy-nosed or soft-furred
wombat.
Distribution: single colony in mid-eastern
Queensland.
Habitat: semi-arid woodland.

Size: similar (possibly slightly larger) size,
weight and appearance to Southern hairy-
nosed wombat, but broader muzzle.
Gestation and longevity: unknown.

[E] Endangered.

▶ **The Common wombat** ABOVE uses its strong
foreclaws to excavate burrows—one reason it is
still regarded as "vermin" in eastern Australia,
where it may damage rabbit-proof fences.
Erosion BELOW reveals the complexity of a
wombat warren in South Australia.

SHIPWRECKED sailors on Preservation
Island in Bass Strait were the first
Europeans to discover wombats. They nick-
named them "badgers" because the animals
were mainly nocturnal and lived in burrows. When the sailors were rescued in
1798 they brought one wombat back with
them to Sydney. This was eventually described as *Vombatus ursinus*, the "bear-like
wombat," after the aboriginal name "wom-
bach" for the slightly larger species found
around Sydney.

At first sight wombats really do resemble
a small bear, or, even more closely, the
marmots of the Northern Hemisphere, with
their thick, heavy bodies, small eyes, massive, flattened heads and similar teeth. Unlike
their closest relative, the smaller arboreal
koala (see p144), wombats are completely
terrestrial and well equipped with short,
powerful legs and long, strong claws (absent
on the first toe of the hind foot) for digging
their large, often complex burrows. Their
dentition ($I1/1$, $C0/0$, $P1/1$, $M4/4 = 24$),
particularly the single pair of upper and
lower incisors which like the other teeth are
rootless and grow continuously, is unique
among marsupials but remarkably similar
to that of the rodents. Both sexes are similar
in size. Wombats have poor eyesight but
keen senses of smell and hearing.

During the Pleistocene (2 million to
10,000 years ago) another two, much larger, types of wombat occurred in Australia.
Today the Southern hairy-nosed wombat is
abundant in arid to semi-arid saltbush,
acacia and mallee shrublands of southern
South Australia from the Murray River in
the east to a few isolated colonies in the
southeast of Western Australia. The rarer
Northern hairy-nosed wombat formerly
occurred at three widely scattered localities
in the semi-arid interior of eastern Australia
but the remaining colony of perhaps only 20
individuals is now restricted to the most
northerly of these, 80mi (130km) north-
west of Clermont, mid-eastern Queensland.
In both cases the areas are characterized by
high summer temperatures, low irregular
rainfalls, frequent droughts, limited free-
standing water and highly fibrous grass
foods containing little water and protein. To
survive in these areas hairy-nosed wombats
have adopted similar strategies to the much
smaller desert mammals. They live in burrows and mainly emerge to feed at night.
The Southern hairy-nosed wombat also has
a very low metabolic rate and low rate of
water turnover, achieved by concentrating
its urine, reducing fecal water loss to very
low levels and restricting respiratory loss of

water by limiting its activity above ground
to periods of more suitable temperature and
humidity. Both species also have a low
nitrogen requirement which, together with
a relatively variable body temperature, low
heat loss, basking behavior and failure to
ovulate during droughts, further econo-
mizes on energy.

The Common wombat mainly inhabits
the wetter, subhumid, eucalypt forests from
southeastern Queensland along the Great
Dividing Range to eastern Victoria. It is rare
now in southwestern Victoria but scattered
populations still persist in the coastal grasslands and some remnant forest areas in
southeastern South Australia. Two smaller
subspecies occur on Flinders Island in Bass
Strait and in Tasmania. The Common wombat is now extinct on Preservation and
Clarke Islands and Cape Barren. Despite
their less dry habitat, Common wombats
exhibit similar physiological and behavioral
adaptations to those of hairy-nosed wombats, although they are less efficient at
limiting water loss. In summer they avoid
environmental temperatures over 77°F
(25°C), above which they begin to lose their
ability to regulate their body temperatures,
by remaining in their burrows until after
sunset. The burrows are up to 20in (50cm)
wide and 100ft (30m) long, often with
several entrances, side tunnels and resting
chambers. In winter, burrow air temperatures rarely fall below 39°F (4°C), and
basking and daytime activity become more
common. The Common wombat also gen-
erates increased body heat in its nocturnal
activities, during which it may travel up to
2mi (3km), and decreases its respiration and
heartbeat rates when resting in its burrow.

Wombats' teeth are highly adapted to
breaking up their tough, highly fibrous food,
mainly grasses such as snow tussocks (Common wombats) and spear grass (Southern
hairy-nosed wombat). Relative to body
weight they eat less than most other marsupials, and a very slow rate of food passage
and microbial fermentation of fiber in their
colons also help them survive on poor-
quality food.

The wombats' social behavior and reproduction are also adapted to saving energy.
Both southern species have highly stable
social relationships involving minimal
close-quarter interaction. When a fight does
occur the aggressor attempts to bite the
other on the ear or flanks while the defender
presents its large exceptionally thick-
skinned rump to the attacker and kicks out
with its hind feet.

The home ranges of Southern hairy

nosed wombats are centered around the warrens, which are often situated around the edges of large claypans, where the thick hard surface has broken away, exposing soft limestone sediments underneath. Home ranges are of 6.2–10.4 acres (2.5–4.2ha), depending on the amount of food present. Common wombat home ranges vary from 12.4 to 57 acres (5–23ha), depending upon the distribution of feeding areas in relation to the burrows, most of which are usually located along slopes above creeks and gullies. Population densities of Southern hairy-nosed wombats can reach 0.08 per acre (0.2/ha), while those of Common wombats may attain 0.2 per acre (0.5/ha), particularly where native forest adjoins open grassy areas.

Southern hairy-nosed wombats are seasonal breeders, giving birth usually to a single young in spring (October–January) in good seasons but none during droughts. Common wombat young appear to be born at any time of the year. Young wombats first leave the pouch at about 6–7 months but may still return to it occasionally over the next three months. Weaning may not occur until they are 15 months old. Southern hairy-nosed wombats are sexually mature at 18 months when they are 23.6–31.5in (60–80cm) in length and weigh 33–44lb (15–20kg), compared with about 23 months for Common wombats weighing some 48.5lb/22kg. Major causes of death include starvation during droughts, outbreaks of mange, predation by dingoes and collisions with road vehicles.

Each species is protected to some degree in the different States, but the Common wombat is still classed as vermin in eastern Victoria, mainly because of its damage to rabbit-proof fences.   JMcI

HONEY POSSUM

Tarsipes rostratus
Sole member of the family Tarsipedidae.
Distribution: SW Australia.

Habitat: heathland, shrubland and open low woodlands with heath understory.

Size: adult male head-body length 2.6–3.3in (6.5–8.5cm), tail length 2.8–3.9in (7–10cm), weight about 0.3oz (7–11g); adult female head-body length 2.8–3.5in (7–9cm), tail length 3–4.1in (7.5–10.5cm), weight 0.3–0.6oz (8–16g); females (average weight 0.4oz/12g) one-third heavier than males.

Coat: grizzled grayish-brown above, reddish tinge on flanks and shoulder, next to cream undersurface. Three back stripes: a distinct dark brown stripe from back of head to base of tail, with less distinct, lighter brown stripe on each side.

Gestation: uncertain, about 28 days.
Longevity: 1–2 years in wild.

▶ **Nothing but nectar and pollen** feature in the diet of the Honey possum, here feeding on *Banksia*. The reduced home range of nursing Honey possum mothers may center on a single such shrub. The many large, compound nectar-rich inflorescences are produced over a long period and may provide all the food requirements for the mother and her young.

The pointed snout and brush-tipped tongue are specializations for this diet, probing deep into the individual flowers for nectar. With its grasping hands, feet and tail, and its small size, the Honey possum can feed on small terminal flowers on all but the most slender branches. While nectar is an easily digested source of energy, pollen grains, the chief source of protein in the diet, are not. The Honey possum's complex stomach has two chambers, but whether these assist in digestion of pollens is not certain.

T HE Honey possum does not eat honey and is only very distantly related to possums. It is an animal all on its own: no fossil history is known earlier than 35,000 years ago and it appears to be the sole surviving representative of a line of marsupials that diverged very early from the possum-kangaroo stem (see p98). Because it is especially adapted to feed on nectar and pollen, it probably evolved at a time when heathlands with a great diversity of flowering plants were widespread, about 20 million years ago. Heathlands exist today in patches around the edge of Australia's arid center; those in southwestern Australia are still very varied and with more than 3,600 species of flowering plant there are always some species in flower to provide enough food for this animal totally dependent on nectar.

These tiny shrew-like mammals have a long pointed snout, and a prehensile tail longer than head and body together. The first digit of the hind foot is opposable to the others and there is a considerable span for gripping branches: all digits have rough pads on the tips.

Honey possums move through vegetation chiefly by fast running; the tail is used for extra support and stability in climbing, and when feeding its use frees the forelimbs to manipulate blossoms. With its grasping hands, feet and tail and small size the Honey possum is able to feed on small terminal flowers of all but the slenderest branches. Teeth are few in number and very small and weak. The dental formula is I2/1, C1/0, P1/0, M3/3 = 22, but the molars are merely tiny cones.

Honey possums communicate with only a small repertoire of visual signal postures and a few high-pitched squeaks, a reflection of their mainly nocturnal activity. The sense of smell on the other hand appears to be very important in social behavior and feeding.

Both sexes mature at about six months. Births may occur throughout the year but numbers of births are at a very low level in mid-summer (December), when few plants are in flower, before reaching a highly synchronized peak of births during January–February. There are two further, less synchronized peaks at about three-month intervals, the minimum time required for the rearing of a litter. A second litter may be born very soon after the first leaves the pouch or is weaned, since the Honey possum exhibits embryonic diapause (see p143), so far the only marsupial outside the kangaroos and wallabies (families Macropodidae and Potoroidae) known to do so.

This timing of births is such that the young are ready to leave the pouch and begin to fend for themselves when food is abundant, in autumn, spring and early summer.

Courtship is minimal; the male follows a female that is becoming receptive (approaching estrus) and attempts to mount her, but only when actually in estrus does she stay still long enough for mating to occur. The young at birth are tiny—about 0.0002oz (0.005g)—and their stage of development is typical of young marsupials. The pouch has four teats, and although litters of four may occur, two and three are most common. The young are carried in the mother's deep pouch for about eight weeks, by which time each weighs about 0.09oz (about 2.5g) and has a good covering of fur, including the back stripes; their eyes are open, but they are very shaky on their feet. A litter of four such young weighs nearly as much as their mother. As soon as they venture out of the pouch, their mother leaves them in a nest (an old bird's nest or a hollow branch) while she forages, returning from time to time to nurse them. After a few days, the young are able to ride on their mother's back but she appears to avoid this if she can—with the whole litter on her back she can hardly move. About one week after leaving the pouch, the young follow their mother while she feeds. They cease to suckle at about 11 weeks, and probably disperse soon after.

Most Honey possums live in overlapping home ranges of about 2.5 acres (1ha), but females with large pouch young have a smaller, more or less exclusive, home range of about 120sq yd (0.01ha). In captivity, females are dominant to males and juveniles, and very aggressive to strangers, especially males, suggesting that in the wild the exclusive area of females with large young may be a temporary feeding and nesting territory. Such females are greatly hampered by their young as these grow, and after they leave the pouch their mother needs to return frequently to the nest to nurse them. Honey possums frequently huddle together, an energy-saving behavior which is found in many small mammals. In cold weather when food is short, Honey possums may become torpid.

The Honey possum is at present not endangered, but in the long term a species with such restricted distribution may need special attention. Most of its habitat is in the wetter areas of a very dry continent, where unreserved habitat is still being cleared for agriculture. In reserves, feral cats and, perhaps, "controlled" burning, also pose dangers.   EMR

BIBLIOGRAPHY

The following list of titles indicates key reference works used in the preparation of this volume and those recommended for further reading.

General

Boyle, C. L. (ed) (1981) *The RSPCA Book of British Mammals*, Collins, London.

Corbet, G. B. and Hill, J. E. (1980) *A World List of Mammalian Species*, British Museum and Cornell University Press, London and Ithaca, N.Y.

Grzimek, B. (ed) (1972) *Grzimek's Animal Life Encyclopedia*, Vols 10, 11 and 12, Van Nostrand Reinhold, New York.

Hall, E. R. and Kelson, K. R. (1959) *The Mammals of North America*, Ronald Press, New York.

Harrison Matthews, L. (1969) *The Life of Mammals*, vols 1 and 2, Weidenfeld & Nicolson, London.

Honacki, J. H., Kinman, K. E. and Koeppl. J. W. (eds) (1982) *Mammal Species of the World*, Allen Press and Association of Systematics Collections, Lawrence, Kansas.

Kingdon, J. (1971–82) *East African Mammals*, vols I–III, Academic Press, New York.

Morris, D. (1965) *The Mammals*, Hodder & Stoughton, London.

Nowak, R. M. and Paradiso, J. L. (eds) (1983) *Walker's Mammals of the World* (4th edn), 2 vols, Johns Hopkins University Press, Baltimore and London.

Vaughan, T. L. (1972) *Mammalogy*, W. B. Saunders, London and Philadelphia.

Young, J. Z. (1975) *The Life of Mammals: their Anatomy and Physiology*, Oxford University Press, Oxford.

Monotremes and Marsupials

Archer, M. (ed) (1982) *Carnivorous Marsupials*, Royal Zoological Society of New South Wales, Sydney.

Augee, M. L. (ed) (1978) *Monotreme Biology*, Royal Zoological Society of New South Wales, Sydney.

Fleay, D. M. (1980) *The Paradoxical Platypus*, Jacaranda Press, Brisbane.

Frith, H. J. and Calaby, J. H. (1969) *Kangaroos*, F. W. Cheshire, Melbourne.

Grant, T. R. (1983) *The Platypus*, University of New South Wales Press, Kensington.

Griffiths, M. E. (1978), *The Biology of Monotremes*, Academic Press, New York.

Hunsaker II, D. (ed) (1977), *The Biology of Marsupials*, Academic Press, New York.

Mares, M. A. And Genoways, H. H. (eds) *Mammalian Biology in South America*, University of Pittsburgh, Pennsylvania.

Marlow, B. J. (1965) *Marsupials of Australia*, Jacaranda Press, Brisbane.

Ride, W. D. L. (1970) *The Native Mammals of Australia*, Oxford University Press, Melbourne.

Smith, A. and Hume, I. (in press 1984) *Possums and Gliders*, Royal Zoological Society of New South Wales, Sydney.

Stonehouse, B. (ed) (1977) *The Biology of Marsupials*, Macmillan, London.

Strahan, R. (ed) (1983), *The Complete Book of Australian Mammals*, Angus and Robertson, Sydney.

Troughton, E. le G. (1941), *Furred Mammals of Australia*, Angus and Robertson, Sydney.

Tyler, M. J. (ed) (1978) *The Status of Endangered Australian Wildlife*, Royal Zoological Society of New South Wales, Sydney.

Tyler, M. J. (ed) (1979) *The Status of Endangered Australasian Wildlife*, Royal Zoological Society of South Australia, Adelaide.

Tyndale-Biscoe, C. H. (1973) *Life of Marsupials*, Edward Arnold, London.

Wood-Jones, F. (1923–25) *The Mammals of South Australia*, 3 vols, Government Printer, Adelaide.

Insectivores, Edentates and Allies

Battastini, R. and Richard-Vindard G. (eds) (1972) *Biogeography and Ecology in Madagascar*, Dr. W. Junk B.V., The Hague.

Crowcroft, P. (1957) *The Life of the Shrew*, Max Reinhart, London.

Eisenberg, J. F. (1970) *The Tenrecs: a Study in Mammalian Behavior and Evolution*, Smithsonian Institution, Washington DC.

Godfrey, G. K. and Crowcroft, P. (1960) *The Life of the Mole*, Museum Press, London.

Meester, J. and Setzer, H. W. (1971) *The Mammals of Africa. An Identification Manual*, Smithsonian Institution, Washington DC.

Mellanby, K. (1976) *Talpa: Story of a Mole*, Collins, London.

Montgomery, G. G. (ed) (1978) *The Ecology of Arboreal Folivores*, Smithsonian Institution, Washington DC.

Montgomery, G. G. (ed) (in press) *The Evolution and Ecology of Sloths, Anteaters and Armadillos*, Smithsonian Institution, Washington DC.

Bats

Allen, G. M. (1939) *Bats*, Harvard University Press, Cambridge.

Barbour, R. W. and Davis, W. H. (1969) *Bats of America*, University of Kentucky Press, Lexington, Kentucky.

Corbet, G. B. and Southern, H. N. (1977) *Handbook of British Mammals*, 2nd edn, Blackwell Scientific Publications, Oxford.

Fenton, M. B. (1983) *Just Bats*, University of Toronto Press, Toronto.

Griffin, D. R. (1958) *Listening in the Dark*, Yale University Press, New Haven.

Kunz, T. H. (ed) (1982) *Ecology of Bats*, Plenum Publishing Corp., New York.

Leen, N. and Norvic, A. (1969) *The World of Bats*, Holt Rinehart and Winston, New York.

Rosevear, J. R. (1965) *The Bats of West Africa*, British Museum (Natural History), London.

Turner, D. E. (1975) *The Vampire Bat, a Field Study in Behavior and Ecology*. Johns Hopkins University Press, Baltimore.

Wimsatt, W. A. (ed) (1970) *Biology of Bats*, Vols 1 & 2, Academic Press, New York.

Wimsatt, W. A. (ed) (1977) *Biology of Bats*, Vol 3, Academic Press, New York.

Yalden, D. W. and Morris, P. A. (1975) *The Lives of Bats*, David and Charles, Newton Abbot.

GLOSSARY

Adaptive radiation the pattern in which different species develop from a common ancestor (as distinct from CONVERGENT EVOLUTION, a process whereby species from different origins became similar in response to the same SELECTIVE PRESSURES).

Adult a fully developed and mature individual, capable of breeding, but not necessarily doing so until social and/or ecological conditions allow.

Aestivate (noun: aestivation) to enter a state of dormancy or torpor in seasonal hot, dry weather, when food is scarce.

Allantoic stalk a sac-like outgrowth of the hinder part of the gut of the mammalian fetus, containing a rich network of blood vessels. It connects fetal circulation with the PLACENTA, facilitating nutrition of the young, respiration and excretion. (See CHORIOALLANTOIC PLACENTATION.)

Allopatry condition in which populations of different species are geographically separated (cf SYMPATRY).

Alpine of the Alps or any lofty mountains: usually pertaining to altitudes above 4,900ft (1,500m).

Altricial young that are born at a rudimentary stage of development and require an extended period of nursing by parent(s). See also PRECOCIAL.

Amphibious able to live on both land and in water.

Anal gland or sac a gland opening by a short duct either just inside the anus or on either side of it.

Ancestral stock a group of animals, usually showing primitive characteristics, which is believed to have given rise to later, more specialized forms.

Antigen a substance, whether organic or inorganic, that stimulates the production of antibodies when introduced into the body.

Antrum a cavity in the body, especially one in the upper jaw bone.

Aquatic living chiefly in water.

Arboreal living in trees.

Baculum (os penis or penis bone) an elongate bone present in the penis of certain mammals.

Bifid (of the penis) the head divided into two parts by a deep cleft.

Biotic community a naturally occurring group of plants and animals in the same environment.

Blastocyst see IMPLANTATION.

Boreal region a zone geographically situated south of the Arctic and north of latitude 50°N; dominated by coniferous forest.

Brachydont a type of short-crowned teeth whose growth ceases when full-grown, whereupon the pulp cavity in the root closes. Typical of most mammals, but contrast the HYPSODONT teeth of many herbivores.

Brindled having inconspicuous dark streaks or flecks on a gray or tawny background.

Browser a herbivore which feeds on shoots and leaves of trees, shrubs etc, as distinct from grasses (cf GRAZER).

Bullae (auditory) globular, bony capsules housing the middle and inner ear structures, situated on the underside of the skull.

Bunodont molar teeth whose cusps form separate, rounded hillocks which crush and grind.

Câche a hidden store of food; also (verb) to hide food for future use.

Cannon bone a bone formed by the fusion of METATARSAL bones in the feet of some families.

Carnivore any meat-eating organism (alternatively, a member of the order Carnivora, many of whose members are carnivores).

Carpals wrist bones which articulate between the forelimb bones (radius and ulna) and the METACARPALS.

Caudal gland an enlarged skin gland associated with the root of the tail. Subcaudal: placed below the root; supracaudal: above the root.

Cecum a blind sac in the digestive tract, opening out from the junction between the small and large intestines. In herbivorous mammals it is often very large; it is the site of bacterial action on cellulose. The end of the cecum is the appendix; in species with reduced ceca the appendix may retain an antibacterial function.

Cellulose the fundamental constituent of the cell walls of all green plants, and some algae and fungi. It is very tough and fibrous, and can be digested only by the intestinal flora in mammalian guts.

Cementum hard material which coats the roots of mammalian teeth. In some species, cementum is laid down in annual layers which, under a microscope, can be counted to estimate the age of individuals.

Cheek-teeth teeth lying behind the canines in mammals, comprising premolars and molars.

Chorioallantoic placentation a system whereby fetal mammals are nourished by the blood supply of the mother. The chorion is a superficial layer enclosing all the embryonic structures of the fetus, and is in close contact with the maternal blood supply at the placenta. The union of the chorion (with its vascularized ALLANTOIC STALK and YOLK SAC) with the placenta facilitates the exchange of food substances and gases, and hence the nutrition of the growing fetus.

Class taxonomic category subordinate to a phylum and superior to an order.

Clavicle the collar bone.

Cloaca terminal part of the gut into which the reproductive and urinary ducts open. There is one opening to the body, the cloacal aperture, instead of a separate anus and urinogenital opening.

Cloud forest moist, high-altitude forest characterized by dense UNDERSTORY growth, and abundance of ferns, mosses, orchids and other plants on the trunks and branches of the trees.

Colon the large intestine of vertebrates, excluding the terminal rectum. It is concerned with the absorption of water from feces.

Colonial living together in colonies. In bats, more usually applied to the communal sleeping habit, in which tens of thousands of individuals may participate.

Concentrate selector a herbivore which feeds on those plant parts (such as shoots and fruits) which are rich in nutrients.

Congenor a member of the same species (or genus).

Conspecific member of the same species.

Convergent evolution the independent acquisition of similar characters in evolution, as opposed to possession of similarities by virtue of descent from a common ancestor.

Crepuscular active in twilight.

Crypsis an aspect of the appearance of an organism which camouflages it from the view of others, such as predators or competitors.

Cryptic (coloration or locomotion) protecting through concealment.

Cue a signal, or stimulus (eg olfactory) produced by an individual which elicits a response in other individuals.

Cursorial being adapted for running.

Cusp a prominence on a cheek-tooth (premolars or molars).

Delayed implantation see IMPLANTATION.

Dental formula a convention for summarizing the dental arrangement whereby the numbers of each type of tooth in each half of the upper and lower jaw are given; the numbers are always presented in the order: incisor (I), canine (C), premolar (P), molar (M). The final figure is the total number of teeth to be found in the skull. A typical example for Carnivora would be I3/3, C1/1, P4/4, M3/3 = 44.

Dentition the arrangement of teeth characteristic of a particular species.

Dermis the layer of skin lying beneath the outer epidermis.

Desert areas of low rainfall, typically with sparse scrub or grassland vegetation or lacking vegetation altogether.

Dicotyledon one of the two classes of flowering plants (the other class comprises monocotyledons), characterized by the presence of two seed leaves in the young plant, and by net-veined, often broad leaves, in mature plants. Includes deciduous trees, roses etc.

Digit a finger or toe.

Digital glands glands that occur between or on the toes.

Digitigrade method of walking on the toes without the heel touching the ground (cf PLANTIGRADE).

Diprotodont having the incisors of the lower jaw reduced to one functional pair, as in possums and kangaroos (small, nonfunctional incisors may also be present). (cf. POLYPROTODONT)

Disjunct or **discontinuous distribution** geographical distribution of a species that is marked by gaps. Commonly brought about by fragmentation of suitable habitat, especially as a result of human intervention.

Dispersal the movements of animals, often as they reach maturity, away from their previous home range (equivalent to emigration). Distinct from dispersion, that is, the pattern in which things (perhaps animals, food supplies, nest sites) are distributed or scattered.

Display any relatively conspicuous pattern of behavior that conveys specific information to others, usually to members of the same species; can involve visual and or vocal elements, as in threat, courtship or "greeting" displays.

Distal far from the point of attachment or origin (eg tip of tail).

Diurnal active in daytime.

Dormancy a period of inactivity; many bears, for example, are dormant for a period in winter; this is not true HIBERNATION, as pulse rate and body temperature do not drop markedly.

Dorsal on the upper or top side or surface (eg dorsal stripe).

Echolocation the process of perception, often direction finding, based upon reaction to the pattern of reflected sound waves (echoes).

Ecology the study of plants and animals in relation to their natural environmental setting. Each species may be said to occupy a distinctive ecological NICHE.

Ecosystem a unit of the environment within which living and nonliving elements interact.

Ecotype a genetic variety within a single species, adapted for local ecological conditions.

Edentate a member of an order comprising living and extinct anteaters, sloths, armadillos (XENARTHRANS), and extinct paleanodonts.

Elongate relatively long (eg of canine teeth, longer than those of an ancestor, a related animal, or than adjacent teeth).

Embryonic diapause the temporary cessation of development of an embryo (eg in some bats and kangaroos).

Emigration departure of animal(s), usually at or about the time of reaching adulthood, from the group or place of birth.

Epidermis the outer layer of mammalian skin (and in plants the outer tissue of young stem, leaf or root).

Erectile capable of being raised to an erect position (erectile mane).

Estrus the period in the estrous cycle of female mammals at which they are often attractive to males and receptive to mating. The period coincides with the maturation of eggs and ovulation (the release of mature eggs from the ovaries). Animals in estrus are often said to be "on heat" or "in heat." In primates, if the egg is not fertilized the subsequent degeneration of uterine walls (endometrium) leads to menstrual bleeding. In some species ovulation is triggered by copulation and this is called **induced ovulation**, as distinct from spontaneous ovulation.

Eucalypt forest Australian forest, dominated by trees of the genus Eucalyptus.

Exudate natural plant exudates include gums and resins; damage to plants (eg by marmosets) can lead to loss of sap as well.

Facultative optional (cf OBLIGATE).

Family a taxonomic division subordinate to an order and superior to a genus.

Feces excrement from the bowels; colloquially known as droppings or scats.

Feral living in the wild (of domesticated animals, eg cat, dog).

Fermentation the decomposition of organic substances by microorganisms. In some mammals, parts of the digestive tract (eg the cecum) may be inhabited by bacteria that break down cellulose and release nutrients.

Fetal development rate the rate of development, or growth, of unborn young.

Folivore an animal eating mainly leaves.

Follicle a small sac, either (a) a mass of ovarian cells that produces an ovum, or (b) an indentation in the skin from which hair grows.

Forbs a general term applied to ephemeral or weedy plant species (not grasses). In arid and semi-arid regions they grow abundantly and profusely after rains.

Fossorial burrowing (of lifestyle or behavior).

Frugivore an animal eating mainly fruits.

Gallery forest luxuriant forest lining the banks of watercourses.

Gamete a male or female reproductive cell (ovum or spermatozoon).

Generalist an animal whose lifestyle does not involve highly specialized strategems (cf SPECIALIST); for example, feeding on a variety of foods which may require different foraging techniques.

Genotype the genetic constitution of an organism, determining all aspects of its appearance, structure and function.

Genus (plural genera) a taxonomic division superior to species and subordinate to family.

Gestation the period of development within the uterus; the process of **delayed implantation** can result in the period of pregnancy being longer than the period during which the embryo is actually developing. (See also IMPLANTATION.)

Glands (marking) specialized glandular areas of the skin, used in depositing SCENT MARKS.

Grizzled sprinkled or streaked with gray.

Gumivorous feeding on gums (plant exudates).

Harem group a social group consisting of a single adult male, at least two adult females and immature animals: a common pattern of social organization among mammals.

Heath low-growing shrubs with woody stems and narrow leaves (eg heather), which often predominate on acidic or upland soils.

Herbivore an animal eating mainly plants or parts of plants.

Heterothermy a condition in which the internal temperature of the body follows the temperature of the outside environment.

Hibernation a period of winter inactivity during which the normal physiological process is greatly reduced and thus during which the energy requirements of the animal are lowered.

Hindgut fermenter herbivores among which the bacterial breakdown of plant tissue occurs in the CECUM, rather than in the RUMEN or foregut.

Holarctic realm a region of the world including North America, Greenland, Europe, and Asia apart from the southwest, southeast and India.

Home range the area in which an animal normally lives (generally excluding rare excursions or migrations), irrespective of whether or not the area is defended from other animals (cf TERRITORY).

Hybrid the offspring of parents of different species.

Hypothermy a condition in which internal body temperature is below normal.

Hypsodont high-crowned teeth, which continue to grow when full-sized and whose pulp cavity remains open; typical of herbivorous mammals (cf BRACHYDONT).

Implantation the process whereby the free-floating blastocyst (early embryo) becomes attached to the uterine wall in mammals. At the point of implantation a complex network of blood vessels develops to link mother and embryo (the placenta). In **delayed implantation** the blastocyst remains dormant in the uterus for periods varying, between species, from 12 days to 11 months. Delayed implantation may be obligatory or facultative and is known for some members of the Carnivora and Pinnipedia and others.

Induced ovulation see ESTRUS.

Inguinal pertaining to the groin.

Insectivore an animal eating mainly arthropods (insects, spiders).

Interdigital pertaining to between the digits.

Interfemoral a membrane stretching between the femora, or thigh bones in bats.

Intestinal flora simple plants (eg bacteria) which live in the intestines, especially the CECUM, of mammals. They produce enzymes which break down the cellulose in the leaves and stems of green plants and convert it to digestible sugars.

Introduced of a species which has been brought, by man, from lands where it occurs naturally to lands where it has not previously occurred. Some introductions are accidental (eg rats which have traveled unseen on ships), but some are made on purpose for biological control, farming or other economic reasons (eg the Common brushtail possum, which was introduced to New Zealand from Australia to establish a fur industry).

Ischial pertaining to the hip.

Jacobson's organ a structure in a foramen (small opening) in the palate of many vertebrates which appears to be involved in olfactory communication. Molecules of scent may be sampled in these organs.

Juvenile no longer possessing the characteristics of an infant, but not yet fully adult.

Kopje a rocky outcrop, typically on otherwise flat plains of African grasslands.

Labile (body temperature) an internal body temperature which may be lowered or raised from an average body temperature.

Lactation (verb: lactate) the secretion of milk, from MAMMARY GLANDS.

Larynx dilated region of upper part of windpipe, containing vocal chords. Vibration of chords produces vocal sounds.

Latrine a place where feces are regularly left (often together with other SCENT MARKS); associated with olfactory communication.

Lek a display ground at which individuals of one sex maintain miniature territories into which they seek to attract potential mates.

Llano South American semi-arid savanna country, eg of Venezuela.

Loph a transverse ridge on the crown of molar teeth.

Lophodont molar teeth whose cusps form ridges or LOPHS.

Mallee a grassy, open woodland habitat characteristic of many semi-arid parts of Australia. "Mallee" also describes the multi-stemmed habit of eucalypt trees which dominate this habitat.

Mamma (pl. mammae) **mammary glands** the milk-secreting organ of female mammals, probably evolved from sweat glands.

Mammal a member of the CLASS of VERTEBRATE animals having MAMMARY GLANDS which produce milk with which they nurse their young (properly: Mammalia).

Mammilla (pl. mammillae) nipple, or teat, on the MAMMA of female mammals; the conduit through which milk is passed from the mother to the young.

Mandible the lower jaw.

Mangrove forest tropical forest developed on sheltered muddy shores of deltas and estuaries exposed to tide. Vegetation is almost entirely woody.

Marine living in the sea.

Masseter a powerful muscle, subdivided into parts, joining the MANDIBLE to the upper jaw. Used to bring jaws together when chewing.

Melanism darkness of color due to presence of the black pigment melanin.

Menotyphlan see Lipotyphlan.

Metabolic rate the rate at which the chemical processes of the body occur.

Metabolism the chemical processes occurring within an organism, including the production of PROTEIN from amino acids, the exchange of gases in respiration, the liberation of energy from foods and innumerable other chemical reactions.

Metacarpal bones of the hand, between the CARPALS of the wrist and the phalanges of the digits.

Metapodial the proximal element of a digit (contained within the palm or sole). The metapodial bones are METACARPALS in the hand (manus) and METATARSALS in the foot (pes).

Metatarsal bones of the foot articulating between the tarsals of the ankle and the phalanges of the digits.

Microhabitat the particular parts of the habitat that are encountered by an individual in the course of its activities.

Midden a dunghill, or site for the regular deposition of feces by mammals.

Migration movement, usually seasonal, from one region or climate to another for purposes of feeding or breeding.

Monogamy a mating system in which individuals have only one mate per breeding season.

Monotreme a mammal of the subclass Monotremata, which comprises the platypus and echidnas. The only egg-laying mammals.

Monotypic a genus comprising a single species.

Montane pertaining to mountainous country.

Montane forest forest occurring at middle altitudes on the slopes of mountains, below the alpine zone but above the lowland forests.

Morphology (morphological) the structure and shape of an organism.

Moss forest moist forest occurring on higher mountain slopes—eg 4,900–10,500ft (1,500–3,200m) in New Guinea—characterized by rich growths of mosses and other plants on the trunks and branches of the trees.

Mutation a structural change in a gene which can thus give rise to a new heritable characteristic.

Natal range the home range into which an individual was born (natal = of or from one's birth).

Nectivore (nectivorous) an animal that feeds principally on nectar.

Niche the role of a species within the community, defined in terms of all aspects of its lifestyle (eg food, competitors, predators, and other resource requirements).

Nocturnal active at nighttime.

Nose-leaf characteristically shaped flaps of skin surrounding the nasal passages of horseshoe, or nose-leaf bats (Family Rhinolophidae). Ultrasonic cries are uttered through the nostrils, with the nose leaves serving to direct the echolocating pulses forwards.

Obligate required, binding (cf FACULTATIVE).

Occipital pertaining to the occiput at back of head.

Olfaction, olfactory the olfactory sense is the sense of smell, depending on receptors located in the epithelium (surface membrane) lining the nasal cavity.

Omnivore an animal eating a varied diet including both animal and plant tissue.

Opposable (of first digit) of the thumb and forefinger in some mammals, which may be brought together in a grasping action, thus enabling objects to be picked up and held.

Opportunist (of feeding) flexible behavior of exploiting circumstances to take a wide range of food items; characteristic of many species. See GENERALIST; SPECIALIST.

Order a taxonomic division subordinate to class and superior to family.

Ovulation (verb ovulate) the shedding of mature ova (eggs) from the ovaries where they are produced (see ESTRUS).

Pair-bond an association between a male and female, which lasts from courtship at least until mating is completed, and in some species, until the death of one partner.

Palearctic a geographical region encompassing Europe and Asia north of the Himalayas, and Africa north of the Sahara.

Palmate palm-shaped.

Pampas Argentinian steppe grasslands.

Papilla (plural: papillae) a small nipple-like projection.

Páramo alpine meadow of northern and western South American uplands.

Parturition the process of giving birth (hence *post partum*—after birth).

Patagium a gliding membrane typically stretching down the sides of the body between the fore- and hindlimbs and perhaps including part of the tail. Found in colugos, flying squirrels, bats etc.

Perineal glands glandular tissue occurring between the anus and genitalia.

Pheromone secretions whose odors act as chemical messengers in animal communication, and which prompt a specific response on behalf of the animal receiving the message (see SCENT MARK).

Phylogeny a classification or relationship based on the closeness of evolutionary descent.

Phylogenetic (of classification or relationship) based on the closeness of evolutionary descent.

Phylum a taxonomic division comprising a number of classes.

Physiology study of the processes which go on in living organisms.

Pinna (plural: pinnae) the projecting cartilaginous portion of the external ear.

Placenta, placental mammals a structure that connects the fetus and the mother's womb to ensure a supply of nutrients to the fetus and removal of its waste products. Only placental mammals have a well-developed placenta; marsupials have a rudimentary placenta or none and monotremes lay eggs.

Plantigrade way of walking on the soles of the feet, including the heels (cf DIGITIGRADE).

Polyandrous see POLYGYNOUS.

Polyestrous having two or more ESTRUS cycles in one breeding season.

Polygamous a mating system wherein an individual has more than one mate per breeding season.

Polygynous a mating system in which a male mates with several females during one breeding season (as opposed to polyandrous, where one female mates with several males).

Polymorphism occurrence of more than one MORPHOLOGICAL form of individual in a population. (See SEXUAL DIMORPHISM.)

Polyprotodont having more than two well-developed lower incisor teeth (as in bandicoots and carnivorous marsupials). (cf DIPROTODONT.)

Population a more or less separate (discrete) group of animals of the same species within a given BIOTIC COMMUNITY.

Post-orbital bar a bony strut behind the eye-socket (orbit) in the skull.

Post-partum estrus ovulation and an increase in the sexual receptivity of female mammals, hours or days after the birth of a litter (see ESTRUS).

Pouch (marsupial) a flap of skin on the underbelly of female marsupials, which covers the MAMMILLAE. The pouch may be a simple, open structure as in most carnivorous marsupials, or a more enclosed pocket-like structure as in phalangers and kangaroos.

Prairie North American steppe grassland between 30°N and 55°N.

Predator an animal which forages for live prey; hence "anti-predator behavior" describes the evasive actions of the prey.

Precocial of young born at relatively advanced stage of development, requiring a short period of nursing by parents (see ALTRICIAL).

Prehensile capable of grasping.

Pre-orbital in front of the eye socket.

Preputial pertaining to the prepuce or loose skin covering the penis.

Proboscis a long flexible snout.

Process (anatomical) an outgrowth or protuberance.

Procumbent (incisors) projecting forward more or less horizontally.

Promiscuous a mating system wherein an individual mates more or less indiscriminately.

Protein a complex organic compound made of amino acids. Many different kinds of proteins are present in the muscles and tissues of all mammals.

Proximal near to the point of attachment or origin (eg the base of the tail).

Pseudoallantoic placentation a kind of placenta shown only by the marsupial bandicoots. Compared with the true eutherian kind of placentation, transfer of food and gas across the chorioallantoic/placental interface is inefficient, as contact between the fetal and maternal membranes is never close.

Puberty the attainment of sexual maturity. In addition to maturation of the primary sex organs (ovaries, testes), primates may exhibit "secondary sexual characteristics" at puberty. Among higher primates it is usual to find a growth spurt at the time of puberty in males and females.

Puna a treeless tableland or basin of the high Andes.

Pylorus the region of the stomach at its intestinal end, which is closed by the pyloric sphincter.

Quadrate bone at rear of skull which serves as a point of articulation for lower jaw.

Quadrupedal walking on all fours, as opposed to walking on two legs (BIPEDAL) or moving suspended beneath branches in trees (SUSPENSORY MOVEMENT).

Race a taxonomic division subordinate to

subspecies but linking populations with similar distinct characteristics.

Radiation see ADAPTIVE RADIATION.

Rain forest tropical and subtropical forest with abundant and year-round rainfall. Typically species rich and diverse.

Range (geographical) area over which an organism is distributed.

Receptive state of a female mammal ready to mate or in ESTRUS.

Reduced (anatomical) of relatively small dimension (eg of certain bones, by comparison with those of an ancestor or related animals).

Refection process in which food is excreted and then reingested a second time to ensure complete digestion, as in the Common shrew.

Reingestion process in which food is digested twice, to ensure that the maximum amount of energy is extracted from it. Food may be brought up from the stomach to the mouth for further chewing before reingestion, or an individual may eat its own feces (see REFECTION).

Reproductive rate the rate of production of offspring; the net productive rate may be defined as the average number of female offspring produced by each female during her entire lifetime.

Resident a mammal which normally inhabits a defined area, whether this is a HOME RANGE or a TERRITORY.

Retractile (of claws) able to be withdrawn into protective sheaths.

Rut a period of sexual excitement; the mating season.

Satellite male an animal excluded from the core of the social system but loosely associated on the periphery, in the sense of being a "hanger-on" or part of the retinue of more dominant individuals.

Scent gland an organ secreting odorous material with communicative properties; see SCENT MARK.

Scent mark a site where the secretions of scent glands, or urine or FECES, are deposited and which has communicative significance. Often left regularly at traditional sites which are also visually conspicuous. Also the "chemical message" left by this means; and (verb) to leave such a deposit.

Sclerophyll forest a general term for the hard-leafed eucalypt forest that covers much of Australia.

Scute a bony plate, overlaid by horn, which is derived from the outer layers of the skin. In armadillos, bony scute plates provide armor for all the upper, outer surfaces of the body.

Secondary sexual character a characteristic of animals which differs between the two sexes, but excluding the sexual organs and associated structures.

Sedentary pertaining to mammals which occupy relatively small home ranges, and exhibiting weak dispersal or migratory tendencies.

Selenodont molar teeth with crescent-shaped cusps.

Sella one of the nasal processes of leafnose bats; an upstanding central projection which may form a fluted ridge running backwards from between the nostrils.

Septum a partition separating two parts of an organism. The nasal septum consists of a fleshy part separating the nostrils and a vertical, bony plate dividing the nasal cavity.

Serum blood from which corpuscles and

clotting agents have been removed; a clear, almost colorless fluid.

Sexual dimorphism a condition in which males and females of a species differ consistently in form, eg size, shape. (See POLYMORPHISM.)

Serology the study of blood sera; investigates ANTIGEN-antibody reactions to elucidate responses to disease organisms and also PHYLOGENETIC relationships between species.

Siblings individuals who share one or both parents. An individual's siblings are its brothers and sisters, regardless of their sex.

Sinus a cavity in bone or tissue.

Solitary living on its own, as opposed to social or group-living in lifestyle.

Sonar sound used in connection with navigation (SOund NAvigation Ranging).

Specialist an animal whose lifestyle involves highly specialized stratagems; eg feeding with one technique on a particular food.

Species a taxonomic division subordinate to genus and superior to subspecies. In general a species is a group of animals similar in structure and which are able to breed and produce viable offspring.

Speciation the process by which new species arise in evolution. It is widely accepted that it occurs when a single species population is divided by some geographical barrier.

Sphincter a ring of smooth muscle around a pouch, rectum or other hollow organ, which can be contracted to narrow or close the entrance to the organ.

Spinifex a grass which grows in large, distinctive clumps or hummocks in the driest areas of central and Western Australia.

Stridulation production of sound by rubbing together modified surfaces of the body.

Subadult no longer an infant or juvenile but not yet fully adult physically and/or socially.

Subfamily a division of a FAMILY.

Suborder a subdivision of an order.

Subspecies a recognizable subpopulation of a single species, typically with a distinct geographical distribution.

Successional habitat a stage in the progressive change in composition of a community of plants, from the original colonization of a bare area towards a largely stable climax.

Sympatry a condition in which the geographical ranges of two or more different species overlap (cf ALLOPATRY).

Syndactylous pertaining to the second and third toes of some mammals, which are joined together so that they appear to be a single toe with a split nail (as opposed to didactylous). In kangaroos, these syndactyl toes are used as a fur comb.

Taiga northernmost coniferous forest, with open boggy rocky areas in between.

Tarsal pertaining to the tarsus bones in the ankle, articulating between the tibia and fibia of the leg and the metarsals of the foot (pes).

Terrestrial living on land.

Territory an area defended from intruders by an individual or group. Originally the term was used where ranges were exclusive and obviously defended at their borders. A more general definition of territoriality allows some overlap between neighbors by defining territoriality as a system of spacing wherein home ranges do not overlap randomly—that is, the location of one

individual's, or group's home range influences those of others.

Testosterone a male hormone synthesized in the testes and responsible for the expression of many male characteristics (contrast the female hormone estrogen produced in the ovaries).

Thermoneutral range the range in outside environmental temperature in which a mammal uses the minimum amount of energy to maintain a constant internal body temperature. The limits to the thermoneutral range are the lower and upper critical temperatures, at which points the mammals must use increasing amounts of energy to maintain a constant body temperature. (cf HETEROTHERMY).

Thermoregulation the regulation and maintenance of a constant internal body temperature in mammals.

Tooth-comb a dental modification in which the incisor teeth form a comb-like structure.

Thoracic pertaining to the thorax or chest.

Torpor a temporary physiological state in some mammals, akin to short-term hibernation, in which the body temperature drops and the rate of METABOLISM is reduced. Torpor is an adaptation for reducing energy expenditure in periods of extreme cold or food shortage.

Tragus a flap, sometimes moveable, situated in front of the opening of the outer ear in bats.

Trypanosome a group of protozoa causing sleeping sickness.

Umbilicus navel.

Underfur the thick soft undercoat fur lying beneath the longer and coarser hair (guard hairs).

Understory the layer of shrubs, herbs and small trees beneath the forest canopy.

Vascular of, or with vessels which conduct blood and other body fluids.

Vector an individual or species which transmits a disease.

Ventral on the lower or bottom side or surface; thus ventral or abdominal glands occur on the underside of the abdomen.

Vertebrate an animal with a backbone; a division of the phylum Chordata which includes animals with notochords (as distinct from invertebrates).

Vestigial a characteristic with little or no contemporary use, but derived from one which was useful and well developed in an ancestral form.

Vibrissae stiff, coarse hairs richly supplied with nerves, found especially around the snout, and with a sensory (tactile) function.

Vocalization calls or sounds produced by the vocal cords of a mammal, and uttered through the mouth. Vocalizations differ with the age and sex of mammals but are usually similar within a species.

Xenarthrales bony elements between the lumbar vertebrae of XENARTHRAN mammals, which provide additional support to the pelvic region for digging, climbing etc.

Xenarthran a member of the suborder Xenarthra, which comprises the living armadillos, sloths and anteaters (see EDENTATE).

Yolk sac a sac, usually containing yolk, which hangs from the ventral surface of the vertebrate fetus. In mammals, the yolk sac contains no yolk, but helps to nourish the embryonic young via a network of blood vessels.

INDEX

A **bold number** indicates a major section of the main text, following a heading: a ***bold italic*** number indicates a fact box on a single species: a single number in (parentheses) indicates that the animal name or subject is to be found in a boxed feature and a double number in (parentheses) indicates that the animal name or subject is to be found in a special spread feature. *Italic* numbers refer to illustrations.

Picture Acknowledgments

Key: *t* top. *b* bottom. *c* center. *l* left. *r* right.

Abbreviations: A Ardea. AH Andrew Henley. AN Nature, Agence Photographique. ANT Australasian Nature Transparencies. BC Bruce Coleman Ltd. J Jacana. NHPA Natural History Photographic Agency. OSF Oxford Scientific Films. PEP Planet Earth Pictures. WWF World Wildlife Fund.

Cover BC. J. and D. Bartlett. 1 BC. J. and D. Bartlett. 2–3 A. J-P. Ferrero. 4–5 BC. R. Williams. 6–7 OSF. P. K. Sharpe. 8–9 A. P. Morris. 10–11 AN. 11*t* OSF. 14 Bodleian Library. 15*t* A. 15*b* OSF. 18*b*

NHPA. 18–19 BC. 20 J. 21 A. 22–23 A. Bannister. 23*b* J. Payne. 25 OSF. 26–7 BC. 28*t* NHPA. 28*b* BC. 29 A. 30 BC. 31 OSF. 32–3 Eric and David Hosking. 33*b* BC. 34–5, 35*b* D. R. Kuhn. 37 A. Bannister. 40*b* D. R. Kuhn. 40–1 A. 41*b* D. R. Kuhn. 44–5 A. 45*b* BC. 46*t* M. Fogden. 46*b* BC. 47 OSF. 48, 49, 50–1 M. Fogden. 52–3 J. 53*b* BC. 54*t* OSF. 54*b* PEP. 55 J. 56–7 BC. 57 A. 58, 59 ANT. 64 AH. 65 NHPA. 66*b* Frithfoto. 66–7 ANT. 67*b* J. 68 BC. 69 G. F. McCraken. 70 A. 71*t* ANT. 71*b* Aquila. 72 AH. 73 NHPA. 74 WWF/S. Yorath. 75*t* ANT. 75*b* A. 78 M. Fogden. 80 BC. 81 R. Stebbings. 82–3 M. Tuttle. 84–5 OSF.

84*b* J. 85*b*, 86, 87 OSF. 88 A. 88–9 J. 90–1 ANT. 91 BC. 92 AH. 93*t* Frithfoto. 93*b* AH. 94*b* E. Beaton. 94–5 G. Mazza. 100–1 ANT. 101*t* A. 102 Tony Morrison. 103 BC. 106–7, 108, 109 OSF. 112, 113*t* AH. 113*c* WWF, Switzerland. 113*b* ANT. 114, 115*b* AH. 115*t*, 116 A. 116–17 AN. 117*t* J. 119 A. 120–1, 121*t* ANT. 121*b* AH. 122–3 E. Beaton. 123*t* ANT. 124–5 A. 126*t* E. Beaton. 126*b* AH. 127 J. 128–9, 132*t* AH. 132*b* A. Smith 133 AH. 134*b* E. Beaton. 134–5 NHPA. 137, 140–1 AN. 142 E. Beaton. 143 ANT. 144 AH. 145 AN. 146–7, 149 ANT. 149*b* BC. 150–1 A. Smith.

Artwork

All artwork © Priscilla Barrett unless stated otherwise below.

Abbreviations SD Simon Driver. ML Michael Long. AEM Anne-Elise Martin. DO Denys Ovenden. CW Carol Wells. DT Dick Twinney.

12*b*, 13*b* ML. 12*t*, 12*c* SD. 16 DO. 25, 28, 36 SD. 39 DO. 60*c*, 61*l* CW. 61*b* SD. 61*r* ML. 62 Graham Allen. 65 CW. 80 SD. 96, 97, 98*r* ML. 98*l*, 99 SD 104 DT. 109 CW. 111, 114, 130, 131, 136, 138 DT. 143 CW. Maps and scale drawings SD.